Not All Was Lost

Not All Was Lost

A Young Woman's Memoir
1939-1946

Irene Bessette

To order additional copies of this book, contact:
Xlibris Corporation
1-888-795-4274
www.Xlibris.com
Orders@Xlibris.com
82816

CONTENTS

Note: The author wishes to thank her relatives in France and Russia who preserved and sent her the photos dating before 1939. While she would have liked to include additional pictures, she could choose only from those miraculously saved by others, as nothing remained from her parents' home in Warsaw.

AUTHOR'S FATHER IN FRONT OF THEIR
PREWAR HOME ON PAWIA STREET.

PREFACE

I have often been asked how people could live under bombardment and through the terror of an occupation. There seems to be abundant information about the inhumanity and unspeakable events under the Nazi regime, but perhaps not enough has been said about the endurance of the ordinary people during the tragic years 1939-1946.

How did people react? Did they ever smile? Did they fall in love? Could they work? Study? How did they endure each day with death so close, so real? And, finally, how did they tolerate the harsh and unsettled conditions right after the war?

In my memoir I have tried to answer these questions. For I was one of the millions who, caught in hellish circumstances, struggled to survive while trying to give some sense and dignity to their lives.

I lived through the bombing of Warsaw, the persecution and murder of Warsaw Jews before their imprisonment in the Ghetto and thereafter. I shared the misery of the Polish Christians enslaved to work for the Germans, and witnessed their confusion and hardship when liberated on French soil. And I lived in recently liberated France that had to rebuild itself. Against this historic panorama, I grew from the adolescence into womanhood.

I survived the war, but could not stay in Poland. For when I returned there in 1946, I realized that Jews were not welcome. It was my personal tragedy; I loved my country but could not stand its hostility. Disappointed and hurt, I left Poland and lost my birthplace of Warsaw for the last time. The first time was when I was imprisoned in the Ghetto, the second when I was deported for a slave work on a German farm. I lost Warsaw then because of the occupiers' cruelty.

But the final loss that occurred in liberated Poland was the most painful and most unwarranted.

In time Warsaw was rebuilt. My life too has been rebuilt, but not in Poland. Looking back many years later, I wonder about the ethnic and religious intolerance and political unrest that force people to leave their country. That loss may inflict as much pain as the onslaught of war or enemy occupation.

The present memoir, written from my new country where I have been happy and successful, is a testimony to the struggle to survive war and alienation from one's own nation without losing self-esteem, faith in humankind, and hope.

One final note of explanation concerning names. Since my marriage to Gerard Bessette in 1971, I have been known as Irene Bessette. This is the name I am using to write this memoir, as this is how I am known to most people. I was born in 1924 to Riva(Helena) Dobrejcer and Jan Borman, both dentists on Pawia Street in the heart of the Jewish section of Warsaw. When we escaped from the Ghetto, we assumed different names and I assumed the name of Bakowska and that this is the name my parents and sister also eventually adopted and used after the war. For simplicity's sake I use Bakowski or Bakowska in this memoir to refer to my family and myself.

ONE

THE LAST VACATION

I was 15 years old in 1939, the year of our last vacation. That summer we went to a resort called Brok, a few hours by train east of Warsaw. The little town was on the river Bug in the middle of a forest of old pines.

We spent most of our time by the river. I did not know how to swim, so I stayed near the bank, watching the children laughing, shouting and splashing in the water. Women in brightly colored bathing suits swam out into the middle of the river, or played volleyball with men on the beach. My pretty sister Karolina, two years older than I, swam with her friends. I observed them wistfully for they did not ask me to join them.

My mother stayed with me in the shallow water, for she could not swim either. I loved being close to her—normally she was busy with her patients or other duties. My father had not come with us, for he and my mother shared a dental practice and took their holidays in turn. He planned to start his vacation in early September, when we returned.

Our hotel had once been a large private house. Now elegant and expensive, it retained some rustic aspect: the guests used outhouses and washed in large basins in their rooms. In spite of its simplicity, it was always full of visitors, mostly from Warsaw. On that last vacation, four of us shared a large, sunny room: my mother, my sister and I, and our guest, my classmate Rena Dworecka.

Rena was such a pretty girl that I felt dull and colorless by comparison. She had shining black eyes, long black hair, cheeks as fresh and rosy as peaches, and full, red lips. An only child, she lived with her parents in a Jewish neighborhood of Warsaw. I was intimidated by her pious, bearded, yarmulke-wearing father, sensing that he looked down on me, for though we were Jewish, we were not a religious family. That did not stop Rena and me from being friends.

Although we were the same age, Rena was much more grown up. I remember that one day she fell ill and my mother kept her in bed and called a doctor. Sick as she was, Rena washed her face, arranged her hair, and put on her most beautiful nightgown. Over my mother's strong objections she also insisted on wearing lipstick, and when the doctor arrived, she looked like a beautiful oriental princess.

I was amazed by Rena's nerve. I was unable to stand up to my mother. I always obeyed her, for I respected her as much as I loved her. I was very attached to my mother and liked going for long walks with her in the forest, talking together. I found the forest at once inviting and intimidating; it excited me, made me feel slightly apprehensive, and somehow nostalgic. I felt an overwhelming power surrounding us. My mother and I were so small among the giant, centuries-old-trees, and yet we too were healthy and strong, children of the same Creator.

We had come to Brok planning to stay for two months, and the peaceful summer days flew by. But all the while strange rumors were circulating. One evening the sun was like a ball of fire and the sky was the color of blood, and the farmers predicted war was coming. There was a chill in the air; people became anxious and uncertain. We cut our vacation short and hurried back to Warsaw.

My father's big leather suitcases were already packed with a new wardrobe of expensive shirts, suits and shoes. He was convinced, as were many others, that the forecasts of the coming war were nothing but talk. Shortly after our return he sent his bags on ahead.

But at the last moment he decided to stay at home. His luggage was gone, never to be found. The rumors had begun to lead to chaos. No one knew when trains were coming or going, nobody was in charge. Law and order were disintegrating.

Last Vacation — Summer 1939

TWO

THE BOMBING OF WARSAW

Friday, September 1, 1939, was a normal working day. On the radio we heard that the Germans had crossed our western frontier. We were told not to worry; we had an army to defend us. There would be a general mobilization, and we would quickly defeat the Germans. People in Warsaw were calm.

At one o'clock in the afternoon my best friend, Bela Eisenstein, came to visit and we sat together, talking and laughing as usual. Suddenly we heard the noise of planes above us and strange, crackling sounds coming from far away. At first we thought that the noise was the sound of our pilots practising their military maneuvers. But the dry crackling became louder and louder, and more frequent.

Abruptly, the radio fell silent, the music stopped. The speaker announced in a strangled voice that the Germans were bombing Warsaw.

It was a glorious sunny day, the air fresh and crisp, the sky blue and cloudless. It meant excellent visibility for the bombers. My parents, their patients (the dental offices adjoined our apartment), Bela and I ran into our small inner hall, believing we were safer there because we were further from the windows. No one spoke. Bela and I held hands. We knew the truth but could not believe it. Warsaw, the open city, was being bombed on the first day of the war.

When the planes went away, we looked at each other in dismay and confusion. What should we do next? Some patients had rushed home; some stayed, trying to joke about the war.

We reassured ourselves: "We are not alone, the French and the English are our allies. They will come to our rescue and the Germans will soon be defeated." We were certain that the Allies would counterattack and that Poland would survive.

We were all in a state of shock. In spite of all the rumors in August, the war had caught us by surprise. The bombing came upon us without warning. We believed that Hitler would not dare to attack Poland. The martial music playing on the radio to keep everyone's spirits up was often interrupted by appeals to England and France for help and by the sirens warning of the German air raids. In fact, the warning had already come with the German planes flying over Warsaw. They began to bomb the city, one neighborhood after another. While one part of Warsaw was turned into hell, another was still leading something of a normal life.

In the stores there was a sudden run on candles, and soon there was a run on food as well. Storekeepers hid their merchandise, anticipating that supplies would be cut off and prices would rise. Anything that was not perishable was hoarded away. As people began stocking up and storing, prices skyrocketed in a day.

This situation led to a good deal of distress for my grandmother, Grunia Achlomov Dobrejcer, who had a philanthropic nature, and had made a habit of lending money without interest to several neighborhood merchants. They lived from one week to the next, returning money only to borrow it again. My grandmother's modest, short-term loans had helped them to survive. But on September 2, when my grandmother went to buy her daily bread rolls, the storekeeper—a poor woman who had borrowed money from her for years—now seemed to barely recognize her, and refused to sell her anything. Perhaps the storekeeper was ashamed to charge her the new, inflationary price, for she sent my grandmother away with no bread.

I was furious, but my mother smiled, and told me that I was young and still had a great deal to learn. Then she went to the store herself, put a large sum of money on the counter, and returned home with the fresh rolls for my grandmother.

Bombs now dropped in the city from morning until evening. The beautiful weather favored the Germans; for the whole month of September, the sky was blue and cloudless, and the nights were clear, lit by millions of shining stars. There was no anti-aircraft defense to chase the bombers away; the unprotected city was laid open for the German pilots to bomb as much as they desired. We suffered countless casualties.

Many people volunteered to defend their neighborhoods. Tadek Luka, the son of our neighbors, stayed on the roof during bombing raids to protect it in case of fire. Tadek was soon joined by Samuel Rotein. They were handsome, one with blond hair, the other chestnut. Tadek was Christian, Samuel was Jewish. On the roof they had only a shovel, a hatchet, and their bare hands to fight any fire. And despite the fact that they were in clear view, they stayed up there day after day, the German planes roaring furiously over their heads — so low that the pilots could see them and laugh. But I admired the two young men. Their heroic example helped me to endure the continuous bombardment.

Every day the city's defenses became more disorganized. Toward the end of the first week of war, the government fled into exile abroad. A rumor spread that the fall of Warsaw was imminent, and that all able-bodied men should leave the city, because the Germans would kill them first.

That created even greater chaos and panic. Thousands and thousands of men decided to run away toward Eastern Poland. Since the Germans were our neighbors to the west and to the north, and had occupied Czechoslovakia to the south, only the eastern part of Poland seemed beyond their reach.

We hoped that our defenses could be reorganized in the East, or at least that the Germans would not advance that far. But the massive exodus was not an organized regrouping of able-bodied men, preparing to fight for their country: this was a desperate flight of a panic-stricken population. Every man ran for himself, trying to keep it a secret from his neighbor. The sad irony was that they would escape the Germans only to be trapped by the Russians—for on September 17, Russia invaded Eastern Poland.

Nobody had foreseen such a calamity.

The exodus began toward the end of the first week of September and continued uninterrupted all night. The men ran totally unprotected, often without money and only with the shirts on their backs. My father refused to leave us, for he knew that for us, Jews, the situation was equally dangerous for men, women and children. I was happy that he stayed with us. But many men did leave their families, and their wives stayed behind with the children—although they were afraid to be left alone, often without financial resources. Other women decided to take their children and go with their husbands, entire families fleeing. The roads were crowded with people and their meager possessions, completely exposed under cloudless skies. And the German planes pursued them relentlessly. They dropped bombs on the crowds and chased the defenseless men, women, and children with machine-guns. The roads were covered in blood and the corpses of people and horses.

Among those who escaped was my father's younger brother, my uncle Henryk. A bachelor, he left with the others, and miraculously, he survived the war.

On September 9 the German army began to encircle the unfortified city of Warsaw. During the siege, when the fall of Poland seemed imminent, prison guards feared that the invaders would shoot all prisoners, and so they let them escape. This was only one of the many humane acts of solidarity that prevailed among us at that time. The policemen became more friendly too, and once they even distributed bread freely in our neighborhood. But sadly, the good feelings did not last. The crushing defeat of our country confused and stifled us.

At first our neighborhood was not badly damaged. During lulls in the bombing we were able to walk in the streets. I saw Polish soldiers and their horses stationed near Krasinski Gardens, out in the open, a perfect target for the bombs. I shuddered when I saw all those young faces and helpless animals. Our government had already left and so had most of the generals and other officers. The soldiers stayed behind, waiting for orders which were never to come. A few days later these men and their horses were turned into a bloody mass of corpses.

Despite the confusion and destruction, people showed great courage in many ways. Under the siege, the hospitals stopped functioning. Emergency operations were done without anesthetic in the less-exposed rooms of the ruined buildings. In basements, in washrooms or storage rooms, or in any place that was thought safe from machine-gunning or shelling, brave doctors and nurses worked to help people wounded by shrapnel and bombs. And, in spite of the relentless bombardments, people continued to carry their injured friends or relatives to these ruins that only recently had been well-run hospitals.

Other were brave in more private ways. My sister's classmate, Inka Szekman, who was studying English, read Shakespeare in the original during the catastrophic days of September, seldom leaving her apartment for shelter. She was not afraid; she simply said that she had no time to waste. Inka had great courage and the power of concentration of a scholar. But she never became one, for she was murdered during the occupation.

Yet, in the midst of the great bravery and the despair of people running from street to street among the burning houses seeking shelter, others robbed the empty apartments, stealing money and jewelry. In their lust for looting, they blessed the opportunity given to them by the war and the bombing. It was as if the social system had been turned upside down. The banks were closed, never to reopen. People carried money in their pockets. Many lost homes and fortunes in a day and became completely destitute. An elderly woman, once a famous actress, carried her whole fortune—all her jewels—with her, hidden in a pillow, when she fled from her burning home. When she finally found a shelter, she sat down in a corner, exhausted, and fell asleep. But when she woke up, her pillow and her fortune were gone. Somebody got rich; she became a beggar.

We did not have real bomb shelters so we had to improvise with the cellars of our buildings. They had floors of beaten earth, and were damp, unheated, and without electricity. In the evenings the planes went away, and we could leave and get some fresh air. The streets were full of couples embracing, whispering softly, holding hands. They seemed to ignore the world around them, living only in the present. Before the war, such public behavior had been unthinkable. I realized then that danger and the nearness of death were powerful catalysts of love. I, too, felt a new strange urge inside; I longed for a boyfriend, as I never had before.

Toward the end of the third week of bombing, we lost hope of saving Poland. Yet Warsaw still continued its resistance, and people obeyed the confused orders coming from the mayor of the city, the civil defense militia, and some military authorities.

One day, for instance, an order was given for long trenches to be dug down the middle of the streets. These trenches prevented what little traffic there was from moving, for by this time the fire engines, the ambulances, the taxis, and tramways had ceased operating. And now the pedestrians too would be stopped. Still, men dug arduously for a few days until common sense or fatigue prevailed.

So life continued, while so many were burned alive or suffocated under the debris of their houses. Sometimes the survivors tried to dig out those who were trapped, but there was no equipment and no help. Slowly, painfully, people died under tons of rubble.

The bombing of our city terrified my eighty-two-year old grandmother. She kept repeating to reassure herself, "I have survived many wars and upheavals, thus I will survive this catastrophe as well."

I was touched by her courage and will to live. I knew how many tragedies and tumults she had witnessed, how often her own life was disturbed. She was a very courageous lady. Orphaned at an early age, she got married at sixteen to Aaron Dobrejcer, a teacher of Russian language and literature. Helen, my mother was their eighth and last child.

My grandmother told me how, during the Russo-Turkish wars (1854-56 and 1877-78) there were outbreaks of cholera in the city of Mogilev, where she was born. She saw people dying like flies, an ugly death caused by continuous diarrhea and dehydration. Her memory of this calamity was so vivid that she shivered any time she heard the word "cholera" — a common swearword in Poland.

Millions of Russians suffered because of the troubled political and economic situation in their country, but my grandparents had to endure as well the severe anti-Semitism. Finally, around 1900, the family was forced to leave Mogilev. They moved to Warsaw, then under Russian occupation. Five older children returned to Russia to continue their studies. Then the Russian Revolution of 1917-1922 closed the frontier between Russia and Poland. My grandmother would never see again her five children, who lived thereafter in the Soviet Union.

My grandparents, and later my parents, resided on Pawia Street, in the middle of Warsaw's Jewish section. My grandmother, a widow since 1917, lived with us and led a quiet, orderly life until the war began. The most upsetting thing for her became the regular exodus to the cellar. She had arthritis and a weak heart, but she still had to follow us down the stairs at the sound of an alarm or planes roaring overhead.

We were fortunate because our apartment building was still intact, and so was our cellar, but it quickly became crowded.

Whole areas of Warsaw were destroyed. Frightened and homeless people left their devastated neighborhoods, seeking shelter wherever they could find it, while others, not yet homeless, ran out of their own homes believing they would be safer elsewhere. Our cellar, like many others, became so crowded that it was hard to find a place to sit. Some sat on the floor or even stood up all day. It was difficult to breathe.

Many refugees tried to bring some of their belongings with them, but space was precious and there was simply no room for luggage. A kind of militia of voluntary watchmen formed to forbid the entry of big bundles to make sure that there was room for as many people as possible. People who had already lost everything were forced to leave behind the few things they carried with them, before they were permitted to enter.

My grandmother's health was deteriorating. My parents placed a narrow camp bed in the cellar to let her rest a little. She sat there most of the time, sad and resigned, and no one dared to push her out even though her bed took up precious space. When the bombing raids ended, she returned with us to our apartment on the first floor. But later, once the sirens began sounding all day long, it became impossible for her to run back and forth, and my parents accepted the kind invitation of our neighbors on the ground floor, Mr. and Mrs. Luka (the parents of the brave Tadek), to stay with them. We believed, as everyone did then, that being one floor down would keep us away from the bombs, and safer.

In 1939 the Jewish New Year, Rosh Hashanah, fell on September 14. Our neighborhood was subjected to intense and vicious bombing until Yom Kippur — the Day of Atonement — on September 23. On September 15, the house next to ours was hit by a powerful one-ton bomb. Our house shook like a leaf for several seconds, and everyone ran away from the windows. The air was filled with smoke and dust, and the thunder of the falling building mingled with human cries. Nothing was left but rubble and an enormous hole in the ground.

By the time this happened, my grandmother had become so weak that she was permanently installed in a bed in the Lukas' home, and my mother, assisted by Karolina or me, stayed near her day and night. When the house next door was crumbling, she was lying in bed, feverish, delirious and unable to run; but she sensed danger and was afraid. She thought the warm, bright sunlight coming into the room through the window near her bed was fire, which would burn our house down. She was very frightened. I sat on the bed with her, my arms around her shoulders, trying to explain and telling her not to be afraid. I held her tightly, repeating softly, "Don't be afraid, Grandmother, this is only sunshine."

She didn't understand me but took my hand and asked me not to abandon her in the fire. Everyone else was hiding in the corridor, and we were alone. I had no desire to leave my grandmother to run for shelter. I felt as if I were nailed to her bed, my arms around her. I accepted the thought of dying with her. It was my first close experience with death. And in the presence of imminent danger I became calm and resigned, accepting the inevitable end. I would not run away to save my life. That was it. It was my fate to die with my grandmother—yet under normal circumstances, when the danger of death was far away, the mere thought of dying would have terrified me. I did not want to die.

A few minutes later we heard the planes flying away, and the room was filled with people returning from the corridor. My mother cried and kissed me, regretting that she had left her mother. She proclaimed me a heroine, though I did not at all feel heroic. I simply loved my grandmother very much and could not abandon her when she was so frightened and helpless.

As time went on, the uninterrupted raids forced us to stay in our cellar all day. At night the bombing stopped, but we were afraid to leave. My parents carried my ailing grandmother from the Lukas' apartment to her narrow camp bed in the basement. The four people who had been occupying it in the meantime did not want to leave. It is true, they were exhausted, but my

82-year-old grandmother could barely stand. They finally moved just enough to give her space to sit down. She sat still, said nothing and did not complain. After a few minutes, these neighbors, who had pretended not to recognize my grandmother, changed their minds and silently moved off. She lay down, and was never able to stand up again. We stood near her and tried to comfort her.

After a few days in the damp, dark, overcrowded cellar, my grandmother developed pneumonia and rapidly went into a coma. A woman doctor gave her some injections, but they did not help. I remember my grandmother's hands moving feverishly, touching the edge of her cover as if she wanted to stand up and leave the bed. But only her hands could move, and her eyes remained closed. The air was oppressive, the light from the candles feeble. Grunia Dobrejcer, whose long life—filled with love—had been devoted to her duties, lay on her camp bed among strangers, more and more of whom were constantly arriving.

But although she was in a public place, she was surrounded by her family: my parents, her son Monos, my sister and I. We were always near her and never left her alone. She lingered in her coma for four days, during which the bombing increased. We could hear the German planes roaring above our heads, and shrapnel hitting houses and people. Warsaw had been encircled and the city was under artillery fire.

My grandmother died on September 24, 1939. My mother's grief overcame her fears about the bombs and our safety. Although Mr. and Mrs. Luka invited us to return to their home, my mother wanted to give her mother the last rites and brought the body to our own apartment. The news of Grunia Dobrejcer's death spread quickly. Amidst incessant bombing, no electricity and no running water, two Jewish women offered to wash, clean, and prepare the corpse for burial.

Our kitchen was occupied by men hammering together the coffin from unpainted wood. Jewish law forbids an elaborate casket, and burial is always in a plain, wooden box, with the body wrapped in a shroud. I was in tears because there was no name on the coffin. I was given a piece of wood and, with my friend Bela's help, I found my school paintbox, painted my grandmother's name, and made sure that the wood was well fastened to the coffin.

My mother had another problem. The cemeteries on the outskirts of town (Okopowa Street), Jewish and Christian, side by side though separate, were under direct shelling. The Germans were stationed right behind them. As it was impossible to go near, people were being buried in the middle of the city, anywhere the ground was not covered with asphalt: under trees, in a square, in a garden. But my mother was determined to bury her mother in the Jewish cemetery at any price. She found two cemetery workers and made them swear they would bury the casket at the Jewish cemetery and nowhere else. The men agreed, and took the money and the casket. My mother felt she could be at peace about her mother's burial.

The day my grandmother died, yet another tragedy occurred. My parents' friend, Janka Elterman, who stayed with us during the bombing, lost her sister, Olga, and her sixteen-year-old niece Nelly when a bomb fell on their building. Their mutilated bodies were buried beneath the rubble. Janka's father, Mr. Tran, was seriously injured. Only her eighty-three-year-old mother, Mrs. Tran, remained unhurt. Although she had just lost her daughter and granddaughter in one blow, her first thought was still to save her husband's life. Even in these tragic circumstances, money helped. The Trans were very wealthy, and Mrs. Tran had money in her handbag. She hired a strong, muscular man to help got her injured husband to our apartment. It was a long walk under heavy bombardment, but at last they arrived safely at our home.

While her husband was being cared for by my father, Mrs. Tran sat in our cellar on my grandmother's camp bed, clutching her handbag. My parents asked me to watch over her. Exhausted, she fell asleep. When her handbag fell to the floor, I bent to pick it up. She opened her eyes, did not recognize me, and grabbed her handbag, looking at me with terror and anger. I tried to introduce myself, but she was afraid and backed away. I was shocked. I had never experienced such fear and hostility directed at me. There seemed to be nothing I could do for her.

Mr. Tran succumbed to his wounds and died three months later, in December 1939.

On September 26, the bombing became sporadic. Then it stopped. We heard that the Germans would use poison gas if Warsaw did not surrender. We had no gas masks.

Warsaw surrendered officially on September 28, 1939, and on September 30, German soldiers entered the city. The surrender had at least ended the bombing, so people were free to leave their shelters in search of water and news of their friends and relatives. The news was nearly always bad.

In our own building, a young mother and her baby had moved in with the janitor's family, the Trojanowskis, on the ground floor. The baby, Ada, was pretty and healthy with blue eyes and soft white skin. Although the mother was weak and hungry, somehow she could still nurse the baby. Then the milk stopped. Ada cried. She was given sweetened water, but she needed milk and there was none. The stores were closed and food had disappeared. She cried more quietly. Then her crying ended. Little Ada died one day before the bombing stopped.

Tragedy also struck the family of my father's friend, Dr. Jerzy Śliwa. His brother-in-law, Andrew Mrozik, after a week of bombing, had complained of a strange noise vibrating in his head. His two girls, one seven years old, another three, were hungry and crying. They had no milk for days. His wife, Ewa, tried to comfort him. But on the sixteenth day of the bombing, while Ewa was asleep in a corner of the cellar, Andrew took the children upstairs and shot them dead, then shot himself. Ewa survived the bombing and the war. It was she who told us what had happened to Andrew.

Two weeks after the bombing ended, my mother found the men she had hired to bury my grandmother. When she asked them to show her the grave, they looked uneasy and embarrassed. They took my mother to the Jewish cemetery, pointed at a spot, and said, "This is your mother's grave." They were lying, and Mother knew it. They hadn't carried the casket to the cemetery, but had buried it in an anonymous grave that would never be found. But my mother, being an atheist, comforted herself that no matter where her mother was buried, she had returned back to the earth and to nature. She felt she had honored her mother by trying to bury her properly.

My mother put up a monument in the place that was supposed to be Grunia Dobrejcer's grave, and for a year wore a black veil attached to her hat, as was the custom. Although not herself a religious woman, she tried to do what her mother would have wanted her to do—simply because she loved her. She respected her wishes and beliefs. I admired my mother for that.

So began our life under German occupation, while we were still crying for people lost during the bombing.

HELENA'S PARENTS — GRUNIA AND AARON

AUTHOR'S FATHER
JAN IN 1921

AUTHOR'S MOTHER HELENA — RIVA
IN 1921

THREE

THE BEGINNING OF THE GERMAN OCCUPATION

October 1939. The sky was clear and bright, but the weather was cold. The streets little by little became crowded again as the bewildered, frightened and hungry people left their cellars, looking in disbelief at the ruin and destruction all around them.

I walked along Pawia Street with my mother. She wore a black coat as well as a black hat with a veil, to show that she was in mourning. Pale, she looked sad and dignified. Friends greeted us warmly, waiting for her to explain for whom she was in mourning. They regretted the death of my grandmother, "that good and generous lady," but they were glad that my father, my sister and I survived. They marveled that our home remained intact. We were very fortunate indeed, because not only was our building not destroyed but my parents' dental establishment remained untouched. Of course, they had lost all their savings since our banks ceased to exist along with our government and all its institutions. But my parents would be able to continue to practise their profession, which meant we would have some food, and coal to heat our apartment.

Warsaw was still without water or electricity. People went to the outskirts of the city to fetch water in buckets, and we lit our homes first with candles, then with improvised carbide lamps that filled the air with an offensive smell. Water was restored eventually, then electricity; but only for a short time — it was cut off again periodically for weeks or months. The streets remained unlit at night, except for the carbide lamps attached to the street vendors' pushcarts.

The Gestapo visited our building early in October, less than a week after the Germans' entry into Warsaw. We were still in shock from the bombing; the streets were full of rubble and smelled of burning and decay. Our apartment remained dark and unheated.

The Germans appeared in our courtyard screaming for Mr. Lewin, the Jewish owner of the building. Finding him in his apartment on the third floor, they punched and shoved him and ordered him to follow them to their waiting car in the courtyard. But while still in his apartment, he struggled free, ran to a window and jumped out into the courtyard, three floors down. He lay there, bleeding heavily and moaning from pain, while the Germans stood by, uncertain what to do with the dying man. My father, in his white dentist's coat, took advantage of their momentary confusion and ran quickly to our neighbor to inject an analgesic. But it was too late to help him. The Germans went away, leaving the body behind.

That was my first encounter with the Germans close up. But I had seen them before, at a distance, when they entered Warsaw. Our friend Mrs. Luka had asked me to go with her to see the aftermath of the bombing. We could hardly believe our eyes: Warsaw lay in ruins. On both sides of the streets were tons of rubble and debris from demolished houses, still warm from the smoldering fires. The air stank of smoke and decay. And the Germans marched endlessly in columns of four or five down the middle of the streets, heads high and triumphant. We did not know what was more painful, to see this victorious march or to look at our destroyed, bleeding city. We held hands, trying to hold back our tears and comfort each other. But Mrs. Luka was a Christian, and did not feel that her life was endangered right now. I, on the other hand, felt deep anguish and a sense of impending doom.

Other people who had ventured out told us that in some parts of Warsaw, the Germans would throw bread into the hungry crowds and watch the people fight for it like dogs. The Germans laughed and took pictures.

Our own apartment had lost its former warmth and security. Grandmother was no longer with us, and the rooms felt empty without her. My parents decided to reduce our living quarters to only one room; we could not afford to heat the whole apartment, and we had to save our candles. We were cramped—my parents, my sister and I—but we felt reassured by each other's presence. However, my parents kept mostly to their dental office, even though they had only a few patients. They closed their second office, and later moved the dental laboratory into the kitchen, which was at least slightly heated.

The sky was safe again, but the streets had become dangerous: the Germans were everywhere. From the beginning, they openly and systematically robbed our neighborhood. Not only were businesses emptied but private apartments as well. Big trucks arrived every day on Pawia Street, and men were rounded up and forced to load them with furniture, until they were filled to capacity. There was no escape from these raids, for the Germans were methodical in emptying one apartment after another. They took furniture, rugs, and paintings; they demanded money, jewelry, and gold. Those trying to hide their valuables did so at the risk of their lives; if discovered, they would either be shot on the spot or taken away, never to return.

One family from our street, the Rosens, hid their gold coins inside the hollow bars of their child's crib, certain the Germans would not disturb the baby. But they ordered the child taken out and carried off the crib, and the Rosens lost all their savings. Their business had already been confiscated, all their furniture was gone, and there was no work to be found. The family was doomed and died later of starvation.

Although the Germans were well organized in emptying the apartments, who got robbed was still a matter of luck. It was like an epidemic: your neighbor might get sick and die, and you might live. My mother feared her new dining-room furniture would be taken any day. If we had known what was to come, we would not have let ourselves worry about mere furniture. But we did not know, and so my mother looked sadly at her new possessions. When she was newly married in 1921, she and my father were poor, and had to use my grandmother's massive and unfashionable furniture. My mother wanted a new suite, and could have afforded one many years earlier, yet she did not know how to go about it without hurting her mother's feelings. But one day, in the early spring of 1939, she made up her mind, hired a reputable cabinetmaker, and ordered a round table, eight comfortable chairs and a sideboard, all in expensive wood. The suite was delivered in June. My mother was overjoyed at finally having the fine furniture she had dreamt of. But now it was October 1939, and the Germans could come and take it all at any moment. My parents tried to damage the sideboard by pouring boiling water on it to make it look less attractive, but the finish was unharmed. Then, my parents' friend Janina Zenkowska, a Christian Pole, visited us and offered to take the furniture, and keep it until the end of the war.

Later, much later, Warsaw went through the bloody uprising of 1944, when from August 1 until October 3 almost all the city was burned and destroyed. But Janina and her husband had moved out of the city before the uprising, taking with them all their belongings, including our furniture. When my parents, exhausted and impoverished, met Janina after the war, she was delighted to tell them that our dining-room suite had escaped the destruction and was waiting to be returned.

In the same month of October 1939 radios were confiscated. First, the Germans ordered the registration of all radios; next day they demanded their delivery to the police stations. We had two radios, but my father had registered only one. Yet he was afraid to keep the second one for fear of being shot if it was discovered. He took his better, second radio into the kitchen, put it on the floor and chopped it to pieces with an axe. Hardly believing my eyes, I watched my father, my peaceful orderly father, committing a deliberate act of vandalism. Whack, whack, and the beautiful frame of good quality wood was disintegrating. Whack, whack, and the expensive radio was gone.

Still we were not entirely cut off from world news; some heroic men and women listened to clandestine radios, and edited, printed, and distributed underground bulletins and circulars.

Most people spent October looking for shelter, food or jobs, or searching for relatives and friends. My father too went out to find out how his friends had fared. He met his colleague Mr. Szmit, whose apartment and dental office were destroyed and who was looking desperately for a place to live for himself and his wife. Their only daughter and her husband had gone to the East with the early September exodus. My father invited the Szmits to share our apartment. They were about fifteen years older than my parents, who respected them socially and professionally as their seniors.

When our dining room furniture had been sent to safety, the waiting room furniture was moved into the dining room; and so the former waiting room was now standing empty. It had two windows and a balcony overlooking Pawia Street—before the war it had served as a salon to receive our guests on holidays. My parents offered this large, sunny room to Mr. and Mrs. Szmit because it was the nicest in the apartment, and also for another good reason: a porcelain stove was built into the wall between this room and ours, which made it possible to heat both rooms at once, saving precious coal and wood. We shared the kitchen and the bathroom. Of course, everybody considered it a temporary arrangement, for we hoped that the war would end soon.

Except for that illusion, my parents were very realistic about our situation. They understood that we had to reduce our living standard to the minimum necessary in order to survive and get by. They did not expect to live a decent pre-war life. The Szmits also tried to be brave about their new situation. Mrs. Szmit kept to her room, but Mr. Szmit was more outgoing. He became my friend, and we talked often during the long winter months.

My parents tried to hide their fears from Karolina and me, for they wanted to encourage us to keep busy and to lead as normal lives as possible. So as soon as the bombing stopped, I ran to see my school on 12 Rymarska Street, about 25 minutes walk from our home. The school was gone, only a mountain of rubble. I walked around it and saw that the adjoining building, which housed the elementary school, was sound. It was possible that we would have our classes there when the schools reopened, and I returned several times to the ruins, hoping to find a notice telling us when and where classes would commence. But the Germans ordered all the schools closed in occupied Poland, even the elementary schools. Later, elementary schools for Polish Christian children were reopened, but not ours. The Jews were considered to be filthy people, who should not be allowed to congregate anywhere at all, because they would spread disease. I felt I had been robbed of my school as other people had been robbed of their homes and property.

Our new situation affected Karolina as well, for my seventeen-year-old sister wanted to continue her studies at the university. Only the previous spring she had passed her final exams and graduated from the lyceum. She was granted her Certificate of Maturity, or Matura, an important step in every student's life. The certificate was an official recognition of intellectual maturity and fitness for a higher academic career. Those who had Matura could, as of right, enter the university. Those who had failed were devastated—every year the newspapers reported cases of suicides by students who were unsuccessful in passing the difficult exams.

In September, Karolina would have enrolled in medical school. She had wanted to become a medical doctor ever since her childhood. However, all her efforts to be admitted to a Polish university had proved fruitless because she was Jewish. Father had promised to send her to Paris in the fall of 1939, but now her dreams for the future came to an abrupt end.

My education was very important to me as well. I had just been granted the newly introduced Junior or Small Matura, which marked the end of the four-year-secondary gymnasium education. I planned to attend the lyceum for two more years to obtain the regular Matura and the entrance to the university.

The memories of my school days in pre-war Warsaw are vivid, especially the daily walks to and from Rymarska Street. We did not have school buses to take us, so we always walked, in fair weather or foul, even in the long, cold Polish winters. In particular, I remember those fine, spring days when I was thirteen or fourteen, walking home from school in the afternoon. I left Rymarska Street for the wide and elegant Leszno Street, where well-dressed ladies filled the sidewalks, and horse-driven droshkies competed with trams on the street. On the right, a garden surrounded a majestic church.

I was daydreaming, thinking about Deanna Durbin, the star of my favorite American films. She was sixteen, a radiant girl who sang and danced, and was never seen at school. Nothing could be further from my rigid schedule of classes, home, homework. But that was supposed to change when I grew up. So I could not wait, I dreamed to be sixteen.

But then I turned right down Karmelicka Street and the bustle and noise of commerce interrupted my dreams. After a while I reached Wièzienna Street, paved with cobblestones like our own Pawia Street. The large metal-rimmed wheels of the horse-drawn country wagons resounded against the cobblestones. Children played and shouted all around. The horses, waiting for their masters, neighed and stamped their hooves. It was chaotic and smelly, full of life. On one side of the street was the tall brick wall of the infamous Pawiak prison; on the other was a row of rental buildings. I liked to look in the stores along the street: a cheap jewelry and watch-repair store, and a restaurant displaying food in the window. The smell of garlic drew me toward the restaurant, but I was too young to go in. I had to be home when our dinner was served at 3 p.m.

Quite often, one poor merchant, a tall Jew with a beard and wearing a czapka, a black, peaked cap, displayed Polish, Yiddish and Hebrew books on an old blanket spread on the sidewalk. I liked to look at them, and if I was with my mother or father, he would be respectful and let me look. When I was alone, he chased me away as if I were a dog.

But in the first days of October 1939, those streets were quite deserted. The traffic lights were dead, there were no droshkies, no taxis, private cars, trams or buses in view. All my life I had taken the street lights, the traffic, the noise, and the people for granted; now I felt as if the city had become a vast countryside where people could walk across the roads in any direction they pleased.

I was so happy to see my best friend, Bela Eisenstein, again. She, her parents and two sisters had survived the bombing, but their third-floor apartment on 34 Pawia Street had been destroyed. A corner apartment, it had been cut in half by a bomb and lay open to the street. The family went to live with another tenant, where they were lucky enough to have two rooms for the five of them. A small, primitive iron stove was installed in the middle of one room. No one complained: they were together, except for the oldest sister's husband, who had joined the march eastward early in September, never to be seen again.

At fifteen, Bela was the youngest child. Her father, now old and tired, had been an accountant with an English firm, the Ceylon Tea Company. But in August 1939, its director had left Poland and the company had been dissolved. Mr. Eisenstein and Bela's two sisters, Ala and Pola, who had also worked there, were out of a job. Fortunately, before the director left, he distributed the company's stock of tea as compensation to the senior employees. Bela's father's share remained intact in the remaining part of their apartment. The price rose astronomically during the Occupation, and the family was able to survive, thanks to their stock of tea. It was considered more precious than gold, and they sold it by the gram.

Bela and I missed the daily routine of going to school. Life seemed empty. Before the war, my parents required me only to be a good student, read and study. I was not interested in sports or music, and I had never had a date. All my life it had been drilled into me that I had to get the Matura and attend university.

It was Bela who, toward the end of November, told me about the underground courses. Small groups of students were being formed to study in private homes, each group limited to four or five students, so as not to attract attention. If the group was that small, it was easier to pretend to be celebrating a birthday or just having a social visit if the Germans noticed us.

My parents were willing to support me in joining such a group. They wanted me to continue my education, and insisted that I should ignore the danger and uncertainty, which we could neither resist nor escape. "Irene, try to be brave and optimistic," my mother said. "There is a chance that we will survive. You understand that it is only a matter of time, because the Germans will certainly lose the war at the end." And my father affirmed, "Remember, my daughters, that we cannot give up. We must carry on our passive resistance, no matter what the outcome."

In fact, I was very privileged to be able to think about my education. Masses of people were already hungry and destitute, deprived of everything, uncertain even of surviving the day. There were others, though, who lived in their pre-war apartments, who were still able to work, or who had some treasure hidden away—gold, diamonds, tea, coffee, sugar, or other goods which could be successfully concealed. The children of such relatively well-off people were looking for useful occupations, and many of my friends wanted to learn hairdressing, dressmaking, or corset-making. We had always appreciated manual skills in Poland, and craft work was popular.

People who had relatives overseas dreamed of joining them after the war. English-speaking countries were most favored, and knowledge of the English language most sought after. Thus, the starving teachers had an opportunity to earn some money while their students dreamed of one day leaving our doomed country.

I joined a study group in late 1939 together with Bela and two other enthusiastic girls, Mirka Nusbaum and Ania Miczacka. We met in Mirka's two-room apartment, while her parents went out during our lessons to leave more room for us. We sat around a table on which we put cards or domino pieces — our masquerade as a social gathering should the Germans knock at the door. Luckily, they never did, for it was entirely possible that once in the apartment, the Germans would have arrested us without even asking what we were gathered for. We were playing with fire, but somehow nothing happened to us.

I loved our classes and our teachers, all distinguished scholars with doctoral degrees. We developed a close relationship, very different from what we had known at our pre-war school, where the teachers stood at a distant podium.

Our biology teacher was Dr. Cygowa, a dignified woman of high scholarly standing. Her husband, Dr. Cygie, taught us mathematics and physics. They had earned their doctorates in Montpellier, France, where they had first met and fallen in love. Now they were in their late fifties, both with gray hair, blue eyes, and a gentle, innocent look like two big trusting children. They were devoted to each other, laughed easily, and treated us, their students, as friends and equals. Dr. Cygowa liked to talk about France, which she idealized, perhaps because she spent the best years of her life there. In those days it was very unusual for a woman to obtain a doctoral degree, and Dr. Cygowa was quite rightly very proud of hers. We met sometimes at the Cygies' apartment in a fine old Polish neighborhood not far from Jerozolimskie Avenue. There was no elevator, and we had to walk up four flights of stairs to arrive at a sunny, pleasant apartment of two rooms, a kitchen and a bathroom. Green plants were everywhere, and the

apartment seemed big enough for the husband and wife who had
no children. Both the Cygies were pale and had black shadows
around their eyes from malnutrition. One day, Dr. Cygowa
opened a pre-war box of delicious milk chocolate candies called
"Krówki" and offered them to us. The four of us each took one
candy; we could not resist. She looked sadly at us, and said that
we were young and needed more calories than we were getting.
She assured us that she was not hungry.

Gustawa Jarecka, who taught us Polish and French literature,
was not from our old school. She was a young woman writer who
had published a number of novels before the war. Her beautiful
blonde hair was arranged in two braids on the top of her head,
and her blue eyes shone with intelligence and integrity. She had
heard no news from her husband since he had run off toward the
East, and she and her two young children lived with her mother.
They supported themselves by selling their belongings, one item
after another. She was the first writer I had ever met, and I was
very impressed by her.

French was taught by the enthusiastic Franka Magidson,
while chemistry was taught by her less vivacious but competent
sister, Ida Magidson.

My favorite subject was history, taught by our excellent Dr.
Brams. It was a new experience for me to sit at the same table
with him, listening to him talk in a calm and composed voice
about other times and other wars. He gave the impression of
being in control, of understanding everything, and for an hour
we could forget the hell surrounding us. When we asked him to
explain our situation, and what the future would be, he assured us
that the Germans would lose the war, and he did not believe the
rumors that Hitler would attack Russia. He considered that too
stupid even for the insane dictator. For once, I dared to disagree
with my teacher, although I said nothing to him. Young as I was,
I knew that Hitler was irresponsible and incapable of any logic.
The war he had started was cruel and senseless, and one could
expect anything from people who let their predatory and demonic

instincts loose with such brute force. But our professor was too sophisticated, too civilized, to accept this. He predicted that after the war, Europe would unite and Germany, France and the other European countries would become friends and partners. There would be a United Federation of European States. I thought that he was dreaming.

One day I asked him timidly whether he had considered how to survive the Occupation, before the Germans became peaceful and worthy European citizens. He was not used to being asked direct questions by his students, and his answer was vague and condescending. I was disappointed. I felt the grip of death close by me and did not care about the future of Europe. I wanted to survive but did not know how. However, this topic was not in our curriculum; we were supposed to follow a regular one and to continue "normal" studies in the hope that the Germans would not have time to kill us all.

Much later, in 1942, Professor Brams, his wife and their young son left the Ghetto and found a place to live in the Polish or Aryan part of Warsaw. He and his wife each assumed a different name, which many people believed was safer in case one partner was caught or recognized as a Jew. The other partner could then get away without being traced. However, the woman superintendent of the building where the Brams lived found it most suspicious that such high-class people would live together unmarried, and even have a child out of wedlock, as at that time common-law marriage was considered a sin. The superintendent suspected the Brams of being Jewish and denounced them, and Dr. Brams, his wife, and their young son were murdered.

I learned about this tragedy after the war. I suspect that Dr. Brams believed, till the last moment of his life, that Germany would one day become an honorable European partner.

Refugees began to arrive in Warsaw in October 1939, right after the Occupation began. Either they were victims of the first resettlements or, having lost all their possessions during the hostilities, they hoped to find more opportunities in Warsaw. The Jews believed they would be safer there with so many others around.

Thus, one day in December, Mrs. Laufer, a dentist from a small town, arrived in our building. She rented one room in a pre-war tenant's apartment for herself, her unemployed husband and their son, Abram, a 30-year-old army veteran. Destitute, she hoped to earn some money by practising dentistry in their single room.

My parents had a lease guaranteeing them the exclusive right to practise their profession in our apartment building, and the arrival of this woman dentist provoked an angry outburst from some of our neighbors. They were concerned that my parents would lose patients to her, and advised my parents to exercise their rights and force her to leave. My mother smiled sadly and answered, "Don't you understand that we are all doomed? This is no time to worry about money and fight for patients. All I want is to buy bread for my family and survive, as does my refugee colleague. May she live in peace, here among us." My mother realized, though others did not, what was happening. Pre-war mentality and aspirations did not change rapidly, and many people continued to believe that we could maintain a style of life similar to what we had before the Occupation. My mother sensed the danger over our heads; she had a foreboding of the coming catastrophe.

Mrs. Laufer was a distinguished and cultured woman with gentle manners and a soft voice. Probably in her fifties, she looked tired and much older, her once-beautiful face wrinkled and her hair gone gray. Somehow, she did not establish much of a practice. She had very few patients, and she and her family often went hungry.

My mother sent her food from time to time—not enough, unfortunately. We ourselves had little food, and my parents shared it with family and friends. None of us ate enough to completely satisfy our hunger, but at least we were not starving.

I often carried food across our courtyard to Mrs. Laufer. One day when I went there I found her sitting wrapped in sweaters in her clean but barely heated room, visibly uneasy at accepting the food. I tried to tell her with my eyes that it was all right. Her warm, brown eyes answered me that she was grateful. She smiled and asked me to thank my mother. We talked little; she was aware that I felt embarrassed. She told me, "Remember, Irene, your parents are good people. Be proud of them. Should you ever in your life experience hardship, may the thought of your parents' kind hearts sustain you."

Her son had been mobilized on the first day of September 1939 and had tried in vain to reach his regiment. The Germans were advancing fast and the Polish soldiers could not stop them, though they fought desperately and with enormous courage. The lack of communication between units soon degenerated into complete chaos. Abram was wandering around the countryside looking for his unit when he met some soldiers whose regiment had been destroyed. They were trying to reorganize, and they gave Abram a uniform and ordered him to join them. The group was hiding in the forest trying to contact the Polish army when they fell into combat with some Germans. The Poles were heroic, but the Germans were stronger. Abram was hit and fell, and two dead soldiers fell on top of him. The Germans left the corpses behind, and Abram's life was saved when he was discovered by Polish farmers. The local doctor cut off his injured leg without anesthetic and Abram was hidden in the village until he could walk with a stick and rejoin his parents. Only then was a primitive wooden leg fastened to his knee. Shortly afterwards, Abram and his parents were expelled with the other Jews from their town, and came to Warsaw.

I met Abram when he was talking with our Polish janitor at the entrance to the building. He liked to stand there during the safer moments when the Germans were not around. I knew that he was only 30 years old, but he looked like an old man. Abram was very gallant to me—maybe I reminded him of a girl with whom he had danced, talked and laughed in his younger years, when he had his two legs, a home and a future. And all I could say was, "Hello, how are you? Nice to meet you." I was shy, as he was, and we did not talk much.

Karolina and I had outgrown our winter coats, and my mother decided to have new ones made for us. An unemployed tailor was eager to do the job, and found nice material for us, but we needed fur for our collars because Polish winters were rigorous. There was a chance to find some fur pieces on Franciszkaîska Street, a commercial artery full of Jewish businesses which somehow had not been destroyed during the bombing. My mother asked me to come with her.

We had been told that the Germans were regularly robbing the Jewish stores on this street. What happened was this: the German trucks arrived daily, early in the morning and the stores were meticulously emptied, one by one. The Jews were rounded up and, with whips, forced to load the trucks. The screaming Germans, in a real or simulated frenzy, kicked and whipped the men, forcing them to empty the seized stores faster. They could not stop to rest for a moment, and their faces sweating, their eyes downcast, the Jews held back screams of pain and continued loading the trucks.

But the district housed such an enormous wealth of merchandise that the Germans could not steal it all at once, so they worked on a few blocks at a time, concentrating on their immediate prey and leaving the rest of the street alone. The owners of the robbed stores stood by, looking helplessly at their misfortune, while the other merchants tried desperately to sell their goods before the trucks reached them. It was no use keeping a store closed, because the Germans would smash and destroy it completely. That was why the stores were open: the merchants hoped to at least save their premises from damage, and perhaps sell some goods before they were looted.

We were afraid to go there, but we had no choice and when we did go, we saw huge German trucks parked in front of the Jewish businesses. Some occupied the whole building, housing textile, fur, or other merchandise on the upper floors, while their main floor stores were transacting wholesale and retail business. But even these main floor stores looked like warehouses overflowing with the merchandise and displaying it in bulk in their windows. They attracted the out-of-town as well as the Warsaw clients because of the quality and quantity of the merchandise and "no frill" prices.

Before the war, the district was bustling with life, the buyers anticipating good buys, the merchants good sales. People were hopeful and excited — money was changing hands. Now the atmosphere was full of terror, grief, and chaos. The street was swarming with Poles from Warsaw and the countryside, often hostile and arrogant, trying to buy goods for next to nothing. The honest people transacted business quietly, politely and often thanked the merchants for the bargain. But the situation attracted masses of profiteers who taunted the merchants ready to sell their possessions for a piece of bread.

We were careful to stay away from the Germans and their trucks, and my mother and I were greeted warmly by many merchants standing in front of their as-yet-unlooted stores. They were her pre-war patients. We easily found two fur pieces and my mother asked the price. The merchant looked sadly at his former dentist and said: "Please pay me ten zíotys [Polish currency, roughly the equivalent of two dollars]. That is less than one third of its value. I know that the Germans will be here soon, but I cannot give it to you for nothing, I have a family to feed."

Just then two Polish men entered the store, grabbed as many large fur pieces as they could hold, shouting, "Jew, give it to us for one zíoty! If you don't 'sell' to us now, you'll give it to the Germans for nothing tomorrow."

The merchant pleaded, "How can you do that to me? Please . . ." But the men continued gleefully, "Jew, give it to us, give it, your time is up!"

My mother paid the merchant requested price and shook hands with him. For a long moment they looked at each other, the merchant's face flushed and his eyes shining from tears, anger, or fever.

In this lawless, chaotic, hopeless time, the American Joint Distribution Committee (known as Joint or AJDC), stood by the Jews and helped us in many ways. The Joint is a Jewish non-profit organization, akin to the Christian Caritas and dedicated to helping needy Jews around the world. In this connection, I will mention only what happened to our relative, Józef Lautenberg. Before the war he was a prosperous manufacturer of men's shirts. My father's sister, Rosa, married Józef's son, Ignacy, who was chief cutter and associate manager of his family business. Józef Lautenberg rightly feared that his merchandise would be stolen by the Germans, so he delivered it to the Joint representative and received a voucher for its value to be redeemed after the war. We had no idea what the Joint did with the merchandise, and giving away goods in exchange for a piece of paper seemed even more chancy that keeping them. But as it turned out Mr. Lautenberg was wise. After the war we met in Paris, where the Joint had its headquarters. Mr. Lautenberg, an old man then, asked me to assist him, and we went together to the Joint office, where he actually did receive money for his voucher.

The apartment buildings in our neighborhood were at that time very different from the ones we see today in North America. Each block was only three or four floors high, built around a rectangular courtyard. In the wealthier areas, these courtyards had trees and grass, but in our neighborhood they were simply covered with asphalt, cobblestones, or plain beaten earth. A large, tunnel-like entrance, opened by a high, ornamental iron gate, led from the courtyard out into the street. This entrance was used by trucks and pedestrians alike.

Every apartment building had a superintendent, who was respected by everybody, especially the children. He was in charge of the courtyard, responsible for keeping it clean and secure. He also closed the big iron gate at eleven o'clock every night, and any tenant who came in later had to ring for him to open it and tip him for his trouble.

When I was a child there had been grass and some beautiful, old trees in the center of our courtyard, surrounded by an iron fence. Although children could not play inside the garden, which was kept locked, they were always playing around it. But I was forbidden to join them, and used to watch wistfully from our apartment windows.

A few years before the war, the green square had been replaced by a huge garage for the trucks of the factory which occupied the whole left wing of our residential section, together with an adjoining smaller courtyard. A wooden gate led from one courtyard to the other. The factory was called Opus, a company that must have employed more than 100 people, working in dry cleaning and the manufacture of men's shirts.

Almost all the windows in our large front apartment overlooked the treeless expanse of Pawia Street and the bare brick wall of the Pawiak prison. Although our view was only of the prison guards' dining room, it was considered more fashionable to have an apartment with windows looking out on to the street, and so these apartments were more expensive. But on the other side of our apartment, the dining room and laboratory windows looked on to the courtyard, which was often even noisier than the street. Air conditioning was then unheard of, and the windows were kept open almost constantly, unless the bitter cold made it impossible. We lived among active, energetic people; the familiar sounds of meat and onions being chopped for dinner, or the laughter and voices of the children playing, still echo in my ears.

But after September 1939, all that had changed. For one thing, a curfew was imposed. Instead of the superintendent closing the gate at eleven p.m., the Germans ordered it closed at nine and sometimes even as early as seven or eight o'clock. At one time, as a special punishment, the curfew was at five o'clock.

In addition, the Opus factory lost its Jewish owners. It was Mr. Lewin, the head of the family business, who had committed suicide by jumping out of the window while he was being arrested by the Germans. The whole property was expropriated shortly thereafter, and a German administrator was put in charge. Fortunately, he was a decent, friendly person. He became my father's patient, and proved himself to be a good and honest man.

In fact, he made it possible for my father to render a great service to Dr. Blumstein, the director of the Gymnasium and Lyceum that Karolina and I had attended. Dr. Blumstein and his wife were refined people — they both held doctoral degrees, he in mathematics, she in biology. But now they felt helpless, for they had lost their apartment during the bombing, and, like many others, had difficulty finding a new one, since so much of Warsaw had been destroyed. But in October there was an apartment vacant in our building, and my father used his influence with the German administrator to let the Blumsteins move into it. The administrator could easily have demanded a huge amount of money for this favor, but he did not ask for a single zíoty. And my father was glad to be able to help Dr. Blumstein — who proved later unworthy of his kindness.

At this time, Mr. Luka, our friend and neighbor from the ground floor, was arrested for being a Christian foreman in a Jewish business. Terror gripped us. Our building was no more a safe place, and different noises came from our courtyard. Every day now, trucks would arrive to load and remove the merchandise and machinery which the Germans were systematically stealing from the Opus factory. They arrived every morning between eight and nine o'clock and stayed until noon. We were usually warned of their approach by the Germans' yelling and the clamor of their heavy trucks. Everyone ran inside, kept away from windows, and was careful not to attract the Germans' attention. But often the trucks arrived so abruptly that they took us by surprise, and some tenants would be caught outside and rounded up, together with any unlucky Jewish men who were nearby. The men were forced to carry heavy bundles or even machines to the awaiting trucks. Many of these men were elderly, some were sick or handicapped, and all were unaccustomed to this kind of work. They were insulted, pushed and mercilessly beaten. We could hear people screaming with pain, whips lashing, the Germans shouting, their dogs barking. The blood left on the ground spoke of the daily horrors in our courtyard.

The Germans always succeeded in rounding up people, for the streets were crowded. People had to attend to their daily occupations: going to work, selling their meager merchandise on the streets, transacting business there, or simply moving from one place to another. They could not afford the luxury of staying locked in their apartments all the time.

One day Adam Birman was caught by the Germans in our courtyard. He was a dental mechanic who did freelance work for several dentists, and visited my father's laboratory regularly to use his equipment. But this time he was grabbed by the soldiers as he was approaching the building. He was pushed and punched in the face, but when the Germans turned away to beat up someone else, Adam, who knew the building well, ran up the back stairway and rang at the kitchen entrance of our apartment. Our maid, Stefa, opened the door. She saw his face covered with blood and his whole body shaking while he wiped his shoes on the doormat. Yet she shut the door in his face, saying, "Wipe your dirty shoes before you enter my clean kitchen." Adam, in terror of being discovered by the Germans at any moment, rang and rang. We came to see what the commotion was about, and my mother opened the door and brought him quickly into the apartment, where he was able to take some tea in our room and rest until the Germans had gone. My father dressed his bloody face, while Stefa looked on and said nothing.

Later, my mother asked her gently, "Stefa, why were you so cruel to Adam? It is not like you to be nasty and hurt people."

Stefa repeated, "I worked hard to wash the kitchen floor, and Adam's shoes were dirty, dirty." Angry and miserable, she added, "Adam should have shown more respect for my work and more consideration for me." She never apologized to Adam nor showed any remorse for her cruel behavior, but she never repeated it either.

Stefa's own story was a sad one. Her father owned a very small piece of land but in order to support his family he had to work for a rich neighbor for long hours every day. And still the family lived in abject poverty. Her mother contracted tuberculosis and died when Stefa, her oldest child, was only nine years old. Her father soon remarried. Stefa's stepmother was supposed to work their piece of land, do the housework, and take care of the children. She always seemed ill-natured, abused Stefa verbally and physically, and expected her to do work beyond her age. Stefa went to school from time to time, and though she could recognize the alphabet, she could not read. She learned to sign her name, but that was all the education she received.

When her brothers and sisters grew up, Stefa's help was no longer needed, and she was forced to leave her father's house and her village. Unmarried and humiliated, called a good-for-nothing old maid at 22, she came to Warsaw in search of work, and found a job as a maid. Her successive employers had been harsh and demanding and paid her very little.

Stefa Redke came to live with us in 1935. She seemed contented in our home. And in 1940, she was a single woman of 33, pretty, graceful and vivacious. (She was also very healthy, and the monastic life of a maid must have been hard on her.)

I liked Stefa and tried to understand why she had so badly mistreated Adam. I asked myself, did Stefa resent the fact that he was a bachelor who didn't seem to be interested in courting her?

When Adam lost his father at the age of four, his heavy-set mother had to support herself, her daughter and her son by selling bagels from a basket on Smocza Street. She sent Adam, her younger child, to the Orphans Home for Jewish Children, known as Korczak's Orphanage. It was a modern, secular orphanage directed by its founder, Dr. Janusz Korczak, who understood the plight of all mistreated children and was totally devoted to his orphans. They found warmth and security in the care they received from the "good doctor" and his assistant Stefania WilczyÆska, who were always available to comfort, listen to and advise their pupils.

The children were taught that they had a right to be understood and respected, and that no one had a right to abuse them. They were also taught that they should be just and honest, forgiving toward themselves and toward others. The democratic rule was applied by the institution of the children's self-government and their court of peers. Children pronounced verdicts — some acted as prosecutors, others as judges or advocates. Physical punishment was never applied in the orphanage. This innovative and advanced approach to the children's education was introduced by Dr. Korczak himself, who was a medical doctor, as well as an exceptional pedagogue and defender of children's rights through his lectures and writings. "Janusz Korczak" was at first only a pen name of Hersh/Henryk Goldszmit, born on July 22, 1878, into a Jewish middle-class family. But when his writing and his ideas became known, people referred to him exclusively under his pen name. Even though he no longer used his father's name, Dr. Korczak never denied his origin nor renounced being a Jew. And later, much later, he accepted deportation from the Warsaw Ghetto to die with his children.

Adam was happy at the orphanage and would have liked to stay there as long as possible. But when the youngsters reached 15 or 16, Dr. Korczak tried to help them to learn a trade and become independent. My father agreed to take on Adam as an apprentice, and he and Adam became friends. Once he was trained as a dental mechanic, Adam devoted his life to supporting his mother and older sister, who was slightly retarded. The three of them lived in a small apartment on Pawia Street, not far from us. Adam never married.

Since the beginning of the war, everyone's main preoccupation had been to buy and stock up on anything that could be preserved. People were acquiring as many non—perishable goods as they could afford, and so merchandise was disappearing rapidly from the stores and prices were skyrocketing. There was a panic run on most staples: flour, sugar, salt, lard, soap, candles and matches. Of course, Stefa had free access to our store of fresh and stocked food: she was one of us, we trusted her, and she was in charge of the kitchen. Yet, one day, we discovered that she was stealing our food. She was not hungry, and did not have any family in the city to give it to; she simply gave away our food, offering it to casual acquaintances.

Why? My mother never confronted her. It was too dangerous to antagonize a Christian girl. She could easily bring disaster to a Jewish family. She could report us to the Gestapo for any real or imaginary non-compliance with the hundreds of orders issued by the Germans. Non-compliance always brought the most brutal punishment: instant death or deportation.

The Germans continued their plundering of Jewish homes, and one day somebody ran in to warn us that two Germans were on the way to check our apartment, looking for the gold which they believed all dentists had. The most incriminating things in our possession at that time were two long bars of ordinary soap; the Germans could use it as pretext to accuse us, the Jews, of the crime of hoarding and speculating. It was too late to leave the apartment and dispose of the soap. What could we do? My parents looked helplessly at each other. Stefa spoke up. "Let me pretend to be sick and to sit on my bed and conceal the soap. The Germans will not touch me because I am not Jewish." My mother objected, "Stefa, you cannot do it. You will be punished if the soap is discovered." "No, I will not, I will say that it is mine and I am a Christian," said Stefa.

We heard heavy footsteps and shouting on the stairway, and the Germans entered the apartment. My father had just the time to leave by the back door. My mother confronted the "visitors." They were big, heavy and loud, and demanded gold. My mother, who spoke German fluently, explained that my father made teeth with porcelain rather than gold. She showed them the "Made in Germany" oven for baking porcelain teeth. Her blonde hair, her professional white coat, and the medical character of the establishment must have impressed the brutes. They didn't touch anything but went from room to room looking around. In the kitchen, they saw Stefa sitting on her bed and loudly asked, "What are you, a pretty Aryan girl, doing in a Jewish home?" Stefa said nothing. They shook their heads with disapproval but did not touch her or her bed. After a few minutes, which seemed longer than eternity to us all, they finally left. Stefa sat on her bed a while longer before she took the soap and gave it back to my mother. She looked like a child proudly presenting her parents with a good school report.

A year later, just before the Ghetto was sealed, the Christians were ordered to leave our area. Stefa cried and refused to leave us. She had no place to go, she said. "You see, once back in my village, without a job, I would be deported for slave work in Germany."

My mother explained, "Please, Stefa, try to understand. You must leave because we are doomed, but you have a chance to survive."

Stefa became angry, "You don't like me, you want get rid of me, you are rejecting me after all these years of faithful service!" My mother took Stefa's hands into her own, dried her tears, and tried to calm her. Finally, she persuaded Stefa that she must leave us, and gave her some food to take with her. Stefa was crying as I embraced her. I never saw her again, though my mother sent her a message after the war. We heard that she was still living in her village, but she never came to see us.

Adam and his family did not survive. They were murdered by the Germans in 1942.

At the beginning of the Occupation, word spread among the Jewish population that we should go into mourning. Women should wear their hair naturally and not go to hairdressers. We should not wear hats, but cover our heads with modest scarves. Movie houses and theaters were closed, while private dances, musical recitals, and artistic performances were all considered improper. We were to lead very subdued lives, and everyone should stay at home as much as possible. We were a nation grieving.

But the consequences of this were very serious. The craftsmen and artists had no jobs and no bread. Business premises stayed empty. Meanwhile our population swelled daily with masses of Jewish refugees desperately looking for jobs. So for the sake of economic survival, the directives were changed. People were instead encouraged to spend money, for today we were alive, and tomorrow we might be dead. It was selfish to keep money; we should share it with others by consuming. It became proper and laudable to use the services of hairdressers, dressmakers, tailors, dentists, doctors, teachers, and artisans or craftsmen.

My mother, now forty-three, returned to her pre-war hairdresser and once again became a steady client. The owner of the salon allowed two refugees to work there, even though there were not enough clients for the three of them. My mother noticed one of them looking at her with imploring eyes. He wanted her to let him take care of her hair. So on her next visit, when the owner was busy with another client, my mother let the refugee cut her hair.

She came home quite upset, unhappy with the result. I reproached her for pitying the man so, for thinking more of the hairdresser's needs than of her own. "Please promise me you'll never let this man touch your hair again," I said. But the next time she went to the salon and the same refugee hairdresser jumped up to meet her, his sad eyes pleading. She let him set her hair again; and although he was not as good as her pre-war hairdresser, she remained his client for as long as he stayed there. She told me, "Try to understand, Irene, the owner of the salon has enough clients to survive, while the refugee, Mr. Paul, has not. He has a family to support and they are hungry."

The days were gloomy during our first winter under the Occupation, but the evenings were worse. The apartment was cold. The electricity had been cut again, and we could afford only one small candle to light the room we lived in. After the curfew, neighbors from our building dropped in to exchange news and talk over the horrors of the day. The passing of a car on the street made everyone shiver, for it could only be the Germans bringing brutal beatings or death. Conversation would stop abruptly. We would listen. When the car did not stop at our building, we were safe for the moment. And so we lived in constant terror, every day bringing more disastrous news.

People grasped at every possible shred of hope, and many thought again of escaping to the eastern part of Poland, now occupied by the Russians. But since September we had no news about the people who had left Warsaw. Many were certainly killed, either by German bombs and machine-guns, or by bandits who would murder them for no more than a watch or a few zíotys. And the women and children who had stayed behind, hungry and without resources, were still waiting for their husbands and fathers to return and protect them. Yet these men, a short while ago responsible heads of families, had become — if they were still alive — only powerless Jews.

Some of the refugees to the East decided to return home because they were starving. Things got worse when the Russians began deportations to Siberia. The refugees coming back thought of their pre-war life: they had no idea of the horrors perpetrated by the Germans, much less of the atrocities that still awaited us. Some could have survived in the East or escaped across the borders to Lithuania or Romania, yet they returned. They did so out of a sense of duty, believing that they would be able to protect their families. Some young people were unable to endure the separation, and chose to live or die with their mothers and fathers, brothers and sisters.

But not many returned, and the clandestine exodus toward the East continued. It was a perilous journey; for one thing, the road became increasingly difficult as the Germans and their collaborators got better organized and watched every possible route. They were looking for fugitives, and those they caught were often murdered after a cruel beating. Men and women were subjected to brutal anal searches for money, diamonds, jewelry, and gold. Women's genitals were searched as well. Some people were caught, beaten and robbed, but left alive and forced to retrace their steps back to occupied territory. Still people ran for the East, and not all were caught.

When the Ghetto was sealed on December 16, 1940, escape to the East became practically impossible. Nonetheless, people continued to try. All hope was lost on June 22, 1941, when the Germans attacked Russia and closed the border completely.

The somber months under the Occupation dragged on. Our family continued to sleep, eat and live in one room. So far we had succeeded in heating it, albeit slightly, along with the adjoining Szmits' room, as well as one dental office and the kitchen we shared with the Szmits. Although many pre-war patients, Jewish and non-Jewish, remained faithful to my parents, our waiting room was now often empty. People had no money; they rarely visited dentists. Wearing their coats and boots, our patients waited in the chilly room, once the bright dining room where we'd had so many joyous meals and gatherings.

Sunday was usually a day off. Thus, I was very surprised when, one Sunday, my father announced somewhat mysteriously that he was expecting two patients. He asked me to stay out of the waiting room. Such an unexpected and bizarre order aroused my curiosity and I kept watch. My father let a woman in and left the room, leaving her alone, waiting. But for whom, or what? I opened the door slightly. She saw me, said my name, and asked me to come in. I barely recognized her as Mrs. Szwedowa, pale, thin, and wearing a widow's black veil. Once a wealthy lady, she was now impoverished, and looked very tired, her hands shaking.

Before the war, she had been an elegant and gracious woman with a beautiful apartment and many friends. But when she lost her husband, her only son, Józio, rebelled. He rejected middle-class values and became politically active. Shortly after the Germans entered Warsaw, he and his friend, Zosia Zatorska, a Jewish girl also from a well-to-do family, decided to convert the German soldiers into peaceful human beings. They distributed anti-war pamphlets appealing to the soldiers' reason and humanity. The two young Jewish idealists, about twenty years old at the time, believed they could convince Germans to change their allegiance — simply by explaining to them the truth about Hitler and the Nazis.

Józio and Zosia were arrested, held in Pawiak prison, and tortured. They tried to commit suicide by swallowing pieces of glass, but to no avail. They were saved, and tortured again.

Like many other mothers, Mrs. Szwedowa spent long hours in cold, windy or rainy weather in front of the entrance to the Pawiak prison. They all brought parcels for their loved ones, even though there was no assurance that the prisoners would ever receive them.

Mrs. Szwedowa had been a patient of my parents for a long time, and knew that a number of Polish prison guards were also among their patients. She asked my father to help her meet a prison guard, a good and honest Polish patriot, who could give her news about her only son and maybe take a parcel to him. Certainly many pre-war Polish guards hated the Nazis and were sympathetic to the Polish prisoners, regardless of their religion. But the guards wanted to keep their jobs and, like everybody else, they were afraid of the Germans. In addition, any one of them might have chosen to became a spy for the Germans. It was very risky to approach a guard.

Nevertheless, my father decided to help Mrs. Szwedowa. He asked a guard, whom he believed to be trustworthy, to come for his dental appointment on Sunday. Mrs. Szwedowa waited for the man alone in our cold waiting room. He came, they talked. He was very understanding. Did she pay him? It is possible, but I truly don't know. Mrs. Szwedowa saw him again, but that was the last time she came to our home. Shortly afterwards, her son and Zosia Zatorska were murdered.

On December 1, 1939, the order was issued that all Jews must wear armbands on their right arm, a blue Star of David on white material. It was a strange feeling to be singled out this way. Many people said that they were proud to wear the star because they were proud of being Jews; yet I felt ambivalent about this "distinction." My parents, who were not religious, had brought me up simply as a Pole and we had many Polish friends. But because of the morbid, virulent anti-Semitism that prevailed in Poland at that time, I could not feel entirely Polish.

In one sense the distinctive armband freed me from any hesitation as to my identity; the problem of who I was had been solved for me. But on the other hand, I felt humiliated and deprived of my right to be treated equally with other Poles. I felt that by wearing the armband I was officially classified as different and inferior. We Jews were branded as animals for slaughter, banished from society, targeted for persecution. We were hated. We were not sure how people would treat us on the street, even though we could still walk freely anywhere in Warsaw. The armbands showed clearly that we were Jews, and that gave free license to anyone to mistreat us.

One day Karolina and I were walking on Marszaíkowska Street, a main commercial artery. It was a bright, sunny April day. The air, though still cold, was fresh and invigorating, and it was a pleasure to walk, with the worst of the winter months behind us.

Suddenly we heard an uproar and saw a crowd in front of us. For a moment we did not understand what was going on. Then we heard people saying that the commotion was being caused by "the sick woman." She was already well known in Warsaw, a big strong woman who was insane, or pretended to be. She was fulfilling her "divine" mission of destroying and mutilating Jewish faces. She wore special gloves with sharp iron nails, and acting in a kind of frenzy, aimed her hands at her victim's face.

Karolina and I were now in the center of an hysterical crowd that was shouting and encouraging the woman, enjoying the anticipation of a bloody spectacle. Surrounded by this hostile crowd, we could not run back without drawing attention to ourselves. We could be caught by the friends of the "sick" woman. Then we saw an empty droshky passing near us. It stopped and the coachman gestured to us, saying, "Young ladies, climb up quickly and cover your armbands." We covered ourselves with our scarves and got into the droshky. It moved forward, slowly, because of the crowd. As we passed the woman, she turned in our direction and I saw for a moment her distorted, feverish face.

I felt faint, and for a moment my heart stopped beating. Then somebody shouted: "Look—here is a Jew!" She turned in the direction of a man wearing the armband with the Star of David and grabbed him. As our droshky moved on, I heard the victim's screams and people shouting and laughing.

On another occasion, a lovely, sunny day in June 1940, I took my nine-year-old cousin, Jadwiga, to Saxony Gardens for a walk. I longed to get away from our crowded, smelly neighborhood and see again trees and green grass—I'd almost forgotten how they looked. And Jadwiga, my Uncle Monos' only child, would also enjoy some fresh air and tranquility and a view of the flowers and trees. Her family lived on Pawia Street, only a few blocks away from us, and though my Aunt Freda was very protective of her young daughter, she gave me permission to take her for a walk. Jadwiga did not wear an armband because children up to 10 or 12 years old were exempted. I covered mine by holding a coat over my right arm. I felt so proud to be taking care of Jadwiga.

We strolled in the park. When we sat down on a bench to rest, we caught the attention of a group of teenagers. The boys said, "Hey, what are two nice ladies doing here alone? You are so pretty, we are in love with you and would like to marry the older one. We will wait for the younger until she grows up." They were merry, joking and laughing.

I was relieved that they were only talking, and didn't come too close. But Jadwiga became frightened. "Irene" she whispered, "I want to go home."

I pretended that we considered the boys' talk innocent fun. "We like you young men very much," I said "and we will certainly return here tomorrow to meet you again. Good-bye for now." As we stood up to go, my overcoat fell from my arm.

The boys saw my armband, and their behavior immediately became hostile. "Jewesses! Oh, blessed Jesus! We wanted to marry a Jewess," they shouted and crossed themselves as if they had met two witches. We hurried away, frightened, before they could attack us.

My mother heard about a bakery in the Polish section of the city that sold fresh bread. It was a long time since we had tasted such a delicacy, and since it was only a 40 minute walk from our home, she and Mrs. Szmit asked me to go buy bread, and possibly a few rolls. I did not like to venture into the Polish section wearing my armband, but I went. It was early in the morning, the day was cold but sunny, and after a long walk I arrived at the bakery.

It was full of people, and I was the only person there with a Jewish armband. The talk stopped as I entered, and the crowded store became very quiet. I felt all eyes fixed on me. People moved away. I tried to look self-assured as I approached the counter, walking slowly and looking straight into people's eyes. I placed my order, speaking clearly and evenly in my educated Polish. I expected to be insulted and thrown out, but that did not happen.

Some people returned my gaze with a look of sadness and sympathy; a few smiled at me, slightly, imperceptibly. But no one said a word.

In my own country, in my own city, I had become a leper. Yet this time I was allowed to return safely home, with a bag full of fresh bread and rolls.

By January 1940 large numbers of Jewish refugees were arriving daily in Warsaw, as they were deported from other parts of Poland in the middle of that cold winter. They were freezing, they were hungry, and they had little hope to survive. We knew that the Germans would lose the war, but we didn't know if we would live long enough to see it happen.

My studies were my salvation. I was now studying intensively the two-year lyceum curriculum in preparation for the Matura, and this helped me to go on living in spite of the Germans. My life was at their mercy — but not my mind. I tried to preserve my inner self, to keep it untouched by the daily horrors.

One evening I was sitting at my desk in our room, doing my homework. Our room was chilly and dark, for blackout had been imposed and the only window was covered by a blanket and a heavy cotton shade and tightly closed drapes. The slightest ray of escaping light could attract the attention of the Germans, and so could be the cause of death. Outside, I knew, Pawia Street was dark and cold but still full of hurrying pedestrians, people peddling all kinds of merchandise, beggars imploring passers-by for a piece of bread. The street lamps were turned off, and the only light came from the smelly carbide lamps on the merchants' carts or baskets. Even this meager light would disappear at the curfew. People tried to take advantage of the safer early evenings, for the Germans usually finished their business before dark and the terror of their possible reappearance at night was still remote.

Mr. Szmit walked into our room. Though he wore a heavy sweater under his woolen jacket, his first act was to station himself by the tiles of the stove, everybody's favorite place. We filled it with wood and a little of our precious stock of coal every other day. The first day, the porcelain tiles were deliciously warm; the second day, they became lukewarm.

Mr. Szmit warmed first his hands and then his back. Then he turned toward me. Wrapped in two woolen sweaters and a heavy skirt, wearing winter shoes, I still felt cold. But Mr. Szmit's big, brown eyes looked at me with a solicitude that warmed my heart. I liked the gentle smile at the corners of his lips. I liked his presence, and felt safer with him there. I enjoyed our long conversations. In the middle of the growing terror of 1940, he was calm and thoughtful. His stories made the past half-century come alive before my eyes.

He had come to Warsaw from a small town in Lithuania a long time ago, growing up in the years before the First World War. He had been brought up in the Jewish tradition, knew the Hebrew Bible well, and quoted from it often. Although he was not a practising Jew, he was a wise man who found in Judaism answers to many life problems. He treated me as an adult; yet, he constantly reminded me that I had a whole life ahead of me. "You will survive, Irene," he reassured me. "Your future will be bright and meaningful."

But I was scared; I felt that my future was as dark as the night behind the window. I feared the coming spring of 1940, the spring I had once so eagerly awaited, the spring of my sixteenth year. Before 1939, I had been impatient to be sixteen, the age of my idol Deanna Durbin. Like her, I had wanted to laugh, dance and have lots of admirers. Now I was frightened of reaching that age. I feared the cruelty of the Germans, who were running our streets. Their sadistic appetite was not abated by the cold, overcast days, nor was their furious energy. How would they behave during the sunny spring? Would any woman be safe?

Mr. Szmit did not share my anxieties. "The Germans do not have women in mind. They yearn for blood and destruction. Murder appeals to them, not women," he said. I was not convinced, and we changed the subject.

We talked about school and education. Mr. Szmit agreed with my parents, who wanted my sister and me to have professional careers. But I doubted my abilities and felt a strange longing for something other than my studies—although I could not describe what it was. I knew the spring would make this inner anxiety, this nostalgic feeling, even stronger.

"Does everyone have to be a perfect, educated professional?" I asked my friend.

He smiled. "Let me tell you the following tale: Many years ago, in Warsaw, before 1914, there was a young dentist who did not like his work. He enjoyed nice clothes, amusing company, good food and interesting conversation. He spent his time socializing, talking and drinking coffee or expensive liquor. His father had to support him and worried about his future. Then, one day, someone decided to open a private school of dentistry in Warsaw. And guess what happened? The likable dentist was chosen as the first director of the school—not, of course, for his professional achievements, but for his good looks and his know-how with people. So you see, Irene, there is a place in this world for everyone, and there will certainly be a place for you, God willing."

I laughed. It was so pleasant chatting with Mr. Szmit. He believed in God: "God will help us," he would repeat. His words took the chill from the cold room. For a brief moment, I was able to forget about the Germans.

But shortly after this conversation a terrible thing happened to my friend. He looked after his son-in-law's business daily, as his daughter and her husband were somewhere in Eastern Poland. He was always back at home at four p.m., before dark. But one day, he did not return on time. Hours passed and still Mr. Szmit had not come home. The curfew was approaching. His wife became frantic and kept watch in the cold corridor next to the entrance. It was nearly nine p.m. when I heard a commotion at our door. Mr. Szmit staggered in, went immediately to his room, and collapsed. His wife followed him and shut the door. What had happened? My father went in to see him.

I learned the truth bit by bit. Mr. Szmit had been caught on the street by a gang of uniformed Germans and forced with other Jews to do sit-ups and other "gymnastics." He could not explain how, at his age of 56, he had been able to do it, in the middle of the street, with the Germans whipping him, pushing him and mocking him. He was terrified. He was mortified.

His life had only been saved because the gang caught some bearded Jews and found more fun in plucking their beards and mutilating their faces. The Jews previously caught for sit-ups had to stand to attention and watch the spectacle. The "fun" lasted for over an hour, while more and more men were seized and subjected to this torture. Finally, the Germans had enough and let the men go.

Mr. Szmit was so crushed he did not leave his room for weeks. My father tried to convince him not to feel humiliated by what the Germans had done to him. His wife, an educated woman and a dentist like my mother, sneaked tranquilizers into his ersatz coffee, and tried to encourage him by talking about the future when they would be reunited with their daughter.

It was his love for his daughter, and a sense of duty toward her, that brought Mr. Szmit back to life; he had promised to watch over her husband's business. But when after many weeks he returned to my room again, I saw an old man with a pale and sunken face. His left eye and lip trembled constantly.

He asked me what I was learning in my underground classes. I told him about Professor Brams hope for a united Europe. Mr. Szmit smiled, and asked me to repeat, again and again, what Professor Brams told us about the future peace and understanding among European countries.

Mr. Szmit did not live to see the future peace. He and his wife were murdered at the end of 1942. His daughter survived the war. Her husband did not.

FOUR

LIFE IN THE WARSAW GHETTO

The summer of 1940 was hot, the air oppressive. Our neighborhood became even more crowded as thousands of bewildered Jews continued to arrive in Warsaw daily. They had terrifying stories to tell of forced resettlements, brutalities and murder. All over Poland, Jewish communities were being closed, their inhabitants forced out or, even worse, deported — destination unknown. Most people arrived destitute, with nothing more than small bundles. They became the first victims of disease and starvation.

The refugees hoped that they would stay in Warsaw till the end of the war — that would come soon — and the Germans would have no time to hurt them further.

We Jews were branded as an inferior race, as carriers of diseases. And the Christian Poles, called Aryans, had to be protected from contact with us. We were already segregated from them by the obligatory armbands. But as early as November 1939, rumors were spreading that we were to be confined in a quarantine zone to prevent the spread of epidemics. This was the reason given for the resettlements and the herding of the Jews into one area. Yet, in spite of persistent rumors, we did not believe in the forthcoming total imprisonment.

The summer passed, and the windy fall arrived. People worried about heating and food. Then, at the beginning of October, the order to create a closed Jewish district became official. On

October 12 the street loudspeakers announced to the public that all Jews must relocate into the Ghetto, and all Aryans must move out by October 31.

Panic-stricken Jews tried to exchange their apartments on the so-called Aryan side of Warsaw for apartments in the Jewish district. The out-of-town Jews tried desperately to find a place to stay within the Ghetto. The entire Jewish population was frantic. As the Aryan Poles could hardly move out in such a short time, the Germans extended the deadline to November 15. On November 16, 1940, the Ghetto was sealed.

I wanted to help Dr. Cygowa, my dear biology teacher, who was unable to exchange her small apartment for one in the Ghetto. There were many more Jews entering the Ghetto than Aryan Poles leaving it. Aryans could easily exchange a small basement apartment for a large one, in a fashionable neighborhood — together with its expensive furniture. The Jews could not sell their furniture, as no one was willing to pay for it. And there was no place for much furniture in their new quarters in the Ghetto.

I ran all around our neighborhood trying to find an apartment for Dr. Cygie and her husband, but I found nothing. Resigned and sad, they left behind their precious books and plants and most of their possessions and moved into one room in somebody else's apartment. They had to share the kitchen and the toilet.

The Ghetto was surrounded by a three-metre-high brick wall. About 400,000 Jews were imprisoned within an area of 307 hectares (about 760 acres) of city blocks. The checkpoints or police stations at the entrances and exits were guarded by uniformed Germans with machine guns, assisted by Polish policemen and unarmed members of the Jewish Order Service or Ghetto police. The latter wore no uniform and were recognized by a special cap, a distinctive armband, a belt and a club or truncheon. Huge signs were posted at the entrances proclaiming that it was a typhus area, through which only vehicular traffic was allowed. No stopping was permitted. In fact, only one non-stop tramway crossed the

Ghetto. Apart from this, entering and leaving without a special permit were forbidden.

For our family, the establishment of the Ghetto was less traumatic because this was already the neighborhood we lived in. Many Jews had lived in Warsaw before the war, most of them in our northern residential area. The Christians living there were mostly policemen, janitors and blue collar workers, and they were greatly outnumbered by the Jewish population.

November 16, 1940, the first day of our imprisonment in the Ghetto, fell on a Saturday. My mother asked me to go with her and look around, and we walked hand in hand. Pawia Street was noisy and very crowded. We were among Jews, with no Aryan Poles in sight, no policemen, no hostile Christian thugs. That made us feel more relaxed and at home. "It would be good to live in our own country," my mother said with a sad smile.

We walked slowly along Pawia Street. Mrs. Fromowa, the owner of the fruit and delicatessen store and an old patient of my mother's, stood in front of her store. She greeted us in a friendly manner.

Suddenly, a German truck appeared out of nowhere. We could see the green uniforms, and hear their shouts. My mother pushed me into Mrs. Fromowa's store and quickly followed me. Mrs. Fromowa immediately lowered the iron shutters and bolted the door. "Let us stay quiet, let them believe that the store is empty and permanently closed," she whispered.

We could hear the footsteps and loud yelling of the Germans, and the barking of their dogs. We listened, afraid to move, to breathe. The Germans passed our store and stopped in the middle of the street. This time they had come not to rob stores but to seize men. The men were pushed into their truck, and were never seen again.

We lived in the Ghetto day by day expecting the worst, yet hoping for a miracle to save us. My family was my refuge, its love sheltered me. I admired my sister and felt inspired by her determination. She had always wanted to be a medical doctor and was overjoyed when, in 1941, a medical school opened in the Ghetto, under cover of a "Course to Fight Against Epidemics."

When I obtained my Matura, I followed in her footsteps, enrolling at the same underground medical school. I simply could not resist my parents' urgings to follow Karolina's example. The school was located just outside the Ghetto, on the corner of ñelarna and Leszno streets, and getting to our classroom was most frightening. We had to pass the checkpoint under the watchful eyes of two German guards. We were entirely at their mercy, but there was no other way to reach the school building.

The dark stairs leading to our third-floor classroom were also frightening. The electricity supply was sporadic, and the stairs were often pitch dark, although the classroom was always lit, either by electricity or by carbide lamps. I could feel secure only once I had passed the police station and the stairway. Being among lively young colleagues and listening to a lecture allowed me the illusion that all was well, and that I was a student at a real university. That illusion was destroyed as soon as I was back on the street. How many times did I see the imploring eyes of starving people sitting or lying on the sidewalk, and children begging for a piece of bread, with no more tears to cry. Guilt, that I was not starving, that I still had my parents and my home, overwhelmed me.

In the classroom we concentrated on our lectures, and tried not to hear the noise and occasional gunshots coming from the street. One day, however, we heard women's piercing screams and cries. Somebody entered the class to say that two girls who tried to enter our school had been taken to the guardhouse and were being raped. No one could help them. We were frozen in our seats. I felt numb, gasping for air. After a moment, which seemed like an eternity, the instructor said, "Let us continue the lecture."

Was he serious? How could we concentrate on our lecture and ignore the fate of these tortured girls? But he repeated calmly, "Let us focus on our studies." Then, I remembered reading about the First World War and the soldiers dying in the trenches. When one soldier fell, the others continued fighting. They did not stop to cry or grieve. They had to be brave. And I understood that we too were fighters—we fought to preserve our minds and our inner self. And, like soldiers, we too had to be brave. The lecture continued.

Walking to my classes one cold winter afternoon, I saw a woman sitting on the sidewalk. Her body and legs were swollen from starvation, and she looked up at me with great intensity. I stopped and put a few groszy (a few cents) near her inert hand. During classes, I thought about her eyes, her swollen body. I wanted desperately to do something for her, at least to talk with her, to apologize for hurrying away. After class, though the curfew was approaching, I made a detour to see the woman. She was sitting in the same place, her eyes staring. But she could see no more, she suffered no more. She had died right there on the street. There was no one even to close her eyes.

I knew that the cadaver would be piled up with dozens of others on a primitive wooden cart, pulled by one or two men. Every day we would see one pushcart after another, full of dangling corpses barely covered by paper or cloth, going through the Ghetto. The Jewish Police were in charge of collecting the bodies of those who had died on the street, and of throwing them into anonymous mass graves in the cemetery.

At home, I studied at night. Our apartment was cold and uncomfortable, but we were not freezing. The street was dark and quiet, for only Germans were allowed outside during the curfew; so the noise of an approaching automobile signaled mortal danger. I would lift my head from my studies and listen. When the car passed our building without stopping, I could return to my books. Another reprieve.

During the day, hungry people knocked at our doors asking for food. Refugee doctors came to see my parents, begging for referrals. Like other forcibly resettled refugees, they had lost everything and had no work. Later, of course, typhus epidemics broke out and doctors were in great demand. They became powerful men.

One day I opened the front door to find a well-dressed gentleman begging for food. He said that he was a refugee from Lódî, a lawyer and a cousin of our well-known poet, Juliusz Tuwim. He stood in front of me, eyes downcast. I had no money but I ran to the kitchen and gave him a piece of bread. He took it and thanked me. I was as embarrassed as he was.

My mother's brother, Monos, ate dinner with us every day. Before the war he had been a teacher and associate director of a high school. He was a man of letters, an Esperantist, who believed in the power of reason and education. But when the schools closed, he lost his job. He had to rely on his savings in Russian gold rubles, which he had accumulated before the war. But because the Germans had been robbing one Jewish home after another, Uncle Monos entrusted his savings to his two brothers-in-law. They owned an apartment house which had a large, well-concealed, built-in safe. Miraculously, the house was untouched in the bombing, and during the first weeks of Occupation the brothers-in-law hid Uncle Monos' savings there, together with their own and those of a few other wealthy merchants. Everybody believed that it was an excellent idea. Then, one day the Germans arrived, and without warning seized the building, and expelled all the tenants on the spot. The owners could not reach their savings, and Uncle Monos found himself destitute. Fortunately, he was hired by the Judenrat (the Jewish Council), as some other jobless teachers or lawyers were.

The Germans ordered the establishment of Jewish Councils in each community to carry out their instructions. These councils became administrative tools for overseeing daily life in the Ghettos; they were completely dominated by the German authorities. But Uncle Monos' salary was not enough to feed himself, his wife, and their young daughter, Jadwiga; they were hungry. So the family split up for meals: his wife ate dinner with one of her sisters, Jadwiga with another, and uncle Monos at our home. One meal a day was not enough to keep them well fed, but they were not starving. It meant a lot in the Ghetto. The food we did eat was of very poor quality and had few calories. The bread tasted of gypsum or chalk, the little meat we could get was blue and watery—everything was a substitute for the real thing. Even those of us who still ate every day were constantly hungry.

I was cooking for the family, and it was not easy. We used a small stove to save our precious coal. There was not much to put into the pot, yet every day people came to the back stairs leading to our kitchen to smell if the food was cooking. They begged me to let them drink the water in which I had boiled the potatoes. I would have obliged them, but there were too many people and not enough water. We looked at each other helplessly. Nobody pushed me, nobody tried to grab the pot; their eyes just implored, "Give it to me, give it to me." They showed no anger because my family and I were eating while they were not. The first time this happened, I gave the pot to the first person at the door, the next time to the middle person, and so on. The drained-off hot water was shared by at least two people, who blessed me. I felt pain growing and growing inside me.

My parents tried to help the people who lived nearby. A deaf-mute barber, a widower, lived on Pawia Street; my parents had known him for years. He had three sons, handsome and healthy boys who had fled eastwards in September 1939. The deaf-mute barber was left alone in the Ghetto; few people required his services. He was hungry and visited our kitchen regularly, though not every day. My mother always gave him a meal, yet every time I saw him, he was paler and weaker. He would eat slowly, sitting in a chair, then close his eyes and lean back, half lying in his chair, his legs stretched out. He was resting, dreaming. As the months went by, he became more and more emaciated, yet he still visited us. Then we saw him no more. My mother went to his place to inquire and was told that he had died of starvation in his sleep. He had been buried in a mass grave.

Before the war, when I was still a child, there was a street merchant a few blocks from us on Pawia Street who sold newspapers, cigarettes, candies, and peanuts from his kiosk. I remember that merchant very well, both for his reddish-yellow hair and beard that reminded me of carrots, and because he was one of my grandmother's protégés. My grandmother would sometimes give me ten groszy (about ten cents) to buy some peanuts for myself. It was an adventure for me. My grandmother would stay behind, watching, but we pretended that I was making the whole transaction all by myself. The man was in his late thirties then, and I was fascinated by his kind, blue eyes.

But the Germans forbade street kiosks in our district. We were allowed only one newspaper, Gazeta ñydowska (the Jewish Gazette) and no more candies, cigarettes, or peanuts. The red-headed merchant sold all his belongings, one by one, to buy food. First, he and his wife went hungry, then they starved. He suffered more than she, for even the process of starvation does not affect people in the same way. My mother kept in touch with the couple and brought them food from time to time.

One day his wife came to our apartment, asking urgently to see my mother. She said, "My husband went to bed yesterday, and today he cannot get up. He told me, 'Go get Dr. B., fast, get the dentist, go quickly, quickly, I am dying'." The merchant's wife was crying as she spoke. My mother took some soup and went to see the man, but it was too late. He could eat no more. He was in a coma, dying of starvation.

Another protégé of my grandmother's was a woman who sold coal by the bucket. I remember her well because she wore a cheap wig, which fascinated me. My grandmother explained that pious married Jewish women shaved their hair, and for the rest of their lives had to wear a wig. I was glad that my mother and my grandmother were not pious.

The coal-seller had two helpers, Moshe and Joe, who had no steady jobs in the Ghetto and were hungry. They were well-built, tall, and willing to work, but they were not very bright. My mother gave them odd jobs from time to time, and one day Joe came to carry some coal from our cellar to the apartment. Before the war our janitor usually did this job, but now he was gone. Our cellar, where my parents stored turnips and potatoes as well as coal, was damp and dark, without electric light or a window, and the floor was just beaten earth. It was reached by a long, dark corridor. I was scared to go there; the blackness and stench of the enclosed, windowless area frightened me.

But my mother was unsure whether she could trust Joe to handle the lighted candle properly, and so she asked me to go with him and hold the candle. I felt very nervous at being alone with Joe deep in this dark basement, far away from everybody. I decided to run if he tried to touch me. An instinctive fear was overwhelming me, intensified when Joe suddenly disappeared. Was he hiding and would he attack me from behind? I stood there, frozen.

Then, somewhere behind me I heard a crunching sound. Hungry Joe was devouring our raw turnips. He ate as fast as he could, afraid that I would stop him because he was stealing our food. I did not stop him. I cried, for Joe, for us.

Occasional jobs could not save the two brothers from hunger. One died of starvation. The other came to see my mother, begging for food. My mother asked him, "Is Joe dead?" He answered, "Joe is not dead. Moshe is dead. I am Joe, I am not dead." He kept repeating over and over again: "I am Joe, I am not dead." He looked so thin and miserable and frightened, trying to reassure himself that he was not dead yet. My mother gave him food, which he wolfed down in our kitchen. Then he was gone, and we never saw him again. His boss, the woman with the wig, told us that he had died in his barely heated room.

On a sunny day in the spring of 1941, I was walking with my mother on Wièzienna Street. Men and women lay on the pavement or sat leaning against the buildings, their bellies swollen from hunger. The children were begging. The evacuees who had arrived from all over Poland were the first to starve, for they'd had to leave everything behind, and could not find work in the Ghetto. But many Warsaw Jews suffered similar plights, for they too had lost their jobs and all their possessions, as a result either of the bombing or robbery at the hands of the Germans.

Suddenly, we heard someone calling my mother's name. It was a woman sitting on the sidewalk, with her swollen legs stretched painfully out in front of her. Her face was feverish, but she smiled at my mother and asked, "Dr. B., do you remember me? My parents and my grandparents were your patients before the war. They used to come into Warsaw to see you. You took care of my teeth in 1938, just before I got married. My husband, my parents and my grandparents were killed and I was transported here. I have nothing left to sell." My mother knelt down and talked with her. Yes, she remembered how pretty and happy the woman had been in 1938. My mother left a few zíotys in her hands and we went away. Two days later I looked for the woman but could not find her. Somebody said that she had died.

The summer did not bring much relief to the poor. Although they were not freezing, they were still dying of starvation.

In the cold autumn of 1941, my mother and I walked through Karmelicka Street, which was full of people begging for a piece of bread. We saw two young boys, about five and three years old, standing against a wall and crying. A note attached to the older boy read: "These are my sons, Abel and Sam. I cannot feed them any more. Good people have mercy on my children and help them." The night and the curfew were approaching. People stared at the abandoned children and shook their heads. Eventually, the Jewish police arrived and took the boys to a shelter. We knew that they would find not much food there.

Everywhere, children were crying, "Give me a piece of bread." Adults begged, "Have pity on me, Jewish child." One woman sitting on the sidewalk cried, "My son is a doctor in America. Help me, help me. I will sign a paper and my son will reimburse you. Don't let me die, my son will repay you." Perhaps this woman received some food parcels from her son, though we knew that many were stolen. And even though some did reach the imprisoned Jews and helped them, occasional food was not enough to keep anyone alive for long.

Hunger, typhus and terror dominated our existence. People tried to survive by selling everything they had. They crowded the streets with their meager possessions in their hands or hanging over their arms. Others became regular petty junk dealers, selling anything they could find: food, used clothing, utensils, candles, coal, and so on. The poorest among them displayed their merchandise in a little box or an old valise; the more fortunate had pushcarts. Thin, hungry men sold armbands, for sewing armbands had become a new opportunity for making a little money. Some of the street dealers did even better. They dealt in gold, foreign currencies and jewelry. I saw them on Pawia Street speaking politely to well-to-do customers, but rudely to those who were down to selling their last possessions. The hungry people were too humble and weak to defend themselves.

One of my father's patients came to see him wanting to sell his gold bridge. My father took out the bridge, and told him how much it weighed and what was the current price of gold. The man smiled and said, "that it is exactly the same weight you had told me years ago, when you put it in my mouth". Then, humbly, his head down, he said: "Please doctor, would you help me? I just cannot go to the black marketeers alone; they will cheat me." My father told me to accompany the man and tell the gold/currency dealers, who were nearby on Pawia Street, that he had sent me. I watched to make sure that my father's patient got the right price. The half-starved man looked at me and blessed me and my family with a prayer for our survival.

I received many blessings from people grateful to my parents. These blessing sustained me when the time came for me to face my own ordeal.

A whole underground life had developed in the Ghetto, in spite of countless orders forbidding everything under the penalty of death. Public or private parties with music and dancing were prohibited, yet my mother, like a number of other people, organized parties in her apartment. She invited a young musician, her pre-war patient, now hungry and unemployed, to entertain our neighbors. He came with his young and pregnant wife, who sat quietly in a corner of the room watching her husband play the violin. My mother offered refreshments, and I watched the hungry, pregnant woman devouring her food. With delight she drank our Ghetto tea, made of recycled tea leaves with added fake color, and sweetened by our impure sugar.

And one day, I was invited to a dancing party by David Frydman, the nephew of my parents' friend Zygmunt Frydman. The party, organized to collect money for poor tenants, took place at the David's building, 46 Pawia Street. It was going to be my first date—my first dancing party with a young man. Nineteen-year-old David was two years older than I. He was good looking, with brown hair, brown eyes, and very full red lips. I was drawn toward him when we were dancing, his arms around me. He tried gently to kiss me, but I turned my head away for I had not been kissed before. He did not realize how shy I really was, and tried again. Finally, he succeeded. I was visibly upset and David understood and did not kiss me again. But before we parted, he promised to call me soon.

Any time the telephone rang, my heart jumped hoping it was David. I talked to him inwardly, "David, please don't feel offended. I acted as a child because it was my first dance, and I didn't know any better. David, you were the first man who kissed me. Please don't be angry, please, please call me." But he never called, for he was caught with other Jews on a street and forced to work for the Germans outside the Ghetto. It was David's uncle who told us what had happened to his young nephew. The day the men finished their assigned work, the Germans ordered them to dig a long and deep ditch. Then, they were ordered to stand next to the ditch with their faces turned toward it. They were shot and their mutilated bodies fell into the ditch. Other Jews were called in to shovel earth over the victims and to bury them dead or alive.

David was dead. But life continued. I had two close friends who lived in our apartment building: Mietek Elcztein, a young man, only one year older than I, and Irka Silnicka, a girl just my age. We could easily visit each other during the curfew. Irka's family—her parents, her younger brother and she—survived at the beginning of the Occupation like my family in relative safety. Irka's father was a printer who had his own shop that survived the bombing. Small orders would still arrive daily. But during the first winter under the occupation, a German truck arrived one day and the workshop was emptied. The printing machine was gone. The family had to sell their jewelry, paintings and clothes, one item after another. They took in another family of four people to share their two-room apartment, their kitchen and toilet. Food was tightly rationed by the mother.

But Irka, who was an accomplished pianist, still had her piano. I spent many evenings sitting next to her while she played softly for me. When she played, the Ghetto and our real life would disappear, to be replaced by dreams in which Irka, beautiful in a silk gown, gave concerts in a great hall. The public applauded and she smiled, while I danced in a white organza dress. In my dreams I was always dancing, on endless green lawns surrounded by huge old trees and flowers of all kinds; or on the beach looking at the changing colors of our Baltic sea, under a blue sky and a radiant sun. I felt light and happy. When Irka stopped playing, the reveries faded. It was quiet around us; the Germans usually did not go out robbing in the evening, but we were never sure when and where they would surprise us by their sudden appearance. We listened for the sound of cars, but heard nothing. We were still together, and alive.

As time went on, the lack of food in Irka's family became increasingly painful. Hunger was the Ghetto's first disease, with typhus close on its heels. Irka's father caught typhus, and he had to lie on a couch in their dining room because their bedroom was rented and the tenants had to walk through his room to get in and out. Fortunately, the tenants were good people, cultivated refugees from the Øódì ghetto.

My parents, their closest neighbors, were consulted, and promised to help by finding a doctor who would not report the disease. If the Germans discovered unreported typhus, the penalty for the whole family would be death or deportation. Reporting meant putting the whole house under quarantine. I don't remember if patients were removed forcibly to a hospital but I remember well the houses that were kept under quarantine, for there were many around us. A Jewish policeman guarded the entrance to the building and no one could enter or leave it—although I heard that the policemen readily accepted bribes to let people in and out of the "contaminated" house. This situation created terrible hardship for the majority of people who had very little money.

The Jewish sanitation personnel sprayed sulphur disinfectants at the entrance to the building, and the nauseatingly strong smell filled the street. All the apartments were disinfected in the crudest manner. That was not all: the residents of a quarantined building were forced to go under police guard to the public bathhouse to be disinfected and deloused, thereby exposing themselves to many other kinds of infection and disease. The whole quarantine business was a mockery of sanitary principles, creating great hardship and humiliation for the people involved.

For those reasons, Irka's family did not report her father's illness, and kept him at home. He was terribly thirsty and hungry, and got steadily weaker. The family nursed him during two weeks of pain, until he succumbed to the disease and died. Irka, her mother, and her younger brother, Adam, fought desperately against the pains of hunger. They survived until the fall of 1942, when they were murdered by the Germans.

Mietek Elcztein, our other neighbor, was the only child in his family and like a brother to me. I had known him all my life, and played with him throughout my childhood. His father lost his livelihood at the beginning of the war, and the family became impoverished. Mietek got a job compiling statistics for the Judenrat, and this helped them to stay alive. But he hated his job, having to interview people who mistrusted both the Judenrat and Mietek, its representative. He was often threatened and was scared, but had to continue to work because he had to eat.

Mietek was very attached to his mother. She had been unwell for some time before the war and had to be on a special diet, an impossible luxury in the Ghetto. Eventually she became ill with an infected liver. She lay in the large double bed, her husband sleeping on the floor near her. She became semi-conscious and often hallucinated, crying and begging for an orange, for some flowers. I don't know how my mother, who visited her frequently, got hold of an orange, but she did. (Many things could be purchased in the Ghetto, but for a very high price.) Then she took her pre-war perfume, Chanel No. 5, and sprinkled Mrs. Elcztein's bed, saying: "I brought you some flowers, you can smell them." But she did not answer, nor could she eat the orange. She was in a coma and died shortly thereafter.

The family unit was broken, and Mietek and his father were inconsolable. The two stayed together until they were murdered by the Germans, some time in the late fall of 1942.

I had a new friend, Adam Himelfarb, who moved with his parents to our building during the first winter of the Occupation. They wanted to stay with their relatives. Adam was a handsome, tall, athletic fourteen-year-old teenager. But I was embarrassed to be intimate with him because I was two years older than he, and so we were just friends.

Mature for his age, Adam had definite plans for the future: he wanted to emigrate to Palestine and work on a farm, even though his father wanted him to become a lawyer, like himself. Since we lived in the same building, Adam could visit me after the curfew. He talked about Palestine with its warm, sunny climate and its modern farms. He longed for freedom and a Jewish homeland, and his dreams sustained him. When the young Zionists were forced into the Ghetto, he continued to work underground for a Zionist resistance movement. He was completely devoted to his cause, and very secretive about it. Adam did not want to involve me in his plans. It was as if he knew that the Germans would one day crush him and his friends, and he wanted to spare me.

Gradually I became more attached to Adam and thought about a life with him some time after the war, when he would be older. But in July 1942, as soon as the Himelfarb family understood our sinister fate and had no illusions that deportation meant anything other than death, the three of them, mother, father, and son, committed suicide. Palestine indeed became Israel, but too late for Adam Himelfarb.

When our street was calm, and the Germans were not around, I used to visit my best friend, Bela Eisenstein. We always enjoyed each other's company, discussing books and making plans for our future after the war. Bela and her family lived in a third-floor apartment facing the infamous Pawiak prison. The Germans ordered the occupants of apartments overlooking the prison courtyard to black out their windows permanently. It was forbidden to look into the prison yard under penalty of death. As we sat and talked together in a dark room, we could hear the agonized screams of the prisoners as they were beaten and tortured and had water hoses put up their noses. We would stop talking and hold hands and wish to sink into the earth. When the screams stopped, we felt so guilty and miserable that we avoided looking at each other.

Often when Bela visited me, she would bring her older sister, Pola. Pola could have had a better and safer life if she had loved Alex, the young Christian man, who proposed to rescue her from the Ghetto and marry her. She had met him just before the war and he fell in love with her. Pola did not feel the same passion for Alex, although she did like him a lot. Even after the Ghetto was sealed, Alex managed to communicate with Pola with the help of a friend, who was employed by a telephone or public utilities company and thus was able to enter the Ghetto. These companies remained in "Aryan" hands till the end.

Alex arranged a pass for Pola to leave the Ghetto. But Pola did not want to abandon her family in the Ghetto, and she knew that her parents would be grieved if she married a non-Jew. Moreover, she was unable to marry a man she did not truly love. So Pola stayed with the family. I heard of other cases of young Jewish women rejecting opportunities of escaping from the Ghetto by marrying a Christian Pole. They were unable to break with their tradition and their family, especially at this time, even though it would have saved their lives. Looking back, I wonder at how shortsighted were parents who did not encourage, or even force, their daughters to leave the Ghetto when they had a chance. Apparently, people were ready to endure all kinds of hardship to stay together and keep their faith. Only they did not realize that their aspirations were futile and that soon their lives would be cut short.

One day Bela and Pola visited me as I was about to unwrap a piece of lard, the only natural fat we could obtain. (Butter was rare and, if available, impure; we could not even begin to guess what it had been mixed with.) I was going to cut the lard into small pieces and melt it, so that it could be stored like gold. But as soon as I unwrapped it, I discovered that it was covered with crawling maggots. I felt nauseated and wanted to throw it away, but Pola stopped me. She asked me at least three times if I was sure that I wanted to throw it away. Then she grabbed it, and ran downstairs. After a few minutes, she came back and told us that she had sold this piece of lard to the small grocer next to our building, who was happy to get it. He would melt the lard together with the worms. No food was ever wasted in the Ghetto.

During this time, though all the libraries were closed under the usual penalty of death or deportation, some clandestine private libraries were established. Karolina's friend, Gienia Sztucberg, ran such an underground, one-person lending library, carrying books from home to home under her coat. She risked her life, but she needed the money to buy bread. Like a trooper, she was resisting the enemy and, at the same time, helping to feed her parents, who were now jobless teachers.

Reading was one of my favorite pleasures, and so I awaited Gienia's coming with great anticipation. It was a joy to see her arrive safely with her hidden books. She was a healthy, joyful young girl, only seventeen when the war began. My mother would offer her a cup of ersatz tea with a piece of bread, which she would eat slowly in order to conceal how hungry she was. Then she would talk about the books she had brought, and what she would be able to bring the next time.

Thanks to Gienia, while I was in the Ghetto I read, among other books, Jalna by Mazo de la Roche and Gone With the Wind by Margaret Mitchell. How much pleasure these two books gave me! I began to dream about Canada with its apple trees, green meadows, and fresh flowers. I longed for this immense, beautiful country filled with clean, fresh air. Often I closed my eyes to let my imagination take me there.

The books I read then were full of life, and reminded me of how beautiful nature was. I envied Scarlett O'Hara, who lived in an open country, who could move and fight to better herself. Instead, I was locked in our airless, foul-smelling Ghetto. Professor Ludwik Hirszfeld had told us in one of his lectures at our underground medical school that we would all die "naturally" of typhus or hunger in the next five years. The Ghetto was one big grave to entomb us all.

But the Germans did not want to wait five years to see us all dead. Gienia Sztucberg and her parents, like most of the Ghetto Jews, were killed by the Germans in 1942.

From time to time, a poor woman would come around and sell us meat, not very appetizing, but we were glad to buy it. She got it from a young Jewish smuggler, for many Christian and Jewish adolescents, as well as children, smuggled food into the Ghetto to support themselves and their families. The woman, like her supplier, risked her life in doing this forbidden trade, but she needed money to feed herself and her five-year-old daughter. She never left the child alone and brought the little girl, wrapped in rags, on her perilous delivery errands. "There is nobody to look after her, and our room is very cold," she explained to my mother.

But one day, the woman came without her daughter. They had been walking down a street in the Ghetto, when she suddenly felt the child's hand slip out of hers. She looked at her daughter and saw blood pouring from her head. A brick had fallen from one of the ruined buildings, and the little girl was killed instantly. She was buried in a mass grave. The mother, who still had herself to look after, continued to sell meat. Nobody was responsible for the accident; nobody helped or comforted the mother. It was just another Ghetto casualty.

There were too many victims to be counted. Hundreds, and later thousands, of people died daily from hunger and disease, mostly typhus. People were camping out on the streets and dying there. The situation became worse after October 1941, when the so-called "Little Ghetto," a smaller, southern part of the Ghetto separated from us by Chłodna Street, was closed to Jews. Thousands lost their homes, and we heard that some 600,000 people were now crowded into the diminished area of the Ghetto. I could not verify this figure, but I remember the dense crowds, the lice, and the stench. We were suffocating. But even while some people were suffering from typhus, or dying of starvation, others still walked the streets and attended to their business, in the intervals when the Germans were away.

The "resettlement" continued, with Jews from Germany, France, Holland, and other countries being forced into the Warsaw Ghetto. Many of them were deported soon after their arrival. We did not know then that deportation meant death.

The terror that surrounded us made us fearful and indecisive. I remember one occasion when I stopped at a shoemaker's shop, on my way home from my underground classes. I had my books and notes hidden under my winter coat, because I would be deported or killed on the spot if my study materials were discovered. I put them on a table at the shoemaker's while I transacted my business. After I had left the store in a hurry, I realized in terror that I had left my books behind. I was not afraid that the Jewish shoemaker would denounce me, but that he might destroy my books to avoid being implicated in my crime.

I ran back and found the man pale and trembling with fear. When he'd discovered the school books and notes, he suspected that somebody wanted to frame him by planting evidence of a forbidden activity. He was afraid to remove the evidence and afraid to keep it under his roof. He was certainly relieved when I took my belongings and left his store.

Hunger and typhus were relentlessly killing us. My father phoned his friend, a dentist, Dr. Jerzy êliwa, asking him for anti-typhus vaccines, which were delivered by smugglers. (Telephones were removed from the Ghetto, but my father, sharp and pragmatic, bribed the Pole who came to the Ghetto to confiscate them. He left ours under the pretext that my parents, as dentists, belonged to the medical profession.)

My father had us vaccinated and shared the remaining vaccines with Aunt Rosa and Uncle Monos and their families. But Uncle Ignacy Lautenberg, Rosa's husband, still became ill. His doctor wrongly treated him for typhus, but he had actually contracted typhoid or enteric fever. When he suffered intestinal perforation, my parents knew that his end was near. Night came; Ignacy was dying in his home. I could not sleep, and prayed for his miraculous recovery. He was only thirty-four years old, and so full of life. But the miracle did not happen and Ignacy died that night, leaving Rosa and their young daughter, Hania.

A new order came at the end of December 1941: Jews were forbidden to wear or possess furs. We were at first given a couple of days, then a week, to surrender all our furs. The news spread fast, and Aryan Poles began coming into the Ghetto to buy our furs.

It was very difficult to enter or leave the Ghetto, but it was not entirely impossible. Jewish and Christian smugglers, who were young, clever and physically fit, did it every day — through the roof-spaces of adjoining houses, through underground passages, through the holes in the wall encircling the Ghetto, or any other way they could think of.

There were also loopholes in the sealing of the Ghetto which allowed people to enter, legally or illegally. (Later, these were discovered by the Germans and eliminated one by one). For example, the High Court building on Leszno Street had two entrances: one from the Aryan side, the other from the Jewish. This allowed people to walk from one side to another through the building. There were also trams, beginning and ending their route on the Aryan side, which ran through the Ghetto without stopping. But it was possible, though not easy, to jump on or off as the tram passed through the Ghetto. Sometimes the conductor could be bribed to slow down the tram so that it was easier to jump. Sometimes a decent conductor would slow the tram down without being bribed. It was also possible, though dangerous, to bribe a policeman at the entrance to the Ghetto and pass through when the Germans were not watching.

So it was not impossible for Aryans to enter the Ghetto and buy furs. And it was a great opportunity for the purchasers, who could name their price to the imprisoned Jews. My aunt Freda still had an expensive, almost new, astrakhan fur coat—perhaps her last, valuable possession. She had wanted to sell it before, but her husband, my uncle Monos, objected. "Keep it," he told her. "At least you will not freeze when outdoors, and maybe, maybe, we will be able to keep it until the end of the war." But now it was too late. There were so many Jews willing to sell, as long as they could get any money at all; and some Polish Christians were ready to pay a fair price, even in these circumstances.

My father's Christian friends, Mr. Grunwald and his wife, were among these people. They appeared at our doorsteps, smiling. They told us they were looking for a couple of fur coats and were willing to pay a reasonable price. While they sat with my parents to chat over a cup of our erzats tea, I ran to my aunt Freda with the good news. She gave me her beautiful fur coat and their fur collars. Mrs. Grunwald kept her word and paid a decent price. I ran back to my aunt and gave her money (we lived on the same street, a few blocks away). She embraced me, grateful. She cried, my proud aunt—now a humble, destitute Jewish woman.

The Grunwalds, friendly and respectful toward my parents, enjoyed their visit. I felt for a moment that everything was all right—like it was before the war—and that we were equal, not branded Jews. That illusion was quickly dispelled when Mrs. Grunwald wanted to use our toilet and there was no running water. In winter the pipes were frequently frozen for days, if not weeks or months. We felt deeply embarrassed and humiliated.

Since the Polish winter is very cold, a fur collar was really a necessity, especially for us, weak and undernourished. Our own fur collars went for safekeeping to Mrs. Koska, a pre-war friend of our lodger, Mrs. Szmit. For years, she assisted and encouraged her needy friend who reached Poland with her husband in 1920, as a penniless refugee from Bolshevik Russia. Mrs. Koska, loyal to her benefactress, had frequently visited Mrs. Szmit in our apartment before the Ghetto was established. She even came to see her a few times after we had been locked in the Ghetto. This time, she came to help Mrs. Szmit, offering to keep her furs in storage, for we all still believed that we would survive the war. My mother, too, gave our own fur collars to Mrs. Koska.

As time passed, our misery intensified. We lived in the stench of unwashed human beings, of urine and of the sulfur used to disinfect the typhus-ridden buildings. Lice were everywhere, and people were dying by the thousands on the streets. Roundups, vicious beatings, and torture occurred daily.

In the middle of this nightmare, Dr. Hanarin, a well-respected radiologist and a good friend of my parents, called on my father one day with a spark of hope. He was very excited and secretive. He wanted to speak with my father alone, and told him that a Jew in the Ghetto could provide, for a price, genuine Argentine passports. Such a passport would entitle the holder to leave Poland for Switzerland as an Argentine national. The whole story had to be kept absolutely secret; the passports would be sold by referral only to a few well-recommended families. The seller assured the potential buyers that he had secured a passport for himself and believed firmly that it would lead him and his clients to safety.

Dr. and Mrs. Hanarin were very enthusiastic about this splendid opportunity. They had a seven-year-old daughter and they wanted to protect her. It was difficult not to be tempted by such a wonderful dream—the price was not even very high. Although my parents were skeptical, my father expressed interest.

There were a few meetings concerning the passports, and my father asked me to go with him to Dr. Hanarin's home for the last meeting. There were, as I remember, five men interested in purchasing the documents, all solid professional citizens like Dr. Hanarin. I waited in the adjoining room, and talked with a young man of my own age, who was also waiting for his father. We both wanted to believe that our fathers would succeed in saving us from the Ghetto. I was drawn toward this handsome and polite young man, even though I had just met him. I wanted to hold hands with him. With death so near in the Ghetto, I ardently desired to love and be loved. I remembered the couples I had seen embracing during the bombing of Warsaw. Perhaps they had felt like me, and believed that the magic of love would shelter them from impending death, or at least make it easier to wait for it. Oh, life could be so beautiful in the arms of the young stranger. But I kept those thoughts to myself, the meeting ended and we parted.

My father had been uncertain about buying these passports; but when he had been told that they had to be registered with the Germans he decided not to purchase them. He refused to have our family's name registered with the Germans. Other people did register their passports and waited to leave, full of hope.

They had been misled: they were taken to the Pawiak prison shortly afterwards and murdered there. We did not hear what had happened to the Jewish seller. Did he join the group in the Pawiak prison? Was he duped, or was he a scoundrel?

In February of 1942, my mother had a most unexpected visitor: Dr. Altman, her classmate from the dental school where they had studied together back in 1918. Dr. Altman had been practising successfully for many years in a small town near Warsaw. The two women were glad to see each other, but my mother was puzzled, "Why did you come to the Ghetto, and how?" she asked her.

Dr. Altman told her story. She, like other Jews in her town, had been confident that the war would end before they were resettled. But the Germans had special plans for them. Unknown to the trusting townspeople, the Germans had decided to experiment on this small community with what later became known as the "Final Solution." One day they arrived in the town and started killing Jews at random, creating terror and panic. Then, in the middle of the confusion, they issued an order that the Jewish population would be transported to another city, and the Jewish Council had to pay for the transportation. All Jews must contribute. Those who disobeyed the orders would not be resettled, but instead, killed on the spot.

The next day the frightened Jews were ordered to come to the marketplace with only as many belongings as they could carry. Those who tried to hide or to remain in their homes were beaten and pushed till they joined the others. Some were shot in their homes.

At the marketplace, the Germans, their collaborators and their dogs encircled the helpless Jews, pushing them toward the big trucks carrying the sign of the Red Cross. The Jews were told not to be afraid and that the trucks would transport them to a safe destination. But Dr. Altman was an intelligent and observant woman, and she did not like the look of the trucks. Why did they close hermetically? There was something sinister about them.

She decided to try to escape with her daughter. So many people were herded into the marketplace, waiting to board the trucks, that she succeeded in finding a place to hide and from there she saw what happened. Again and again the trucks were filled to capacity, and driven from the marketplace to the forest outside the town. She learned later that they were, in fact, mobile gas units. All the people inside were gassed by poisonous fumes and their bodies thrown into a waiting pit.

Dr. Altman succeeded in bribing her way out of the doomed town, but she had no place to stay with her daughter, or anywhere to go except the Warsaw Ghetto. She paid dearly to reach it, but believed herself to be safe with us, since it was inconceivable that the Germans would be able to kill the whole Ghetto population. She hoped that time and our large numbers would be the two factors that would save us, and that the Germans would soon be defeated. She had escaped with a certain amount of money and gold, so she and her daughter had settled in a rented room and hoped to survive the war.

I felt faint when Dr. Altman had finished telling my mother her nightmare story. I thought that I was losing my senses. It could not have happened, it was utterly unbelievable. It was beyond human comprehension, beyond anything one could imagine.

Dr. Altman was remorseful that she had upset me. She and my mother tried to comfort me, saying, "Don't be afraid, Irene, we are safe here." I wanted to scream, "That's not true, we are all doomed here, we are condemned to die soon." But I understood that Dr. Altman herself needed reassurance. She had to protect her young child, and needed all the strength and hope she could muster.

So we lied to each other, and denied the truth to ourselves. On July 22, 1942, five months after Dr. Altman's arrival, the mass extermination of the Warsaw Ghetto began. Dr. Altman and her daughter were killed in August.

FIVE

THE FINAL SOLUTION

Most people doubted the stories Dr. Altman and others told. After all, she did not see the mass graves, she only heard about them. The inhabitants of the Ghetto desperately maintained their hope that the war would end soon and that the Germans would never attempt to kill an entire nation. Besides, the Jews remembered the Germans as highly civilized people, and could not believe in their sudden and complete metamorphosis. Nonetheless, the rumors about brutal mass murder were getting more persistent. As 1942 went on, the atmosphere became heavier and the fear about our fate stronger. We heard more and more often about people disappearing, about the annihilation of entire communities. And yet the illusion persisted that the Jews were only being resettled, not murdered.

But on Wednesday, July 22, 1942, a decree that the Judenrat (Jewish Council) was forced to sign, announced that all Jews living in the Warsaw Ghetto would be evacuated. Only those working for the Judenrat office and administration, the Jewish Police, the hospital or the sanitation department were exempt, along with those working in German factories or workshops. People reprieved from the order of evacuation could stay in the Ghetto with their spouses and children. But they could not protect their fathers, mothers, brothers or sisters.

Furriers, tailors, dressmakers, cutters and others able to handle needles and sewing machines were the first to find employment in the German workshops and get their exempt-from-deportation papers. In just one day, they became a very special, privileged group, with seemingly a fair chance to survive the war. But the unfortunate ones who did not belong to this group would be deported.

Although we still hoped that "deportation" meant only transportation to work in the Eastern territories, we sensed the impending torture and death. Yet, our minds still could not accept the possibility of the mass murder in such a systematic and absolute way. It was simply unbelievable.

Adam Czerniakow, the president of the Judenrat, committed suicide on July 23, 1942, being unable to stop the mass deportation. But his death did not prevent the Judenrat from complying with the German orders. We had no help, no arms, no strength against the Germans. The Judenrat had to feed the Germans as one feeds a hungry beast: with our blood, with our people.

The official plan for resettlement was to transform the Warsaw Ghetto into a setting for German workshops. We heard that at least six thousand non-exempted people, classified by the Germans as "unproductive," were to be deported daily. The deportation was to be carried out by the Jewish Police, supervised by the German authorities and assisted by their associates, a mixture of displaced Lithuanians, Latvians and Ukrainians.

The "unproductive" population would be escorted forcibly to the Umschlagplatz, as the transfer area was called. The mere sound of the word "Umschlagplatz" filled everyone with terror; it signaled deportation, it foreboded death. This "transfer area" consisted of two adjacent squares located on Stawki Street in the northern part of the Ghetto, next to the railway tracks. On one square stood a building which had once housed a school but now was occupied by the Jewish police and a newly established first-aid station run by the Judenrat.

Even starving, emaciated people wanted to avoid evacuation and hoped to survive the war, but the beggars, the sick, the handicapped, the elderly, and the children were at the top of the list of "unproductive." The first transport of deportees left the Ghetto the same day the decree was announced.

At the beginning, the victims were being rounded up off the streets. The streets were full of ragged, hungry children begging for a piece of bread. Chased, the children cried, "Let me go, have mercy, let me go, let me go." Some tried to kick and fight, but in vain. They were put into open horse-drawn trucks, primitive sinister vehicles with folding steps at the back. The vehicles were often pulled by two horses and were big enough to carry a great number of children. These wagons moved through the Ghetto from one street to another, searching for children. It was easy to see them approaching, but the children were promptly rounded up and could not escape.

The blocks occupied by the German workshops of Schultz and Többens were, for the time being, ignored by the hunters. We lived in one of these blocks. I felt safe in our apartment. One day I was there alone. I sat on the floor of my old bedroom and fixed my eyes at its familiar blue walls, trying to recall some pleasant memories. But the piercing cries of the children reached me through the closed window. They were being seized not far away, and they cried and screamed and moaned and begged, "Pity! Mercy!" But still, they were loaded into the wagon.

I felt pain, rage, and guilt because I could do nothing to save them. Although I moved as far as I could from the window, the plaintive voices penetrated into my room. I wanted to reach for my mother, and ask her to tell me that it was only a bad dream, but I realized then that she could help me no more. I was on my own, utterly alone to face our agony. Sitting on the floor, I pushed my body against the wall. I wanted to enter the wall, to disappear from this world.

The children continued to be taken to be slaughtered, mercilessly, irrevocably.

Later, when fewer children were left in the Ghetto, those torn from their parents, or dragged from their hiding places, went together with the adults into the hastily constructed vehicles used for transportation to the infernal Umschlagplatz.

There, the Germans directed and supervised the loading of the victims into freight or cattle trains. The Jewish policemen were ordered by the Germans to assist them. The policemen were forced to round up people on the street, search for them in their homes, and deliver them to the Umschlagplatz, where the defenseless people were pushed into the trains. Many criminals from Lithuania and Latvia had been freed from their prisons to assist the Germans with the deportations. These helpers often appeared unexpectedly on the streets to terrorize and brutalize people. At the Umschlagplatz, wearing uniforms of a different color from those of the Germans, they kicked, whipped and often shot at people as they loaded them into trains.

Some Jewish women were seized and forced to clean the quarters of Lithuanians and Latvians. We heard rumors that after a few days of these women's presence, some of the criminals felt sympathy for them and, as a result, became less enthusiastic about their brutal tasks. They were promptly shot and replaced by others still immune from human feelings.

Special units of Germans, well-trained and devoted to the Nazi doctrine, circulated through the Ghetto in small private cars to supervise the "action" and give the orders. They ordered all the killings, including those of the Lithuanians and Latvians who had lost their zeal. The presence of these special units (called Einsatzgruppen) was not so much visible as constantly and overwhelmingly felt.

Our building at 38 Pawia Street continued to be fairly safe from roundups for deportation. This was because the Opus shirt and dry cleaning factory, located there, had been given to the German industrialist, Mr. Schultz, who operated it as a workshop. Those who worked there were exempt from deportation. Their families quickly joined them to remain together on the Schultz's workshop premises. But hundreds of other people tried also to stay there, albeit illegally.

The Ghetto was less crowded now, and it became possible to find apartments. The Jewish supervisors and managers quickly moved into the vacant apartments in our building. They looked down at the "unproductive." They felt secure in their new positions. They trusted the Germans. They felt important and powerful. They could give or refuse the working papers, entitling other Jews to remain in the Ghetto.

But I did not trust the Germans. I felt death so near, so imminent, that I could barely breathe. Yet I had to dress in the morning, feed myself, face my family, and pretend that I believed in our survival.

We lived in a protected building, so we too were privileged, at least for the moment. We did not have to run in search of a hiding place as thousands of people did. We tried to go out as little as possible because the streets had been turned into traps where Jewish policemen waited in ambush for victims and took them away to the Umschlagplatz. We could also be seized on the street by the Gestapo or their collaborators, who might kill Jews on the spot, as hunters would shoot animals.

One hot day in late July, I was looking down on Pawia Street, kneeling down, hidden behind the ornamental columns around our balcony. The street was not crowded any more; there were just a few hurrying pedestrians. In the distance I heard a peculiar noise. A four-wheeled, horse-drawn vehicle, with narrow planks for seats, was approaching on our cobblestone street. It stopped two buildings away from us, at number 34.

People with blanched faces, immobile with terror, were sitting on the plank seats. Four Jewish policemen were in charge. Two of them stayed to guard the prisoners, and the other two entered the building. Then I saw two of my teachers, the sisters Franka and Ida Magidson, coming out of the building escorted by the policemen. Franka, my French teacher, climbed into the vehicle; her sister Ida helped her up and, as soon as she was seated, put a small valise and a blanket into her lap. The sisters kissed each other goodbye as if Miss Franka was only going for a trip to another town; but her once vivacious and cheerful face was now gray. She looked like a frozen doll. The vehicle turned right into Lubeckiego Street and disappeared. Ida stood alone on the street for a while, then slowly went inside her building.

Although I did not know then about the death camps and gas chambers, I felt horror gripping my throat. Somehow I knew that I would never see the lively Franka Magidson again. Ida probably had working documents which protected her, while her sister was unable to obtain them. But later Ida too was deported, and perished.

During the time of "resettlement," the Jewish policemen, tools of the Germans, would run around like madmen looking for people. They would encircle whole blocks of buildings, searching inside the courtyards and apartments and dragging people from their hiding places. All the residents were seized, and the buildings were left empty. It became increasingly difficult for the policemen to fill their assigned quotas, and those who failed to do so could be shot or deported, or forced to bring their own children to fill the quota. They lost all control; they became beasts. In a desperate and insane effort to save their own lives, some policemen would deliver their mothers, fathers, brothers, and sisters to the Umschlagplatz. But it did them no good; the Jewish policemen were later shot by the Germans.

On Sunday, August 2, 1942, my Uncle Monos came to visit us. Karolina and my father were out, and the Szmit family had left us a month earlier to move into a recently vacated apartment. We had no patients on Sundays, and so my uncle, mother, and I were at home alone. Suddenly, there was a knock at the door, violent, loud, abrupt—unmistakably a German knock. Panic seized us. The knock came from the front door, so my mother pushed her brother toward the back door. My uncle just had time to escape before, a minute later, three uniformed Germans were in our apartment.

They were loud, aggressive, fat and coarse. They wanted to see my father, who luckily was not in. Their next question was about gold, just as it had been two years earlier when the Germans first came to our apartment and our maid Stefa had guarded our contraband soap. My parents were dentists and so must have gold, they insisted. As before, they ran from one room to another searching, while my mother patiently explained to them, in her educated German, that my father made teeth of porcelain, not gold.

My mother was wearing her white lab coat. She had put it on instinctively as soon as she heard the threatening knock at the door, hoping that her professional attire would impress the ruffians. My blonde, handsome mother, a graceful lady with a serious, intelligent face and large blue-gray eyes, inspired respect and deference. She looked poised and calm; but I, standing next to her, sensed how frightened she really was. I did not understand the German language and tried to deduce the intruders' intentions from their behavior. Would they hit us? I watched them intently. If they had beating in mind, their voices would become louder and louder, they would go into a sort of frenzy and then they would begin pounding us.

I looked straight into their eyes, not leaving them for a moment, trying to send the three Germans a silent message: "Don't touch my mother." I adored her and was ready to die defending her. I felt very tense inside, but forced myself to hide my fear—inspired by scenes from a film in which early Christians were thrown into a Roman arena full of lions. The martyrs had looked straight into the lions' eyes, giving them a silent order to stop, not to advance.

The Germans finally did at last leave without hurting us.

The next day, Monday, August 3, 1942, the blow finally hit us. Around 1 p.m., several Jewish policemen entered our apartment simultaneously from the front and the back. This time my father was unable to slip away. The police told him that the B. family was under special arrest, and had to leave the apartment, under their escort, immediately. We understood that we were being taken to the Umschlagplatz. Numb with terror, we listened to the orders to pack some belongings, as quickly as possible, and to put them into folded bed sheets or pillow cases.

Our neighbors heard of our predicament and, knowing that it was only the Jewish police and that there were no Germans around, some of them tried to reach us. Among them was Dr. Blumstein, the director of our secondary school, for whom my father found an apartment in our building in the fall of 1939. A tall, impressive, patrician-looking man with erect posture and commanding manners, he prevailed upon the policemen guarding us to let him enter our apartment.

He approached my father, "Dr.B. may I help you in any way at all?" My father smiled at him and handed him a little box of gold scraps which he kept in his pocket. He had hoped that this gold would save his life if he were caught on the street; he could try to bribe his way free.

"This gold is useless to me now. But please give it to my sister Rosa Lautenberg. She will need it, she is a widow with a six-year-old child." "Pan Dyrector" took the box, saying, "Don't you worry, I will personally deliver this box to your sister. Take care of yourself and trust me." However, my cautious father asked the policemen, who knew us well, to let his sister know that the Director had the gold for her. Ill at ease because they were arresting us, they promised to do so. They treated my parents with respect, but nevertheless continued to carry out their brutal task.

My mother told the policemen that our newly engaged, part-time cleaning woman, Fela, a Jewish refugee, was not a member of the family and so should be set free. But to our surprise, Fela threw herself upon my mother's knees, embracing her. "Please let me go with you, don't leave me alone," she begged. She kissed my mother's hands, "Your family is all I have now. I don't know what I will do without you, please don't abandon me." The policemen seemed not to care whether Fela stayed with us or not. They were hurrying us as we threw things into our improvised bags. We were allowed to take only as much as we could carry. Fela helped my mother, taking the heaviest bundle, and then another one, relieving my mother of almost all her load.

The moment of departure arrived, with Fela carrying a great deal of our belongings. We left the apartment and were put into rickshaws that were waiting for us, three-wheeled vehicles with two seats in front of the peddling driver. Each of us was escorted by a policeman. But Fela was nowhere to be seen: she had disappeared with our bundles. My mother smiled sadly, as if she were amused by Fela's ruse. She whispered to my father, "Jan, it doesn't matter. I don't think we will need our things where they are taking us. It really doesn't matter." My father shook his head, "It's done anyhow; maybe it will help Fela to survive."

The four rickshaws, with policemen in front and behind, were ready to turn on Lubeckiego Street toward the Umschlagplatz. The street filled with people waving to us and crying openly. "Dr. B., Dr. B., if you are being taken away, no one will escape! We are all doomed, it is the end of us!" The crowd became dense. Emotions ran high. Some screamed, "Dr. B., may God be with you, may God protect you."

I looked at this crowd from my rickshaw as if I was witnessing our funeral. People stood there to express their affection, their compassion and, finally, their grief for our Jewish fate.

The Umschlagplatz was so crowded that we found ourselves against a solid wall of humanity. It was impossible to move, and our guards led us to the main building, clearing the way ahead by pushing people brutally aside. We held hands and walked sideways, one after the other, to get through. Before the war the main building had housed a trade school, and the room we were taken to had been the director's office. It was now dirty and completely bare, the only remnant of its former glory a brass plate attached to the outside door saying "Director."

Left to stand or sit on the bare floor, we tried to guess what was awaiting us: interrogation, torture, or deportation with the others? We were not alone; two other dentists' families were already there. Obviously, the methodical Germans had decided this time to reserve special treatment for three well-known Jewish dentists and their immediate families. Why? We did not know and never found out. My parents' colleagues greeted us sadly. We found out that they too had been visited the day before by Germans asking for gold. The Germans had pushed them around and behaved in a most brutal way.

There were five young people in our room: two boys in the one family, a young man in the other and Karolina and I. Two Jewish policemen were posted at the door to prevent us from escaping. But where could we escape to? On the square outside there were thousands of people waiting to be pushed into freight trains.

The Jewish policemen guarding us were ill at ease and defensive, for they had been my parents' pre-war patients. Some were poor, and my parents had taken care of them and their families without charge for years. They were even more embarrassed and more polite to us. One of them, a handsome young man with blond curly hair, had lived on Pawia Street with his widowed mother, and my parents treated both of them without charge since he had lost his father many years earlier.

The young man felt a debt of gratitude to my mother. He spoke with another policeman from Pawia Street and the two men approached my parents with a proposal. "Please listen to us. Since the arrest order was for the B. family, if Karolina and Irene were to be married, they would change their name, and thus could regain their freedom. So, please let us marry your daughters. We assure you that we mean a marriage of form only." They were very serious, their sole desire being to save the two of us. It would be a matter of a few minutes to find a rabbi who would perform the marriage.

My parents, sitting on the bare floor, turned to Karolina and me in shock, asking us to decide. My kind, caring father looked miserable; he was unable to protect us, unable even to decide what would be best for us.

We said no without hesitation. We wanted to remain with our parents. Our love for them was greater than our desire to survive.

We had almost no food but we did have some water, so we were better off than most of the immense crowd massed at the Umschlagplatz without food or drink. Some of this agonized multitude peered at us through our barred window, for it was unusual to see prisoners inside. One person who saw us was my classmate, Henia Zawoznik, who was there with her father and younger sister. (Their mother had been deported previously.) Henia and her father begged me for water. My mother asked our guards for some, and passed it through the window to my friend. People around started crying out, "Give us some water, water, water, please." We could do nothing but move away from the window and cover our ears, so as not to hear the screaming of the crowd and the shouting of the police.

The people's despair mounted, and some of them managed to get into the building. They saw the sign on our jail, and demanded to see the director. The Jewish policemen guarding us tried to explain that there was no director there, only prisoners, but the people did not believe them. A small riot broke out. When we heard the commotion and my mother learned what was going on, she asked that the door be opened. The policemen opened it and the people saw us sitting or lying on the dirty floor. They understood, bowed their heads in sadness and quietly went away.

I was hungry. I dreamed of warm milk with sugar. I had never liked it before, but now all I could think of was a glass of pure, white, warm milk. The craving was painful. I tried to distract myself and looked around at our companions. Karolina was talking with the young man, her fellow-prisoner, as they sat in a corner of the room. They were holding hands, timidly, trying to hide from the rest of us the beginning of a new-born affection. Karolina's face became alive, her eyes shining. The two young prisoners enjoyed a moment of reprieve. Again I marveled how quickly a bond can be formed between two young healthy people who, close to death, still cling to life and yearn for the fortifying feeling of love.

In the outer corridor there was a room with a row of dilapidated toilets without doors, which we could use only with our guards' permission. I asked one of the policemen to let me go to the toilets. He escorted me there, but refused to wait outside the dirty room. He insisted on coming inside with me. I was horrified — a young, shy girl, not yet a woman — I could not use a toilet with a man watching me. Finally, he relented and turned his face toward the wall, promising me he would not watch. But I felt deeply humiliated and angry with him. There was no possibility that I would escape, since there was no window and only one door. I was furious at all these policemen who took us and guarded us at the Umschlagplatz. But what could I do with my anger? We were powerless.

I said to myself, "I will not show my anger, I will try to conceal my real feelings and I will talk to our jailers calmly, even kindly."

Shortly after I returned to our room, I tested my new resolution. I spoke to the policemen with a smile. "I understand your predicament. You are Jews yourselves, and yet you have to perform your dreadful tasks. It is nice of you to be so polite to us. We appreciate that." The reaction was immediate: the policemen smiled back at me and promised to help as much as they could. My imprisonment became more bearable when the policemen were civil.

It was August 4, the second day of our detention. Through our window we could see the endless stream of people being brought to the Umschlagplatz for transportation. The thousands of Jewish victims, herded together at the Umschlagplatz, had to stand as if glued together. There was no room to sit and no one got food or water. People were pushed, shouted at, beaten and terrorized indiscriminately. They were suffocating from the heat and stagnant air, filled with the smell of sweat, urine and excrement. They were faint with terror, hunger and thirst. We could hear the oppressors' endless shouting mingled with the painful moaning and crying of the victims. Some of them wanted to be put into the trains quickly in order to escape this living hell. Not many could imagine the true destination of their journey.

The arrivals at the Umschlagplatz stopped in the early afternoon. Around 3 p.m., after the victims had been loaded into the freight trains, the place was empty. The transport for the day was gone; tomorrow a new one would arrive. It was then that I noticed a group of gypsies sitting together on the ground. Were they left over from that day's transport, or had they been brought too late and left for the next day? One thing was certain: they would be loaded into the trains tomorrow.

As for us, locked in a room, we were still waiting, not knowing what horror awaited us. At least we had water brought to us by our jailers—only because we were in the building, and not far from the faucets. We were given a little watery soup, all the nourishment we were entitled to. The two other families with us had grown-up children who were able to bribe policemen and send them small packages of food, and they shared them with us. They were fine people, gentle and gracious. My parents were younger than the other dentists, and knew them by reputation only. My parents were rather shy and kept to themselves, while the two other couples knew each other well and kept close.

We were distressed that nobody thought of sending us food. We knew that my mother's brother, Monos, and my father's sister, Rosa, had very little money and enough worries of their own. They had to fight for their lives. Still, it hurt to be so completely abandoned. My parents did not complain. They looked at Karolina and me with infinite love and sadness. We could not have eaten much anyway; we were too terrified by what was in store for us and so revolted by what we saw around us that our stomachs were tied up in knots. I felt very weak.

On the morning of our third or fourth day at the Umschlagplatz, three policemen rushed into the room. They told my mother, "Janusz Korczak and the children went to the trains!" In spite of all the Ghetto's horrors and the mass deportation of Jewish children, it was unbelievable to all of us, including the policemen, that Dr. Korczak's orphanage had been liquidated.

Dr. Korczak had taken care of some 200 children in his orphanage. (That was where our friend, Adam Birman, the dental technician, had been brought up.) He defended his children selflessly against the famine and cold in the Ghetto, begging the Jewish Council for help and soliciting donations from private citizens. He managed to receive enough assistance to prevent children from starving and freezing. Most of them would have survived, thanks to him, if they had escaped deportation.

We listened as the policemen described to my mother how the 64-year-old Dr. Korczak and the children had arrived at the Umschlagplatz, marching in order and singing. The Germans and their helpers, who usually loaded the trains by whipping and pushing people, had stood motionless, the whips inert in their hands, looking silently at this unusual scene of the children from the tiniest to all ages walking behind their elderly leader. First Dr. Korczak, then his assistant, Stefania WilczyÆska, and finally the trusting children, had quietly entered the freight train; and the policemen had closed the doors behind them.

Dr. Korczak had many Christian friends and admirers. When the liquidation began, his friends had urged him to escape from the Ghetto, but he refused to leave his children. He said that he would never abandon those who needed him. And he kept his word. This selfless and courageous man became a legend. He chose to die with the children he could not save, and Stefania WilczyÆska perished with them.

Later on that fateful day two Jewish policemen, visibly embarrassed, came to see my parents. They said, "Don't be upset. We were not sure if we should tell you, but we decided that you should know. Your apartment has been completely emptied. Everything you owned and all your equipment has been confiscated by the Germans. Three huge moving vans were loaded with your property, and took it away."

My mother looked at them, surprised, "You were afraid to tell us that? Don't you realize that we are facing death and will have no use for the belongings we left in Pawia Street?"

It was strange that the policemen did not understand the simple, grim reality that we were all condemned to die. My mother did.

On the morning of the fifth day of our imprisonment, two men appeared in our jail. They looked arrogant and ugly. One of them had a red, ulcerated nose, possibly deformed by syphilis. We were horrified at the sight of these hoodlums.

The red-nosed man shouted: "The B. family step out and remain on the other side of the room."

We were being singled out—a bad omen. But the man winked at my father and said in a low voice, "Don't be afraid." We were watching, and we saw the wink and heard his words, which somehow alleviated our terror. Bewildered and shaking, we were quickly bundled out of the room and into two waiting rickshaws, and whisked out of the Umschlagplatz.

Only then were we told that we were free for now but would have to stay in hiding. My parents asked that we be taken to our friend Janka Elterman's apartment. She and her mother were happy to see us. "You are now with us, you have escaped the deportation, you may relax," they reassured us. But we did not feel saved, for the deportation continued.

It had been Janka Elterman who thought of bribing the two
Jewish men (who worked for the Gestapo) to save us. She collected
ransom money from our friends, mostly from Józef Lautenberg,
my Aunt Rosa's father-in-law. The men were paid handsomely
for taking us back to the Ghetto, where, they expected, we would
be caught again with the thousands of others and deported for
real the next time. No one would ever discover that they had
been bribed. The two other dentist families who were imprisoned
with us at the Umschlagplatz were put into the freight train and
deported shortly after our release. We grieved for them and
felt guilty that we had escaped, and we hoped that, in spite of
everything, they would survive.

We became like automatons, unable to smile, programmed
to watch for any sign of danger from our unpredictable, terribly
efficient captors. The gigantic roundups continued, and six
thousand or more Jews were herded daily to the Umschlagplatz
and shoved into the trains.

We saw no way to escape our fate. But Janka Elterman was
cheerful, with infinite confidence in my father's ability to protect
us. She counted also on my parents' gratitude for her effort in
rescuing us.

Janka had come to live with us in September 1939. Her husband
brought her to my parents' apartment before he joined the Polish
army as a colonel and medical doctor. He asked my parents to
take care of his wife in his absence. They had no children. My
parents kept their promise and watched over Janka and her
widowed mother, Mrs. Tran. When they were forced to move
into the Ghetto, my father found an apartment for them near us
on Pawia Street. It was to this apartment that we came from the
Umschlagplatz.

We stayed with Janka and Mrs. Tran for two days. There for
the first time I saw my parents as homeless and impoverished.
The impending danger of deportation and our present situation

made me feel as if I was losing my mind. Everything seemed unreal.

Mrs. Tran's presence cheered me up a little. Janka's 86-year-old mother had little chance of survival in 1942, yet she was calm and her mind remained young and alert. She talked often about her favorite authors, amazing me by remembering passages from Shakespeare. Our tragic situation did not change her disposition or her faith in Judaism and in God. Her stoic acceptance of our fate was soothing. She looked at me tenderly, sorry for my destroyed youth and my uncertain future, and I felt comforted being near her.

We liked staying with Janka and her mother in their small but comfortable apartment. Unfortunately, their building was wide open and unprotected from the roundups, so my parents decided to return to our own building. It was safer from the selections because of the presence of the Schultz workshop. However, only the tenants and workshop employees had the right to be there, and we had lost our status as tenants. Yet the Jewish guards let us enter the building. Of course, we found that our apartment had been requisitioned and the doors locked, and we stood there helplessly while my father tried to locate the newly appointed Jewish superintendent. When he found him, the man refused to let us in and told us to go away. My parents argued: evening was approaching, it was getting dark and the Germans would probably not come at night. Thus, they would not discover that the superintendent had disobeyed them. Finally the superintendent relented and let us enter our home secretly, on the condition that we would not stay there for long.

As the policemen at the Umschlagplatz had warned us, the apartment had been sealed and stripped. Everything in it had been confiscated: my parents' dental equipment and laboratory, our furniture, paintings — absolutely everything would have been loaded into trucks and sent to Germany. There was not a single chair left. We did, however, find some of our clothes and linen left in one wall closet. Most importantly, my parents' savings in gold coins was still untouched in their hiding place.

At this time Aunt Rosa heard from a friendly Jewish policeman that we were back. She wanted to see us but it was very risky to be on the streets because of the continuous roundups, so the policeman accompanied her through the few blocks she had to pass from her apartment to our building. The guards at the entrance recognized her as our relative and let her in.

We were so happy to see each other again, still unhurt, still alive. Then Aunt Rosa told us the unbelievable story of Dr. Blumstein's behavior. The day after our arrest, she had approached him and asked to give her the box. "What box, what do you mean?" Dr. Blumstein had asked.

"The box with gold my brother gave you for me," my aunt replied.

Dr. Blumstein denied any knowledge of such a box. "Go away, foolish woman," he said. "I have nothing for you."

A little later my father confronted Dr. Blumstein and asked the reason for his behavior. He replied, "I was sure that you would return. Your sister became hysterical and I decided to keep the box for safekeeping. I was afraid that the poor woman would lose it."

"So please give me back my box," my father said in a stern voice. Only then did Dr. Blumstein reluctantly hand the box back to my father. And so it was: the man we trusted and believed to be our friend, this apparently outstanding citizen, given the opportunity, brazenly robbed a widow and her little orphan daughter.

Our bare apartment was the only place we could stay, albeit furtively. We spent most of the day in the courtyard, sneaking into our apartment at night. One day, when we came inside for a few minutes to rest on the bare floor, one of the high-ranking Jewish policemen who had taken us to the Umschlagplatz only a few days before caught us. He demanded three pieces of gold from my father, threatening, "Not only I will take you back to the Umschlagplatz, I will report you for illegally entering your requisitioned apartment." My father bargained with him. Finally, he gave the policeman two gold coins for his silence. The policeman was satisfied and left. Years later, I heard that he and his wife had survived the war and moved to Paris.

I reflected then, as I did during the bombing of Warsaw, how the time we were living in brought out people's true characters. While some people were greedy and cruel, others were brave and remained loyal to their family and friends. Mrs. Frankel was one such a person. She was visiting her friends when their building was suddenly sealed off by the Jewish police and the selection began. Mrs. Frankel had working documents, but her friends did not. The policeman ordered her friends to come down to the waiting truck, and told Mrs. Frankel, "You can stay behind in the apartment. You don't have to go down with us."

She answered, "We have been friends for years. I cannot turn my head away from them now. I will go with them, and I will not abandon them in their distress."

Mrs. Frankel was unable to take advantage of her new status as the "exempted Jewess with the papers." She could not dissociate herself from her friends. Thus, she went to the Umschlagplatz with them and they were deported together.

The Jewish policemen, who told us this story, were astonished at such loyalty and selflessness.

Mrs. Heller was another example of courage and loyalty. She was a young and good-looking "pure Aryan," a German Christian woman married to a Jew. Her husband had been deported from Germany in 1940. She joined him and went with him to the Ghetto. My mother met her there when she became her patient.

Mrs. Heller's brothers were Nazis, but they promised to forgive her "mistaken" marriage if she came to her senses and left her husband. She refused to do so. But later, when she realized that all the Jews would be murdered, she told her brothers, "Enough is enough, I have made a grave error and I am sorry. I don't want to see the man I called my husband ever again." They believed her, and found her a home.

She smuggled her husband out of the Ghetto and hid him there. She took great care that her Nazi brothers, who visited her from time to time, did not discover her concealed husband's presence; he remained hidden in the house till the end of the war. It was then that Mrs. Heller met my parents again, and returned, with her husband, as their patient. She laughed when she told the story, as if what she had done was the simplest and most natural thing.

During the days of August 1942, the deportations continued relentlessly. Whole blocks of apartments were sealed off and emptied by the Jewish policemen. Each day they had to fill their quotas of people to deliver to the Umschlagplatz. By then all the unemployed people who had no working papers were in hiding, as were the old, the sick, and the remaining children. The Jewish policemen entered courtyards and private apartments, dragging out anyone they could find. Later, they would even take people who had working papers, if they caught them outside working hours. The Germans too were present everywhere with their helpers, shooting at random and terrorizing the population.

The Schultz's workshop in our building, and that of the other German industrialist, Többens—located on Nowolipie Street, only a few streets from us—were operating at full capacity. The workers, protected by their papers, hoped to be employed there until the end of the war and the Germans' final defeat. Eventually my father managed to obtain working papers at the Többens workshop, but the rest of us were in constant danger of deportation. For this reason, Mother, Karolina and I remained at our old address, 38 Pawia Street, the site of the Schultz workshop, afraid to leave it.

The courtyard, packed beyond capacity, became the center of our lives. Luckily, the summer weather was pleasant in this month of August 1942, but wandering around the courtyard made us very tired as we had little to eat. So we were pleased when Mrs. Cukier, a neighbor who had been my parents' patient for many years, invited my mother, Karolina, and me to spend some time in her apartment. We had already forgotten how to sit on comfortable chairs in a furnished home.

The Cukier family was so far intact. They had prepared a hiding place near their apartment to escape with their six-year-old daughter if there was a selection raid. And, of course, they hoped that there would be no selections on the premises of the Schultz workshop.

Once when we were visiting around lunchtime, the little girl grew hungry and started to cry. Mrs. Cukier gave me an unfriendly look, her eyes signaling "Get out!" I moved to another room but could not help being aware that Mrs. Cukier was trying to hide from me that she was giving her child some bread and butter. Was she afraid, I wondered, that I would grab the food? Or was she afraid to show that she was rich enough to buy food? For food could be purchased in the Ghetto till the very end, for a very high price.

I could hardly believe what was happening: only a couple of weeks earlier, I had been "dear Irene" to Mrs. Cukier, who admired my clandestine studies and complimented me every time she saw me. Now, she saw us in a different light. We had lost our apartment and our belongings. Thus, I was no more the daughter of well-to-do and highly respected neighbors; I was a pauper to be kept at a distance. After this I no longer accepted her hospitality.

In the evenings people could relax a little, for there were no selections at night. They talked, exchanged news, and hoped for a miracle to rescue them from death. Most people in the courtyard were "illegal" — they had no working papers. Even though the night was safer than the day, the "illegals" were afraid to leave the courtyard to sleep in their homes because they could not be sure of getting into our building again the next morning. They slept in the cellars, in unfinished attics, in the workshop — any place they could find. With each sunrise and new day, people again lived from one minute to the next, praying to God for mercy and devising some new scheme of where to run, where to hide, or how to get "papers."

After spending the night on the bare floor of our former apartment, we would go out into the courtyard early in the morning. Mornings were a peak time for selections. The dense crowd of "illegals" was nervous and full of apprehension. But when noontime arrived and there had been no selections, not even a German visit, it was then a good half day. We tried to relax.

One day I was overjoyed to see Bela and her two sisters arriving at our courtyard haven. Bela and I hugged each other, marveling that we were both still alive. Her parents, who had no papers and were too old to obtain them, were hidden in the cellar of a building which housed a German workshop. But the three sisters were able to buy false temporary working papers, and so they dared to venture outside to buy food for their parents. They had to deliver it secretly; if discovered, the parents would immediately be seized and transported to the Umschlagplatz.

I confessed to Bela that I was choking with fear and with the pain of what was happening around me. I had no hope of surviving, yet I did not want to die; I wanted desperately to live, even if I had to become an emaciated beggar. I was so curious about life. I wanted to become a woman, a wife and a mother before I went to the grave.

Bela tried to encourage me, and we parted, embracing each other and hoping to meet again the next day. But the next day Bela and her two sisters were caught and deported.

Her parents waited in vain for their daughters to return, and they too perished a few days later.

One evening after my father finished his day at the workshop on Nowolipie Street, he came to see us at the courtyard with some good news. "I will tell you first, my dear girls, that you will get proper papers to work at the Schultz workshop. And there is hope for my sister Rosa. Her father-in-law, Józef Lautenberg, has come up with an interesting idea how to get his family out of the Ghetto."

Mr. Lautenberg had been born in a village called Zakrzówek, not far from the city of Kraënik. There was no industry there, only some farms around the village, and a few Jewish families living in the village. It was not even close to the railway; to reach Zakrzówek, one had to take a train to the city of Lublin, change to a local train to Kraënik, and then take a horse-drawn country wagon. The village was not even shown on maps, and Mr. Lautenberg firmly believed that the Germans would never discover its existence. He believed that if we could join the local Jews, we could probably stay with them until the end of the war.

Wanting to investigate this possibility by himself before taking his family, he had found a Jewish smuggler who could get him out of the Ghetto and take him to Zakrzówek. There were six in his family: his widowed daughter-in-law Rosa and his six-year-old granddaughter Hania; his son Gustaw with his wife Lily; Lily's mother Mrs. Fryd with her boyfriend.

My father suggested that Mr. Lautenberg take my mother, Janka Elterman, and Mrs. Tran with him on this exploratory trip. Whatever the danger, there was no hope for old Mrs. Tran if she were ever discovered by the Germans; and my father had tried in vain to obtain papers for Mother and Janka Elterman. The sooner these three women left the Ghetto, the better.

Mr. Lautenberg agreed, and decided that while he was gone, his daughter-in-law, Rosa, and little Hania should either stay with us at the Schultz workshop or with his son Gustaw at the Többens workshop, both considered safe from "selections." A wealthy man, he gave Rosa a small bag of precious stones which she hung around her neck under her clothes.

Then the courageous Józef Lautenberg left the Ghetto for Zakrzówek, taking the three women with him. He was full of hope that all would be all right, and promised Rosa to come back for her and Hania in a few days.

Early the next morning, my father succeeded in bringing Janka Elterman and her mother into our building where they were to wait for the smuggler. Mrs. Elterman, very nervous and frightened, had left her home in such a hurry that she had forgotten to take some of her less-expensive jewelry hidden in a box. As soon as she realized what had happened, she became very anxious to recover her treasure. But she was afraid to go out because of the morning selections, and so she tried to get me to go instead. She appealed to my conscience, saying that she had saved us from the Umschlagplatz, pointing out that if she had her jewelry she could share it with us. "We shall need a lot of money to survive," was how she put it. I looked like a young, innocent girl, she urged, and would be able to get through the streets to her apartment without attracting much attention. Besides, it was my duty to contribute to our welfare; she and her mother were now part of our family, were they not?

I could not resist her pleading, even though I was afraid to leave our building to face the dangerous streets. But I did as she asked: I ran to her building further along Pawia Street, went into her apartment, took the jewelry, hid it in a bag under my clothes and left the building.

The street was swarming with men in uniform, Germans and Lithuanians, Latvians and Ukrainians They were sealing off whole blocks of houses, looking for people like hungry wolves for prey. This is the end for me, I thought. But, pretending not to be afraid, I walked on without stopping, passing between the men in uniform.

And I was not arrested.

Were they so preoccupied with their planned "action" that they did not want to waste time on my unexpected appearance? I don't know. But I do know that Janka Elterman risked my life for a few gold pieces. She did not thank me when I gave them to her; suddenly they had become unquestionably "hers," not "ours." But Janka's attitude was not important to me then. For I was thinking about my mother and our separation, and that she was leaving the Ghetto for a safer place.

While we waited for Józef Lautenberg's return, Karolina and I began working at the Schultz workshop sewing by hand around a table with five or six other women. Our supervisor was a young German Jewess who took the work very seriously. Although she and her mother had been deported from Germany to the Ghetto not long ago, she remained a trusting and patriotic German.

From the beginning I disliked the workshop and could not sew. My gnawing hunger and the shop's dust and stuffy air were more than I could tolerate. I had fainting spells and felt nauseous and frequently had to leave the table and lie down in a corner. Karolina, who was stronger and more composed than I, did not leave me for a moment. The woman supervisor must have seen what an inadequate worker I was, but she said nothing, only shook her head and looked at me with pity. Karolina tried to encourage me, but I could not overcome my malaise. It was not until the early evening, when we could go out into the courtyard again and breathe the fresh and pleasant air, that I would recover.

One evening I met Mr. and Mrs. Mitnik in the courtyard. When we met people we had known before the war, there was always a feeling of celebration, of joy in finding out that some friends were still alive.

I liked and respected the Mitniks, who I knew through my Aunt Rosa. When I visited them with my aunt in those bygone days, I was impressed by their kindness and hospitality. They were intellectual and artistic people, with elegant and tasteful furniture and beautiful paintings. Kind, quiet, and well educated Mr. Mitnik was a dedicated and enthusiastic Esperantist. Mrs. Mitnik was devoted to their only child, a little girl named Stela who was then around three years old.

Stela was a beautiful and unusually graceful child, with golden hair, very large brown eyes and smooth, rosy cheeks. She was intelligent and well-spoken for her age, and very affectionate. I had often met her with her mother, holding hands and strolling together through the Saski Gardens. She was always with her mother, rather than with a maid or a governess, as was customary in our pre-war middle-class families. I would often see Stela happily skating for hours in a public park, while her mother stood by and watched her.

But now, in the courtyard in this early evening of August 1942, I did not see Stela with her parents. Mrs. Mitnik explained that, some time ago, Stela had been sent for safety to their ex-maid who lived in the country. The maid was poor and had been glad to have the Mitniks pay her to look after the child. But now — Mrs. Mitnik began to cry — they had no more money left; and the maid had sent word to the parents that she would not be able to keep Stela much longer if there were no payments forthcoming.

Mr. Mitnik looked pale and desperate. "Somebody will help Stela," he tried to reassure himself and his wife.

The Mitniks did not have papers themselves. They had sneaked into our courtyard to gain some time, hoping for a miracle to save them from deportation, but they had reached the end of their resistance. They were mentally crushed, and no longer able to protect their child. Shortly after our meeting, Mr. and Mrs. Mitnik were deported and perished.

But many years later, after the war, I heard rumors that Stela was alive. The maid had sent her to a convent, where the Catholic sisters had adopted and protected her. In 1946, an uncle came from abroad to search for Stela. But the convent sisters concealed her, and neither her uncle nor anybody else could find her. It was strange to think that the once-beloved, bright Jewish child had perhaps become an austere nun.

Minutes before the curfew on the same day I met the Mitniks, my father came to take Karolina and me to his quarters at the Többens workshop on Nowolipie street. It was safer for him to sleep on his workshop's premises, and he had been lucky to find a place there.

Five of us shared the single room: the three of us, and Mrs. Franka Zíoto and her daughter, Krystyna. Since there were only two beds (though plenty of bedbugs), Mrs. Zíoto and Krystyna shared one bed, while the three of us shared the other. Karolina and I slept in our clothes; not only were we embarrassed to be sleeping in the same bed with our father but we also feared the possibility of a German raid.

I missed my mother very much. This was the first time that she had not been with us at night, and the presence of Mrs. Zíoto in the same room as my father embarrassed me. But I liked Krystyna, a healthy and energetic 16-year-old. Her big brown eyes seemed full of promise; I felt that she did not deserve the premature death awaiting us all. I wanted to be friends with her, but she was devoted to her mother and cold to me.

My father tried to smile for Karolina and me, to encourage us, but he was very tired and frightened. And my private world was disintegrating too, the ground shifting from under my feet. We had survived so far, but we were in the middle of a mass deportation: six, seven, even ten thousand people were disappearing daily. Those who had not yet been deported knew that they would not escape, and yet, at the same time, hoped to survive. Until the last moment, everyone hoped to be spared. We truly did not know what the Germans had prepared for us: the gas chambers and the scale of the mass murder. Would we have behaved differently if we had known the truth? Can human beings accept impending execution, without a hope that a miracle will save them at the last moment?

We slept badly in our bug-infested single bed, frightened and fully dressed as we had been during the bombing. Early the next morning Karolina and I went to our jobs. The Schultz workshop was at the address where I had lived all my life, but nothing was the same. Our nice apartment had become an odious hide-out which we could enter only secretly and with great fear, and I felt constantly dirty, hungry, and tired.

At the workshop courtyard, my Aunt Rosa and her daughter, Hania, came to see us. (I believed that Rosa had finally got temporary working papers, for she and Hania managed somehow to circulate between the Schultz and the Többens workshops, as did my father.) But six-year-old Hania was not well; she had been coughing for some time, and it now became clear she had the whooping cough. She was frequently seized by paroxysms which left her weak and distressed. Her fearful eyes were full of tears, though she tried bravely to hold them back. In her plaintive voice she would call out, "Mama, Mama," and cling closer to Rosa, not leaving her for a second.

Rosa was beside herself, desperate and restless; she would have done anything to help her sick daughter, and her heart was torn every time Hania had a coughing fit. She could think of nothing but finding food for her. She even had the money to buy it, but food was not easy to find at this time, and she decided to stay at the Többens workshop for the next few days, with her brother-in-law and his wife, Lily. The mother and her child, exhausted and helpless, moved out from our place to the Többens workshop to await an uncertain tomorrow.

Karolina and I continued to appear at the worktable in the Schultz workshop. One woman there, who sat near the window, had with her a young child, a boy around five years old, whom she tried to hide between the window and the table. He cried frequently and wanted to sit on his mother's lap. We all hoped that the Germans would not come in and deport or kill him on the spot. We tried to comfort mother and child and were afraid that the supervisor would chase the boy away, but she did not.

The women would talk around the worktable, remembering the better days of the past. One woman mentioned the B. family, the dentists, who had lived in this building with their two young daughters. Two others remembered the family as well. Suddenly, everybody seemed to have known the young daughters, and everyone marveled at how nice and well bred these girls had been. One would think the women were talking about a couple of princesses.

After a while I could not restrain myself, and said, "I am one of the two sisters you are talking about."

The women laughed. One said, "You must have a great imagination. I saw the sisters before, and you don't look at all like either of them."

The other women looked at me disapprovingly as if I was an impostor, and Karolina smiled and signaled to me not to insist. I stayed quiet, perplexed. I felt that something very serious was happening to me but I did not realize then that I was beginning to lose my identity.

In the late afternoon we would meet our friends in the courtyard. They were more Karolina's friends than mine, for they were at least her age, twenty, and some older. One of them was her old friend Sol. He belonged to a secret Jewish resistance movement.

Well before the beginning of the "Final Solution" on July 22, 1942, Sol warned Karolina that our lives were in mortal danger and begged her not to reveal to anyone that he was involved in the Jewish resistance. Now he and his group of young men were preparing themselves with renewed determination to fight. They agreed to include the two of us in their action.

August 12, 1942. Karolina and I were at our worktable at the Schultz shop. The day had moved slowly until around noon when we heard loud German voices shrieking orders, "Get out fast." The Jewish supervisors, their faces ashen, pushed us downstairs.

No one expected a selection on our premises, yet a selection it was. The woman from our table tried to hide her little boy in a box probably prepared in advance for this purpose. But the child began to cry hysterically:

"Mama, don't leave me here, mama! Take me with you, mama, I'm afraid, I'm scared, mama!"

The woman's face became red and twisted as she tried to force him into the box. She looked in anguish at the rest of us, leaving the room to go downstairs. She had good papers, she could pass the selection; but her son would not. The last time I saw her she was trying to lock little boy in the box. But she did not leave him.

Hundreds of people came out of the shop and assembled on the street in front of our building. We were formed into a long line down the middle of Pawia Street, four or five in a row. Germans with whips in their hands were walked alongside guarding us, while those in the front directed people either to the right or to the left. The right side meant you would stay in the Ghetto; the left side, you would go to the Umschlagplatz and to the trains.

While the selection was going on, some Poles were watching us from the windows of the guards' dining room in the Pawiak prison. They were just on the other side of the street, so close to us, yet we faced our death while they were safe. They were laughing and hurling insults at us.

I ignored them. I didn't want to waste my energy being angry at them. I wanted to observe what was going on around me with my eyes and ears open, to concentrate on how to pass the selection. There was no other way out.

We were not restrained while waiting our turn, and so people were moving from one row to another to be closer to their friends. Some people moved to the front, close to the Germans, and some moved to the back rows, hoping, I thought, that the selectors would eventually get tired and not bother with the people at the back. That seemed logical to me. However, I saw that the bosses were taking their own elderly parents from the back of the line to the front. Something told me that they knew what they were doing and that there was a good reason for not remaining at the back.

Karolina and I were standing more or less in the middle and I took her hand and led her toward the front. She was surprised, but followed me.

I had a full view of the selection process. I saw our German Jewish woman supervisor presenting herself for the verdict with her old mother. The German in charge brutally pushed the mother to the left. The young woman spoke to him confidently, obviously explaining something to him in her excellent German. Then I heard a groan and saw her pain and disbelief as she too was pushed to join her mother on the left side.

The German officer was tall, with a long whip in his hand and he stood with his legs wide apart as though he were mounted on a horse. Because I was small, my eyes were nearly level with his groin and when he ordered a person to the left, I could see his penis swelling inside his trousers.

At this very moment images of horror films I had seen, in which men turned into monsters, came into my mind. I was appalled then, yet at the same time, I felt pity when I saw the Wolfman becoming a wolf. And now in front of this German officer, I asked myself, as I asked myself when watching a horror film: why had these men not been given a chance to be fully human? What had they done that God had punished them so cruelly by turning them into real monsters?

And I prayed silently, thanking God that this had not happened to my family, for we were human.

Our turn came. Karolina and I tried to be very calm, looking straight into the monster's eyes and not saying a word more than necessary. We presented our temporary working papers. We were directed to the right.

While I stood there, I saw our neighbor, Halinka Herszhorn, a pale and emaciated young girl, facing the German selector. She was pushed to the left.

I, who'd had well-to-do parents and a more comfortable existence than hers, now stood on the side of life, looking at her on the side of death. Our eyes met. She recognized me, smiled and raised her hand, as if blessing me — and all of us, while saying adieu.

Her waving hand, her gentle innocent eyes of a child, and her whole being were telling me, "I surrender to my fate; there is no hatred in my heart. Go on living, I wish you well."

The Germans shouted the order to turn around and march. Halinka, her delicate face reflecting inner calm and infinite goodness, looked at us for the last time. I followed her slender, slightly hunched frame as she marched toward the Umschlagplatz, until she disappeared around the corner of the street.

The selection continued a little longer; then, suddenly, it stopped. All the people in the back rows were taken to the Umschlagplatz without having had a chance to present their papers; the people in the front were left standing on Pawia Street. My premonition of the danger of staying at the back was correct.

When we returned to our worktable, the woman and her boy were nowhere to be found. Were they shot in the courtyard or were they taken to the Umschlagplatz? I didn't ask.

Later that day Pawia Street was quiet, with no Germans in view and no trace of the noon-time selection. I joined my sister Karolina, who was chatting with her underground resistance friends. They spoke in hushed voices, careful not to be overheard. Karolina was warming to their ideas, and it seemed to me that she had become a little taller.

The curfew was approaching when we were found by Gustaw Lautenberg, our Aunt's Rosa's brother-in-law. The sweat was running down his face; he looked haggard and could hardly breathe. "Rosa and Hania were caught and deported," he gasped. "I could not save them."

Karolina and I almost fainted. Our beautiful, thirty two-year-old Aunt Rosa, and little Hania, with her whooping cough, had been taken to the freight train. What agony was imposed on the sick, coughing child in a windowless wagon, packed beyond capacity. And what agony for her helpless mother! It was inconceivable, it could not be true, it could not have happened.

But it had; Rosa and Hania were gone.

Gustaw told us that there had been a selection at the Többens workshop on Nowolipie Street at the same time as the one at our workshop. Our father had not been there; Gustaw had met him afterwards and had to tell him that he had just lost his sister and his little niece. Gustaw felt so guilty about what had happened that he ran to tell Karolina and me in person, as if we could absolve him.

I too felt guilty. I knew there was nothing I could have done to save the child and her mother but that did not alleviate my guilt.

Our father was crying when he came soon afterwards to take us back to his sordid room on Nowolipie Street for the night. He looked at Karolina and me with infinite love. He knew that our time to be deported was approaching, and did not know how to save us.

The next day, Gustaw Lautenberg came running again to see Karolina and me on Pawia Street. The man who had taken Józef Lautenberg to Zakrzówek had come back. He had come to take Rosa and Hania and the rest of the Lautenberg family to Zakrzówek, as arranged — just one day after Aunt Rosa and Hania were deported. If only the selection had not taken place the day before, they would still have been alive; they would leave the Ghetto today.

The smuggler had purchased six false travel passes, but now that Rosa and Hania were gone, he refused to take a load of only four people. He could not afford losing money, he said. He demanded that Gustaw find two trustworthy and non-Jewish looking people to replace Rosa and Hania; otherwise, he would take another family.

Gustaw considered Karolina and me the most suitable candidates for this venture and asked us if we would be interested. He needed an answer as soon as possible, so it was fortunate that our father happened to be with us. He looked at us, uncertain as to what to say and how to advise us. On the one hand, the journey was risky and the future in Zakrzówek uncertain; on the other, this seemed a unique opportunity for Karolina and me to leave the Ghetto. Fortunately, he could pay for our passage, for the smuggler asked a modest sum. He wanted to use all his passes. Finally, it was decided that Karolina and I would join our mother in Zakrzówek. Father, certain that his papers would protect only him, had constantly worried about us. But now he felt relieved, for he believed that, once out of the Ghetto, we too would be safe. There was no time for a sentimental good-bye. We had to separate—we hid our tears. We had to be strong if we wanted to survive.

Later the same day, Karolina and I spoke with our resistance friends. We were embarrassed to tell them we wanted to run away, and save ourselves. But to our surprise, they approved of our decision without reserve and encouraged us to escape as soon as possible.

"We will continue to fight, even if knowing that the Germans will destroy us in the end. You must understand that there is no hope for us here in the Ghetto. But there is hope for you, if you leave," they said, smiling at us in warm friendship. Suddenly I felt very close to these men. I wanted to stay with them, to remain friends with them forever.

But the next day, Karolina and I left the Ghetto.

HANIA IN 1938

ROSA (ROZIA)
IRNE'S AUNT, HANIA'S MOTHER
MURDERED IN 1942

SIX

FLIGHT TO ZAKRZÓWEK

The six of us, accompanied by our guide, left in the morning. At the police station at the Ghetto exit, our guide presented documents stating that we were a group of Jews going to work for the Germans in a place outside the Ghetto. This was not unusual, for Jews continued to work for the Germans on the Aryan side, even after the Ghetto was sealed.

We walked quickly through the police station, hid our fear, and followed our guide without looking around. He had instructed us, "Once outside the Ghetto, cover your armbands with your coats. Do not remove them, just cover them." We did not want to attract attention, even though we had "good papers." At the same time, we had to protect ourselves against the shady characters who specialized in "recognizing" the Jews and making a living out of blackmail. Thus we had to play safe. We acted as non-Jews for the general public, but we remained Jews, protected by our false papers, if intercepted. For we could also be stopped by the gangs of Polish children who waited outside the Ghetto wall and amused themselves by catching Jews sneaking out of the Ghetto. If a man or woman looked lost and uncertain near the Ghetto wall, it aroused the children's suspicions. They encircled their victim and chanted loudly, "Jew, Jew, we caught a Jew," until they attracted the Germans' attention. If the person caught was in fact Jewish, he would be savagely beaten, then shot dead on the spot or deported never to be seen again. Sometimes a "lucky" Jew was not killed but just thrown back into the Ghetto after a severe torment and beating.

We walked through the Warsaw streets and arrived safely at the train station. Nobody stopped us. Our guide had bought our tickets in advance, and we boarded the train to the city of Lublin without being asked any questions.

We entered into a single train compartment occupied already by the Christian Poles, or Aryans, as they were then called. Four of them sat on one bench, and a man sat alone on another across from them. Each bench was designed for just four people. We were greeted in a friendly manner, and the man sitting by himself moved over and sat with his four companions. People were used to the overcrowded trains and tried to make room for others. The six of us—Gustaw, his wife Lily, her mother, Mrs. Fryd, with her boyfriend, Karolina and I—managed to squeeze on our single wooden bench. Our guide stood outside in the narrow corridor, ostensibly looking through the window, in fact, watching for the approach of the train conductor. The other passengers did not know that we were Jews, as we still hid our armbands.

The conductor, a Christian Pole, entered the compartment to check the tickets. Our guide and leader had already intercepted him and given him a small bribe not to give us any trouble. But I believe that in any case he did not want to hurt us. He looked like a decent man. After a few polite words with our leader, he asked, "Who are they?" He wanted to look at the six runaway Jews whom he was unable to distinguish from the other passengers. The leader indicated us with his hand, and we uncovered our armbands to identify ourselves.

I watched the reaction of the Christian Polish passengers with great apprehension. I had been brought up in the Polish language and culture, loving Poland, respecting its customs, obeying its laws and its government. Poland was my country, and the Polish people were my compatriots. Thus, their anti-Semitism hurt me deeply and caused me great pain. While the German atrocities frightened and repelled me, they did not touch my sense of self-worth. To me the Germans were like savage beasts pursuing us. Would I think less of myself because tigers or hyenas were ready to eat me alive? I would run away, I would hide, I would do anything to escape from them, but I would not be morally or emotionally wounded by them. However, I felt differently about my Christian fellow citizens. I needed, I wanted to be liked and accepted by them. Their rejection would hurt me profoundly.

But the attitude of the Christian passengers was sympathetic and not at all hostile. They started talking with us, and urged us to throw away our armbands and our Jewish identity. They asked us, "Do you know what is awaiting you, what the Germans are preparing for you?" We replied truthfully that we did not know. Our new friends told us about the concentration camps, the torture and death in store for all Jews. "You have nothing to lose, you will surely be murdered, so get rid of your armbands and mingle with the rest of us, the Polish people."

I listened attentively to every word they said. The three men and two rather young women looked straight into our faces and, at one point, fixed their eyes upon me. "But you don't look Jewish at all. You would not be recognized. You have a chance to survive, child. Run away, run for your life!"

Those five people seemed truly to care about my survival, repeating over and over again that I could be saved and survive as a Pole. They persuaded me that all Poles did not hate us, did not wish us to perish. The world was not totally ugly; there was a place in it for me. Heartened by their concern, I felt my will to live returning.

We sat quietly thinking about our uncertain future. Karolina and I talked a little and held hands. The journey to Lublin went smoothly. But as soon as we filed out of the train and on to the platform, we saw Germans with pistols and machine-guns in their hands. There was a great deal of commotion, and Karolina and I were pushed ahead by the crowd and separated from the rest of our group. Instinctively we slipped our armbands into our pockets.

We were in the middle of a roundup of Polish people. Train stations were often subjected to roundups, because it was easy to catch food smugglers there and to detain a large number of people in one swoop. The situation we found ourselves in was very dangerous: we could be sent to a concentration camp or be shot in a nearby forest or, at best, transported to work in Germany. Karolina and I would certainly perish once our Jewish identity was discovered.

We were all herded together and surrounded by armed Germans, hundreds of frightened people waiting to be put into three huge, open trucks standing in front of us. Karolina and I looked around and observed what was going on inside our captive group. We had survived a roundup in the Ghetto, where we were saved by moving closer to the Germans. Should we do the same now?

Many people became hysterical. They could not endure the dreadful waiting and moved to the front to get it over with quickly, one way or the other. A few people in the crowd were obviously professional smugglers who clearly had some experience of how to behave under the circumstances; this was not their first roundup. They stayed as far as possible from the Germans, constantly turning about, moving back, and hiding behind other people. We followed them, acting as they did.

The roundup seemed to last forever, but eventually it was over. Three trucks, bulging with people, moved away slowly. The rest of us stayed behind. We knew that sometimes the Germans machine-gunned the people for whom there was no room in the trucks; one was never sure how to behave with them. But this time they departed, leaving us free on the street.

The cries from the seized Poles faded into the distance. Those of us who had escaped began to go our own ways. The train discharged new crowds, totally unaware of the recent tragedy. Life became "normal" again.

We found our friends still sitting undisturbed in the train. They scoffed at Karolina and me for being stupid enough to be caught. I was angry at them for not rejoicing at our deliverance and did not ask how they had escaped. It is possible that they saw or were warned at the last moment, that the Germans were preparing a roundup. They may have got back into the train and stayed there until the Germans marched away.

The train to Kraënik was due the next day. We spent a night in Lublin in a private home prearranged by our guide. From Kraënik we boarded a horse-drawn farm wagon shared with other people.

Finally, we reached Zakrzówek. Karolina and I followed Gustaw and his family, who joined Józef Lautenberg.

How tragically surprised he was when he saw my sister and me instead of his beloved granddaughter, Hania, and his daughter-in-law, our Aunt Rosa. He had prepared a place for them, he had done all he could to protect them—but they were gone.

He tried to control his grief, and politely took Karolina and me to our mother.

She did not expect us, and could not believe her eyes when we appeared. We restrained our joy; we told her about Rosa and Hania.

Thus, our new life began. It was now mid-August, 1942. We moved in with our mother, Mrs. Tran and her daughter. They had rented one room from a very poor Jewish family, happy to earn a little extra money from us.

I remember them well: one daughter, a spinster, cleaned, cooked and baked for the family and took care of her very old father. It had been a long time since I had seen a Jewish patriarch, almost a biblical Jew, living openly in his own house, enjoying the sun and fresh air and, above all, his family's love and respect. They had a farmer's ancient oven in the kitchen wall, and every week the daughter baked delicious bread and rolls, followed by a special Jewish dish for Saturday.

There was no ghetto in Zakrzówek; the Jews lived in harmony alongside the Poles.

Soon after our arrival, the Jewish community elders came to greet and welcome us. They asked about the latest news, as if we knew more than they did. (Jews asked each other constantly about news at that time, hoping to hear some secret information that the Germans would soon be defeated.)

They told us that they were paying gold to the Gestapo stationed in Kraënik for not deporting them. Zakrzówek was a small village, so inconsequential that it was not even shown on the Germans' maps. The Gestapo men hoped that their bosses in Berlin would never discover it, so they could enjoy a steady income for a long time. They were honest enough to tell the Jews that once Zakrzówek was discovered and the order for deportation came, they would have to obey, and the Zakrzówek Jews would be liquidated. They promised, however, that they would try to warn the Jews about the deportation as soon as they received an order from Berlin.

The elders in turn promised that they would let us know about the deportation or resettlement the moment the Gestapo informed them. They believed that we would be able to save ourselves, since we had already been resourceful enough to come all the way from Warsaw.

Soon the young Jewish men of the community came to greet us as well. Karolina and I—educated young women from Warsaw—were quite an attraction and they treated us with great interest and respect. We were "ladies," chaperoned by our mother, doctor of dentistry, and the aristocratic, venerable Mrs. Tran.

One of the most urbane and well-spoken of the Jewish young men was Edmund, a couple of years older than the others. He had no faith in the Gestapo protection of the Zakrzówek Jews, and was trying to find a way to save at least some people. He was very impressed by our bold escape from Warsaw and took a great interest in us.

Edmund fell in love with Karolina, who liked him a great deal. All the men were crazy about my beautiful sister. As for me, I was most attracted to a handsome young man named Muniek. He had beautiful, large eyes of a most unusual color, very light brown turning to green when they reflected the sun's rays. I could never stop admiring Muniek's eyes, and began to like him a lot.

We often walked together through the countryside, passing fields of golden wheat and blue flowers, open green pastures, tall trees with leaves already turning yellow. Occasionally we came upon lovely streamlets and brooks. The view, mingled with the murmur of water, the singing of birds and perfumed fresh air, made me drowsy.

How far I was from the sordid Warsaw Ghetto; how close I was to Muniek. I was a healthy, 18-year-old woman and for the very first time in my life, I felt irresistibly attracted to a young man. We sat under an old tree whose branches, like a large umbrella, shaded us from sun. Then we lay down next to each other, holding hands and barely talking. I felt light and happy — totally relaxed. I wanted to be closer to Muniek, I was waiting for him to make a move. But he remained still.

And then we heard the merry and loud voices of the young Polish children approaching us. They were laughing and singing, "We will tell the priest on you, ha, ha, ha — You are naughty, naughty, ha, ha, ha — do it, we are waiting, ha, ha, ha."

We stood up and slowly moved away. Thus, nothing, absolutely nothing, physical ever happened between Muniek and me, mostly because of his gentlemanly behavior, but also because of the lack of opportunity.

The young men visited us daily, and we talked endlessly. The evenings were sweet and warm. Yet, in spite of all our wishful thinking, we never forgot that we lived under German rule where death was always imminent.

The Jewish young men tried to contact the Polish partisans in order to join them, either immediately or as soon as the "Final Solution" was brought to the village. Zakrzówek was surrounded by old forests where the partisans were said to be hiding, but if they existed, they were unwilling to meet our young friends and did not want to help. The young, healthy Jewish men were sitting ducks awaiting death. They could find no arms, no shelter, no help of any kind to resist the Germans.

I said to myself, "If I survive the war, I will certainly hear a lot about the partisans' heroic exploits. Everybody will claim to have been a partisan, a fighter against the Germans. Why don't they take the young Jews into the forest or give them arms, so they can defend themselves and their village? Where are the partisans now? Who are they?"

As we learned later, they were men and women of different backgrounds and beliefs. Some acted on their own. Many were violently anti-Semitic.

Besides Janka Elterman, who lived with us, Mrs. Tran had a married son, Julius, who had two young daughters. Julius, having obtained the false papers of an Aryan Pole, worked somewhere in Austria where he hoped to survive the war.

By pure chance, Julius' wife and the two girls lived under assumed names very near Zakrzówek. The wife, Marta, pretended to be the widow of a Polish officer and told people that she had moved to this area because the cost of living in Warsaw was prohibitive. In other words, Mrs. Tran's daughter-in-law was hiding as a Christian Pole.

She and her husband were assimilated Jews and fraternized a great deal with Christian Poles. They had lived in the Ghetto only for a short time with Mrs. Tran and Janka, then they appealed to their Polish friends, who provided them with false identity papers, and helped them to escape from the Ghetto.

Janka Elterman decided to contact her sister-in-law to get from Marta the name and address of her sponsors and protectors. Janka wrote her a letter, being very careful not to give her away, and asked for an appointment. Marta fixed a meeting at night at the Zakrzówek cemetery. Eventually she gave Janka the name and address of her protectors, the Pawlo family, and also wrote to them begging to help Janka and us.

My paternal grandmother, my father's stepfather and his two half-sisters had lived all their lives in Lublin. They had survived the massive deportations of March 1942, and remained in Lublin illegally, for they did not have proper working papers. My parents were in touch with them, and my mother managed to inform her mother-in-law that we were in Zakrzówek.

One day a woman came to see my mother, affirming that she was sent by my grandmother. We did not know how the woman escaped from Lublin and reached us, but we knew that the most daring entrances into or exits from the ghettos happened sometimes.

The woman said, "Mrs. B., how would I know your name and address if not from your mother-in-law? She, and nobody else, had sent me. She is starving and is begging you to send her some money."

I watched as my mother, now a poor refugee herself, gave one half of her money to the woman. I don't think my paternal grandmother ever received that money, because soon after the messenger left, my 57-year-old grandmother was murdered. A man who had escaped at the last moment from the Lublin ghetto, and found a refuge in Zakrzówek, as we did, witnessed the agony of my paternal grandmother.

He told us, "She hid with her husband and their two daughters. The husband was caught first and deported. The next day her two daughters were taken. She remained in hiding grieving and crying for her family. Then, two days later, she was found, deported and murdered."

I saw before my eyes the face of my gentle and loving grandmother. I didn't cry, I thought about her agony, I felt crushed. Before she met her brutal death, she had had to endure the loss of her daughter, Rosa, her granddaughter, Hania, and her son-in-law, Ignacy; and, at the end, she also lost her husband

and their two daughters. I will always remember her cruel fate, and my mother's futile generosity.

One sunny, glorious day in the second week of October 1942, about two months after our arrival, a couple of Jewish men ran up to our house to tell us that it was the end for the Zakrzówek Jews. They were to be "resettled," that is, murdered. The Jewish community had received this information from the local Gestapo, and the two men urged our group to run away from Zakrzówek, to save our lives. They appealed to my mother, "Don't let your daughters die. You have a chance—go back to Warsaw."

Later, our other friends came, in spite of the death sentence threatening them. They repeated, "Run away, you have a chance, run away!"

The Jewish men again tried desperately to contact the partisans and join them—in vain. The partisans, if they existed, had vanished deep into the forest. The men said that they would stay and die together with their families.

Karolina's friend Edmund came to help us. He could do nothing for himself or his family—they had nowhere to go, and nowhere to hide. But he knew an honest and trustworthy farmer's family who could assist us for a short time.

Christians who helped the Jews were shot, if discovered, and, naturally, not many were ready to risk their lives. But Edmund had convinced the farmer's family that we would very soon get Aryan papers and would return to Warsaw. We just needed to stay in hiding for a few days, until we obtained these papers. Edmund's friends, the Sobolewskis, agreed to hide us at their small farm in the countryside, very close to the village.—without asking for any money.

Now the problem was how to get those false papers. We had the address of the Pawlos, and we hoped that they would help us. But one of us had to go back to Warsaw, get the papers and bring them to Zakrzówek. Who would do it?

There was general confusion in our little group. Janka Elterman announced that she had to take care of her old mother and would stay put. So my mother pointed at me and told me to go to Warsaw and meet the Pawlos. She believed that I was more "Polish/Aryan" looking than Karolina, and thus would be able to travel, get the documents, and bring them back to Zakrzówek.

Edmund told us that if the Jews had to leave Zakrzówek before I returned, he would take my mother, Karolina, Janka and her mother to the farmer's family. He explained to me very clearly where the Sobolewskis' farm was and how I could find it coming from Zakrzówek.

Józef Lautenberg decided that he would act for his own family. He would definitely go to Warsaw for help. With his long mustaches, his proud blue eyes, his erect posture and his commanding voice, Józef Lautenberg could easily pass for a Polish nobleman.

SEVEN

REACHING FOR HELP: BACK TO WARSAW

The journey back to Warsaw without any identity papers was very risky. I did not even know how to get from our home to the Kraënik train station and, what was worse, I had to walk there. It was too dangerous to travel in a farm wagon; the Polish passengers might suspect that I, a stranger, was Jewish, running away from the imminent deportation.

My mother told me to follow Mr. Lautenberg, but he did not like the idea for he was afraid that I might be recognized as a Jewess. He did not wait for me and I had to run all the way to the station, trying not to lose sight of him. When we arrived and for a moment stood close to each other, Józef Lautenberg was visibly disturbed. He was a good and generous man who wanted to help me, but prudence told him to remain calm and think about his immediate family's survival.

Before we got into the train, his last words were, "Has it been worth it, has it been worth it?" I was not sure what he meant. Did he question whether it was worthy to remain a Jew, in spite of all the hardships it might cause? Did he doubt the worth of his loyalty to Judaism when circumstances now forced him to turn away from a distressed and frightened, though distant, relative?

We entered two separate compartments. I was now totally on my own, making the perilous journey to meet the Pawlo family, uncertain of how I would be received.

From Warsaw station I went directly to Dr. Jerzy êliwa's home. He was polite but could offer me no place to sleep. Thus, the first night I slept at the home of his friends, who were willing, as a favor to him, to risk their lives in sheltering me.

The next morning I went to see the Pawlos. A distinguished-looking lady opened the door. It was Mrs. Pawlo, the mother. I introduced myself, and she told me to wait in the entrance hall. Then she returned to the apartment and closed the door behind her. After a few minutes, which seemed to me like an eternity, I was invited into the living room where I met Mr. Pawlo, the father, a fine gentleman, and the two brothers, Zenon and Czeslaw. They looked very much alike with dark blond hair and blue, kind eyes behind large spectacles. Zenon, taller and a little older than his brother, was the leader. He was in his early thirties.

It was a pleasant family, and their apartment looked so elegant and comfortable that I longed to sit down and have a chat with them.

Instead, Zenon asked me to follow him to the next room. He did not invite me to sit down; standing, I explained the reason for my visit. He listened attentively and regarded me with profound compassion and sympathy. I was moved and tried hard to control my tears; at the same time, I felt somehow elated and warmed. I found Zenon very manly and attractive.

Calmly, he explained to me that one of his friends might be able to prepare the identity papers, called "kennkartes," for a modest price. Unfortunately he could not produce many documents and consequently had to assess carefully who would get the papers. We required five kennkartes, and that was a big order.

"I cannot ask for a kennkarte for Mrs. Tran, who is a very old lady and has already lived a full and long life," Zenon said. "We have to save a younger person. We are ready to risk our lives but only for people with a reasonable life expectancy."

He had a point; he was being logical. But in my mind I pictured our small group waiting for me in Zakrzówek. I saw Mrs. Tran's face, so very old, yet so bright and hopeful. How could I look into her eyes without a document for her? What would I tell her? After all, didn't we obtain the Pawlos' address thanks to her daughter-in-law? When the moment of departure arrived, and we had to leave Mrs. Tran behind, how would we do it? Would we run the moment she looked the other way? Would she cry and call after us?

I knew that if I survived the war, I could not live carrying such guilt. I had no choice; we must all get papers, or I would return to Zakrzówek to die with my family. Thousands of people, unable to rescue their families, chose to die together with them, even though they could have saved themselves.

I explained to Zenon, "Please understand, I cannot accept less than five kennkartes. If you cannot help me, I will go back to Zakrzówek to join my mother and sister." Zenon tried to convince me that I was wrong, but he agreed finally to get papers for all of us. I would have to wait a few days, and in the meantime find a place to sleep, as well as seek a shelter for the five of us on our return from Zakrzówek.

I met with Zenon several times while I waited for the documents. We met on the street or I was received briefly in the corridor of the family's apartment. I was never invited again into their living room, because Zenon's mother was nervous about my coming to their home. She felt that I didn't look Aryan enough and so could bring disaster to her family. But her two sons, Zenon and Czeslaw, were fearless and totally committed to defying the Germans. They believed that helping the Jews was an act of resistance as valid and patriotic as any military action.

"We are fighting the Germans our way, quietly and privately; we don't belong to any political party nor do we seek fame, or recognition for our deeds," the brothers said. "We are risking our lives without hesitation to defend the honor of Poland and our Christian values, and to help innocent people who are persecuted. We are following our conscience, we don't need the orders of a political leader to do it."

Did I hear them well? Yes, I did. They were truly admirable men, their words real and sincere.

Zenon worried about my father who still worked at the Többens workshop, sharing the insect-infested room with Mrs. Zíoto and her daughter Krystyna on Nowolipie Street. "Irene, we must get your father out from the Ghetto. His life is in great danger," he urged. He and Czeslaw worked for an electric and gas company and had a pass to enter the Ghetto. Zenon decided to use his pass to reach my father. I spoke to him about the young Krystyna Zíoto. I vividly remembered her soft, brown eyes looking at me intently, while she said simply, "Do not forget us." These were her last words just before Karolina and I left the Ghetto. I did not forget Krystyna, but all I could do was ask Zenon to help her.

Zenon and Czeslaw had an empty apartment on Dluga Street where they offered to hide my family. I went with Zenon to see the place. There were a couple of straw mattresses on the floor and practically no furniture. The neighbors knew that the apartment was empty, and my family would have to be extremely careful not to be detected.

Either Czeslaw or Zenon began to visit the apartment regularly, every evening, in order to establish a routine for the benefit of the neighbors. They would be used to seeing them when the brothers would later visit my hidden family there. Nevertheless, the fugitives would have to remain almost motionless by day, the danger of being discovered always present.

When we crossed the street, Zenon gently took my elbow to guide me. I wanted the street never to end, so much did I enjoy feeling his closeness. Yes, I fell in love with Zenon. I marveled at his immense courage in helping us. "Are you not afraid of being shot by the Germans for helping us?" I asked.

"Oh, you wouldn't believe it, but I am only afraid of being killed by a bomb. Death does not frighten me otherwise." And he repeated calmly, "I am not afraid to face a firing squad for what I am doing. But I am truly afraid of being killed by a bomb."

Well, there was no bomb threat on the horizon, and I sincerely hoped that no harm would come to Zenon for his helping us.

It was a painful and humiliating time for me; I was carrying a death sentence for anyone who was willing to assist me, yet I needed help and could not avoid contacting people. I hated to impose myself on Dr. and Mrs. êliwa. Mrs. êliwa was pregnant; my presence also endangered the life of her unborn baby. Yet the êliwas let me spend a couple of hours at their home every day.

The rest of the days were long and empty. I walked around Warsaw feeling like a stranger in the city where I was born and had spent all my life. I walked aimlessly to pass the time. I had very little money for myself because I had to pay for the kennkartes and for the expenses related to our journey back to Warsaw. So I walked the streets on an empty stomach, and the people who were risking their lives to save me did not think of offering me a cup of tea or something to eat.

But I did not feel entirely despondent; I felt as if my family were with me — they were always present in my mind. The memory of their faces, movements, words, and of their love nourished and sustained me.

Each night I slept at the home of one of Dr. êliwa's friends. In letting me in, albeit for only one night, they subscribed to the belief that Poles should help the persecuted Jews.

Since I had very little money, I was glad when I suddenly remembered that in the fall of 1939 my father had sent his new X-ray machine and the dental chair to his Christian colleague, Mr. Kosak, whom he believed to be a friend. Dr. êliwa suggested that I visit Mr. Kosak and ask if he would buy my father's dental equipment or sell it for us.

I knocked at Mr. Kosak's door and asked for him. He seemed very angry when he saw me. He chased me away, threatening, "Don't you ever come back here, I will march you straight to the Gestapo if you ever show your face here again."

Before I left Zakrzówek my mother had given me the address of our pre-war neighbor Mrs. Luka, who lived now on Okopowa Street. She greeted me warmly and offered without any hesitation to shelter my mother, Karolina, and me when we began our new lives under assumed names. I was overjoyed, because finding a place to stay had proven to be even more difficult than getting Aryan identity papers. It was a tremendous stroke of luck for us.

Encouraged by this good news, Zenon and Czeslaw confirmed that their empty apartment on Dluga Street would be at our disposal and promised to hide Janka Elterman and her mother there as soon as they arrived.

In the second week of October 1942, the kennkartes were finally ready. Zenon handed me the five documents, telling me solemnly, "From now on, you are another person and must forget who you were before."

Then he cautioned me, "You must be very careful not to fall into a German trap; they have experience in tricking people into revealing their real identity."

"Be aware, Irene," Zenon said. "During the interrogation of a suspected Jew, the Germans will hit the victim unexpectedly and hard from behind. A Christian Pole will cry out, 'Jesus Maria,' while a Jew will call, 'Oh my God.'"

"Forget the word 'God,' Irene. Never call God for help, never. Repeat over and over again 'Jesus, Maria and Saint Joseph,' until these words enter into your bloodstream, your mind, and your heart."

Zenon described another German trick in which the interrogators handed the victim a pen and said, "Please write." The victim would instinctively begin to write his or her real name.

"Irene, remember your new name," Zenon urged me. "Your real name must be forgotten and banished forever from your memory. You must forget your past and cling to the new identity we have invented for you. You are now a different person and must accept that completely."

I wanted to stay alive. I willingly accepted that I must forget who I really was until the end of my life. It was a heavy price to pay for my survival, but I did not realize it at the time.

With the papers now in my hand, I had to return to Zakrzówek and bring my family back to Warsaw. Zenon suggested that a Christian/Aryan Pole should accompany me and carry the papers. If I were caught, he or she would continue the journey and deliver the precious documents to my family; they would still have a chance to be saved. Again we had to act like brave soldiers: if one is killed, the others continue to fight.

I told Zenon about Mr. Koski, the husband of Mrs. Szmit's devoted friend, Mrs. Koska. She was a very clever woman and managed to support her family although her husband never had a steady job. The Szmits thought highly of Mrs. Koska, and so I trusted her and went to visit her. She invited me into their kitchen, which the family used as both a kitchen and a living room. Their small apartment was spotless. Mrs. Koska, pretty, vivacious, and dark-haired, was a gracious hostess. She offered me a glass of hot tea and we chatted amiably. I felt relaxed and was enjoying my visit when the door opened and her teenaged daughter, Emilia, her only child, came in. She looked at me, her eyes widening with terror. "Go away, go away," she cried out hysterically, "I am young, I don't want to die."

Emilia knew that any Pole who helped a Jew would be killed by the Germans; she did not want to be murdered on my account.

While Mrs. Koska tried to calm her, Mr. Koski entered the apartment. He was not at all disturbed by my presence and did not understand the reason for the excitement. "The only difference between a Jew and a Pole is that a Jew has to purchase a kennkarte on the black market, and then all his problems are solved," said Mr. Koski. "Irene, once you have the document, you are no worse off than we are — that is all there is to it."

It would have been useless to argue with him. But his wife had a better understanding of our situation and knew that we needed help. She asked her husband to accompany me to Zakrzówek. He was not working at the time and agreed—for a price—to travel with me.

We boarded the train on the way to Zakrzówek. Mr. Koski kept the papers in the upper part of his boots. In the train, as we sat together, he tried to put his hand under my skirt, and I tried desperately to keep his hands away from me without offending him. He had our precious identity papers, and I could not afford to antagonize him, but the idea of any physical contact with him was truly disgusting to me. I had never been touched by a man and I could not force myself to endure Mr. Koski's advances. His hands were as persistent as mine were defiant, and neither of us said a word.

We arrived at Lublin, where we had to spend the night before we could take a train to Kraënik. We went to Mr. Koski's friend's modest guest house. I was very frightened and unsure what to expect. When Mr. Koski ordered one room with a double bed, I had to think very fast about what the landlady would think of me if I made a fuss. A girl from a good family, a prude, had no business traveling with Mr. Koski at night, so what was I doing with him? Who was I? A runaway Jewess, of course. I could not let the landlady discover my secret.

On the other hand, the idea of being in the same bed with Mr. Koski was so abhorrent to me that I could not accept it, even if I risked my life. In despair, I raised my voice, looked directly into the landlady's eyes and said with conviction, "I don't want to share the bed with him. I want my own bed, away from him. Do you understand that? That is the way I want it, do you understand?"

The landlady was surprised by my attitude and afraid of any disturbance in her house. She tried to pacify me, "All right, all right, you will have your own bed," she said with a little smile around her lips. I slept well that night without being molested or disturbed in any way.

In the morning, very early, we sat at the long table in the dining room of this bed-and-breakfast establishment before catching our train to Kraënik. A few other guests were already sitting there. Three tall men in paramilitary uniforms had long rifles hanging on the backs of their chairs. They were Volksdeutschen, that is, Poles who had German ancestors and opted for German nationality. The men seemed pleased to see us, especially me, a young woman, and began telling us about their work, which was to chase Jews trying to evade deportation. They had been called for duty in this area where deportations were in progress. They bragged of their talent for smelling a Jew from a distance and never failing to recognize one. They smiled at me, trying to impress me with their work and their "gift" for detecting Jews.

"You know, Miss, we can smell a Jew a hundred kilometers away. No Jew can escape us." The men chuckled, confident of my admiration. They were gallant and courteous toward this young Polish lady from Warsaw, an unexpected and appreciative audience for their exploits.

But I was wondering where my family was now. Had the Zakrzówek Jews already been deported? What had happened to the old patriarch and his dutiful daughter, to all our friends?

Nevertheless, I smiled at the men and repeated, "Is that so? You are fantastic, no one can even be compared with you." They enjoyed the company and the breakfast, while I was struggling not to choke, not to vomit. I looked discreetly at Mr. Koski who seemed not to be disturbed at all.

We took the train to Kraënik and then the country wagon to Zakrzówek. Mr. Koski sat close to me and tried again to force his legs and his hands under my skirt. I said nothing but closed my thighs firmly and pushed his hands away from me. A strong and healthy eighteen-year-old girl, I fended him off without showing any emotion on my face. I hoped that my mute rejection would hurt his pride less and be forgiven.

While fighting Mr. Koski's advances, I tried to listen to our fellow travelers. They were saying that all the Jews from the area, including Zakrzówek, had been deported and none were left. Many had been shot on the spot; they mentioned some names and I recognized that of the old man, the patriarch, who was our landlord. Some people seemed happy about the deportation and killing of the Jews, while others just reported the news as current events without malice or regret.

Mr. Koski was so busy trying to feel my body that for a while he did not pay attention to the general conversation. But finally he too heard the news. He became uneasy; he was in my company, holding our false Aryan documents, while the tracking and pursuing of escaped Jews was in progress.

I realized that my family would no longer be in Zakrzówek and that we would have to find them in the countryside, as Edmund had prearranged. My mind raced to find a means of facing our new situation. I thought that the Germans and their collaborators would be looking for Jews running away from Zakrzówek and possibly toward the train station, but they would never suspect people arriving in Zakrzówek. What Jew would choose to come from the train right into their hands?

I decided to pretend to be a carefree young lady visiting all the way from Warsaw, unconcerned about the local problem of runaway Jews. I had to keep my head high and my face serene and smiling.

Our horse-drawn wagon arrived at Zakrzówek and all the passengers got out. Immediately I saw the Volksdeutschen standing in the middle of the village with vicious-looking dogs at their side, big whips in their hands and rifles over their shoulders. They watched our wagon attentively. Mr. Koski began to tremble, frozen with fear and hesitant to go on. He wanted to go back. I took his arm and said quietly, "There is no way to turn back. That would attract the Volksdeutschen attention. We must go on." Mr. Koski followed me and I went directly toward the Volksdeutschen with a smile on my face, giving them a little wave. "We just came from Warsaw. How can we reach the village?" I asked brightly. "I don't like to walk at night, but the trains are so unreliable nowadays and we have arrived so late."

The Volksdeutschen went out of their way to be courteous and polite to me, explaining how we could reach our destination, calling me "Panienko" — that is, "Miss" — full of smiles and putting on their best behavior.

"Isn't it dangerous for us to walk there at night?" I asked. They reassured me, "Nothing is going to happen to you, Miss. We are here, watching. We will protect you, don't worry."

I thanked them, grabbed Mr. Koski by the hand and slowly walked away into the forest. Well, we had escaped and, for the moment, danger was behind us. Mr. Koski recovered and tried to squeeze me again.

In the forest we felt safer and walked in the dark until we arrived at the farm where my family was supposed to be hiding. I knocked at the door, and a woman opened it a little. "What do you want?" she asked grudgingly.

I answered quietly, "I am looking for Mr. Edmund's friends, Mrs. B. and her family."

"Never heard of them. Go away."

"Well, you certainly know Mr. Edmund?"

"I don't remember any such person."

I knew that she was lying because she knew Edmund well, but I had no proof that my family had arrived at her home. I did not know what had happened to them. So I tried to prolong our conversation to get some information from her. In spite of her unfriendly manner and her repeatedly telling me to go away, she didn't close the door but continued talking to me.

"You must remember Mr. Edmund," I said. "He must have told you about Mrs. B. and her friends, such as Mrs. Fryd."

Mrs. Fryd was Lily Lautenberg's mother who lived with her boyfriend. They pretended to be a married couple.

"What are you talking about?" the woman said. "What Mrs. Fryd? Is she a married woman?"

Well, she was not. That was a big secret, because at that time living together without a marriage license was a sin, a disgrace. So I said, "You can say they are married, but I would not." My words produced a most unexpected effect. The farmer's wife opened the door wide and said, "Come in, come in."

I found myself in the arms of my mother and my sister. Janka Elterman and Mrs. Tran embraced me and kissed me warmly. They were sure that the papers would save our lives, that we were on the road to safety. But I knew that we still had the whole struggle of survival before us and thousand of problems to solve.

We had barely reached the second half of October 1942.

We had to wait a few days until the Volksdeutschen and the other headhunters pursuing the Jews were gone. We were hopeful of escaping once again, because we all had places to stay in Warsaw.

Mrs. Sobolewska, the farmer's wife and our hostess, liked Karolina and wanted her to remain on their farm. She understood that Edmund, the Sobolewskis' friend, would be happy to see Karolina again. Edmund's family had been deported, but he was hiding in the forest trying to join the Polish fighters. Karolina eagerly awaited news of him and gratefully agreed to remain with the Sobolewskis.

Mrs. Tran became difficult, refusing to wear the medallion with Jesus on the Cross or with Virgin Mary. "No, no, I am too old to bow to another religion, I cannot do it," she lamented. But it was unthinkable that a Polish woman of her age would not wear a saint's medallion on her neck. Janka finally persuaded her mother to make a concession to the Christian faith for her sake. Old Mrs. Tran grimly and reluctantly agreed to wear the gold chain with the medallion.

Our hostess gave me a bouquet of flowers to carry prominently to make me look like a happy traveler. She instructed me that at the station I should wave to the German soldiers in the passing trains. We tearfully said goodbye to our new friends and left for Warsaw.

In Warsaw, after a safe and uneventful journey, the new phase of our fight for survival began. Now we had to concentrate on not being recognized as Jews. Some of us would have to remain hidden, while others would venture out, ignoring the risk of being caught on the street. Hiding at home did not guarantee safety; a neighbor or a janitor or anyone else could detect an illegal presence and denounce both the Jew and the Polish host. That was why, in the three months that followed our arrival in Warsaw, we had to move from one apartment to another, changing our hiding place.

As soon as we arrived, we all went to our temporary homes. Janka Elterman and her mother went to the empty apartment on Dluga Street, my mother and I to Mrs. Luka's apartment on Okopowa Street. I felt strengthened by being near my mother. I felt loved and needed; my life was worth fighting for. While my mother stayed at home, I went out often. I enjoyed being outside the sordid Ghetto, walking freely without an armband and released from the stigma of being Jewish. But one day when I was running errands late and it was almost curfew time, I became too audacious. I took a tram to reach Okopowa Street, and when all the passengers got off and hurried home, at one point I was left alone with the conductor. What was more imprudent, I did not know the area and had to ask when to get out.

He gave me a probing look as if he could see through me. "Miss," he said "what are you doing on the street so late? You should stay home, you should be more careful." He understood, he knew. But I was young and my newfound freedom made me trusting again. No one had betrayed me so far. I looked straight back into the man's eyes and asked once more for directions. The tram was now on Okopowa Street. I gave a house number close to the Lukas' address and the conductor stopped there, although it was not a regular tram stop. His parting words were, "Be careful, and good luck."

My mother and Mrs. Luka, pale and trembling, were waiting for me near the entrance door. They scolded me, and I promised to be more careful in the future.

Zenon Pawlo visited my father in the Ghetto and my father instantly befriended him. Both my father and Karolina were very much liked by everyone, but my father attracted people even more than she did. Men and women alike were drawn to him and easily became life-long friends. Later the entire Pawlo family became very close to him. But for the moment, my father was still imprisoned in the Ghetto, and Zenon had to convince him to get out. My father was a proud man who liked to help people and abhorred asking favors from others. Even the sordid life in the filthy Ghetto seemed to him preferable to begging his friends to hide him at the risk of their lives.

"I cannot endanger the lives of others. Let me be, let me die like a man, not as a beggar," my father pleaded in his letters smuggled by Zenon.

Like so many others, my father still harbored the illusion that the Germans would have no time to murder him and that the war would end just in time to save his life. So many Jews believed in a miracle or in the promises of the workshop owners, Többens and Schultz. My father shared the optimism of his co-workers that they were needed and that Többens would keep them alive in his own best interest.

But Zenon knew better. He was adamant. "Irene, your father must leave the Ghetto at once. I may be unable to save him later. You must do something to convince him to move."

I wrote a dreadful letter to my poor father, accusing him: "You are being very selfish, Father. You have abandoned us, you don't care about us. We need you, stop hiding and come to help us." My father felt deeply grieved by my accusations, but they worked. He took the plunge and, false pass in hand, left the Ghetto escorted by Zenon.

But as soon as he made his decision and before he left the Ghetto, my father thought about Mrs. Zíoto and her daughter who would be left alone. He asked Zenon if he could rescue them as well. Zenon promised to help and, with the assistance of Zenon and another friend, Krystyna and her mother survived the war.

Finally, around October 22, 1942, I saw my father again. Zenon took him to his apartment on Dluga Street to hide with Janka and her mother. He brought me there to meet him.

Zenon politely greeted a few neighbors who saw us entering the apartment. It was no longer empty and we could move around. But we were still careful and only whispered.

My father looked thin, pale, and sick. He had lived through the massive roundups in the Ghetto. He could not talk about his pain, and trembled when I questioned him about our relatives and friends.

"What happened to Uncle Monos, Aunt Freda, young Jadwiga?" I asked. "Were they protected because Uncle Monos worked for the Judenrat?"

"No," my father replied, barely audible. "Monos was taken first, and Freda and Jadwiga remained in hiding. They were deported later during yet another large-scale raid." His voice trembled, and there were tears in his eyes. "Mr. and Mrs. Szmit were also deported, but I believe their daughter escaped. Yes, Irene, everybody you knew is gone. Please stop asking me questions. I feel so guilty, so miserable."

My father knew that Zakrzówek was not far from Lublin and that we should have some news about his mother. He did not dare to ask me and I did not volunteer to tell him the truth. He was a broken man. But in a few days, I hoped, my dear father would improve and I would tell him what happened to his mother.

He did recover, and when he asked me about his mother, his half-sisters, his stepfather, I told him. He uttered a painful groan, his head went down, his back bent, and he remained silent for a long time. In my distress, I told him over and over again, "Father! Mother, Karolina, and I are alive. We need you, we love you."

"My mother is alive?" he asked as if awakened from a bad dream, a spark of hope in his gentle, blue eyes begging me to say that he had misunderstood me only moments ago.

"No, father, my mother, Karolina's and my mother, your wife, is alive," I said.

"Ah, yes, yes," Father said and fell silent again. After a few minutes he seemed to wake up, looked at me intensely, then turned toward me and held me tenderly close to him. Eventually, he forced a smile and said, "Don't worry, my child, I will be all right, I am here with you. I will find a way to save you."

Life in the apartment on Dluga Street was very uncomfortable. Night and day, the fugitive tenants could barely move for fear of being detected. They were forbidden to run the tap water or flush the toilet. Every evening, Zenon or Czeslaw visited the place after they left their office.

Zenon, kind and understanding, often took me with him so I could see my father. Opening the entrance door loudly, he walked noisily into the apartment so as to be heard by the neighbors. Then, assured that they knew that he was in the apartment, he ran the water for the kettle and for the bathtub, which he had previously emptied, and took care of the toilet. He flushed it several times, emptying everything that had been accumulated there in the previous 24 hours. This action embarrassed me the most, and I admired Zenon even more for his tactful, matter-of-fact approach to our problems. He never used big words, he expected no thanks, but quietly, skillfully, and with great determination did what he believed was right.

Zenon was the first man with whom I was in love. It was a delight to see his thoughtful, intelligent face, to feel his presence. How much I wanted to tell him these simple words: "I love you, my dearest Zenon." But I could not do so, for it would have embarrassed him. I was not an eligible young woman; I was an outcast, a runaway pariah. He, my hero, would not court me. Did he sense how I felt? If he did, he was too considerate to let me know it.

My father left the apartment on Dluga Street after a very short stay and found refuge at the dental office of his old friend Mr. Grunwald. A few days later Janka Elterman and her mother found another temporary hiding place and they too left the apartment on Dluga Street.

I continued to live with my mother at the Lukasas. Mrs. Luka was kind and friendly and we would have liked to stay there until the end of the war. But one day, at the beginning of November, 1942, we had a surprise: Mrs. Sobolewska and Karolina arrived from Zakrzówek. They were pale and troubled and seemed very sad. They brought tragic news: Edmund had been killed with the other young Jewish men hiding in the forest.

The young Jews from Zakrzówek had asked in vain for the partisans to help them and a few dozen Jews had decided to act on their own. They managed to escape into the surrounding forests, where they tried to form their own small resistance unit. Edmund was one of the leaders, hopeful that the group would somehow survive the rigorous winter in the forest. But this was not to be: the men were ambushed and murdered by a Polish partisan band.

Mrs. Sobolewska and her family could not believe the horror perpetrated by the Poles, and they were afraid to keep Karolina any longer. There were bloodthirsty people in the village ready to kill the Jews and anyone who assisted them. The farmer's family felt terrified and helpless; they did not want to send Karolina alone on the perilous trip to Warsaw. She was delicate, she did not belong in the everyday crowd of travelers and could be recognized as "different," that is, as a Jewess. Mrs. Sobolewska risked her life to bring Karolina safely to the Lukas. My mother asked her how much she should pay for Karolina's board and traveling expenses but Mrs. Sobolewska refused to take money.

The three of us were too many to live at the Lukas's. Mrs. êliwa offered to take Karolina to her parents, Mr. and Mrs. Zaleski, who owned an elegant variety store in Warsaw. The Zaleskis, very fine people in their fifties, liked Karolina and could not understand why she should be hidden in an apartment.

"She is young and pretty, let her go out in the fresh air and enjoy herself a little," they said.

Karolina was overjoyed at such a prospect and asked if she could help in the store, since she had no desire to walk on the streets more than was necessary. She was welcomed in the store and liked it there. It was now the beginning of November 1942, and the weather was cool. Mrs. Koska returned our fur collars which she had kept for us since her last visit to the Ghetto in December 1941. Thus, Karolina had a winter coat with a fur collar like other people, and she walked every day from the Zaleskis' apartment to their store. Her life began to be more normal and she began to breathe more easily.

But one afternoon, as she walked home a man accosted her. "Jewess," he said, "Give me money or I will take you straight to the Gestapo." Karolina had no money, and even if she had, it would have been dangerous to acknowledge that she was in fact Jewish. She had to think very fast; she was bright, but her situation was dangerous and she had very few options. When she denied being Jewish, the man was rude and insistent, speaking in a low voice, using coarse, obscene language and repeating the words "Jewess, Jewess." The fact that he kept his voice low so as not to attract attention led Karolina to believe that he was not a regular German agent but a Polish extortionist trying to get money from her. She boldly told him that she worked in the family store and he should let her go. But he insisted she take him to the store; if she was not Jewish, he said, there was no harm in letting him see it.

She had no choice and brought the man to Mr. Zaleski. He understood the situation immediately and tried to intimidate extortionist, threatening him with punishment by the resistance men if he did not go away. But the man had been in the blackmail business long enough to recognize that he had found a real victim. After bargaining as much as he could, Mr. Zaleski paid the man a substantial sum. So ended my sister's freedom—and my parents' modest resources became seriously depleted after they insisted on reimbursing Mr. Zaleski.

Karolina joined us back at the Lukas's apartment. Again we were too many, so we had to look for another place to stay. My father was still staying at the dental office of his friend, Mr. Grunwald. My mother never dared to go out on the street, and now Karolina too was condemned to stay inside. But my father and I went out and did what we could for the family.

My father got in touch with some of his pre-war Christian patients, but they all declined to receive us. Dr. êliwa came to our rescue once again, and spoke about us to his adoptive mother, Mrs. Szaloska. She had known my father for years and liked him; he had been a good friend of her now-deceased husband. With his unique talent for dealing with people, my father was tactful and most respectful while helping the impoverished but proud widow. Now we were fighting for our lives, and we were the ones who needed help. Mrs. Szaloska agreed to shelter my mother, Karolina and me, at least for the winter, in her bungalow near Warsaw in a secluded area surrounded by big trees. She lived alone with a faithful woman servant and received few visitors.

The move of the three of us from the city to Mrs. Szaloska's bungalow was dangerous. We had to take a small commuter train filled with people who knew each other, while we, strangers, might easily be suspected of being Jews. For the same reason, it was risky for us to walk from the station to Mrs. Szaloska's bungalow.

Dr. êliwa and his wife, who was now visibly pregnant, decided to accompany us. They were well known and respected by the local people, as was Mrs. Szaloska.

We arrived safely at Mrs. Szaloska's bungalow. Her maid and companion was an unmarried, ageless country girl. Mrs. Szaloska was a benevolent but exacting mistress; the maid had to obey her absolutely, and was rewarded by an unusual mixture of maternal kindness and contempt. Such a relationship was not uncommon in pre-war Poland, where the master looked down on the servant as the rich condescended to the poor.

As soon as we arrived, Mrs. Szaloska informed my mother that she had neither food nor coal in the house, and asked for the money to buy provisions for the whole winter. She assured my mother that she wanted to keep us for as long as necessary, meaning until the end of the war. My mother gave her the money, but that was not enough. She had to continually pay more, until Mrs. Szaloska had bought all the provisions she wanted for the coming winter and thereafter. Yet she was never satisfied, always complaining that food and coal were expensive and scarce.

Our meals were meager, and we were hungry. I was less able to put up with the hunger than my sister and my mother, and I had fainting spells. My good mother, who always had a healthy appetite, gave me half of her bread and I took it, unable to resist. Mrs. Szaloska criticized my mother for being so generous and me for being so voracious and spoiled. She talked every day, and at every meal, about her brother who was a prisoner of war in Germany.

"He has to be content with little food and his water is rationed. We are very lucky to be here in this comfortable home," she said, looking at us accusingly.

The bungalow was nice indeed, although it was poorly heated. The trees outside were picturesque and the air was pure and refreshing. I longed to go out, but could not risk being seen, so the three of us stayed inside.

Then came the Christmas of 1942. Mrs. Szaloska decided to show us a real Polish Christmas, insisting that Dr. êliwa come with his wife and my father to spend Christmas Eve at her bungalow. There were not enough beds to accommodate all these people, and in the rather chaotic assignment of where everybody was to sleep, Dr. êliwa was directed to share a bed with my mother and me. We were in the middle of the war and the occupation, and such a strange arrangement did not look bizarre at the time. These were our trusted friends, who had risked their lives to help us. We could at least trust Jerzy êliwa, and if necessary, share our bed with him.

But in bed, it did not take long before I felt Jerzy's hand coming in my direction. I defended myself with my youthful strength without uttering a word or a murmur. Fortunately Jerzy had had a long day before he joined us. We had eaten Christmas Eve supper very late; he was tired and soon fell asleep.

In the morning when we assembled in the dining room, Dr. Sliwa looked uneasy. He inquired how his wife had spent the night, reporting that as for himself he had spent an awful night, full of terrible nightmares. He had felt restless, he complained, tossing and moving constantly in his sleep.

"Oh," I said airily, "I had a most unusual night too. I slept like a log. The Germans could have come into the house and I would not have heard them. I can't remember the last time I slept so deeply."

Dr. Sliwa imperceptibly bowed his head. He understood that I would not give him away.

Two days later we heard a commotion in the kitchen. The maid had just come from town and reported that there were many Germans around looking for hidden Jews. She had heard that a few Polish families had already been killed, together with their Jewish guests. Panic struck Mrs. Szaloska; she feared the Germans would search the houses one by one, and she asked us to leave her house as soon as possible.

We had to move again, our provisions for the winter left with Mrs. Szaloska. Where would we go this time? Our money was dwindling and so was the list of our friends. But we had to move quickly, as Mrs. Szaloska was very nervous, although it was obvious that the Germans were not searching the houses one by one and we could have stayed with her a little longer.

My father's last hope was to contact his pre-war patients, Walenty and Julia Kielba. Julia was the great-aunt of the charming Janina Zenkowska. It was a large and fine family, all of them patients of my father. He called on the Kielbas and asked if they could hide my mother and Karolina in their detached house in Bernerowo, near Warsaw. Sympathetic and courageous, they received him with open arms. They agreed to shelter my mother and Karolina, and asked only that my father pay for their food, if and when he was able to. My mother and Karolina were safe, at least for the time being. Another place would have to be found for me.

My father, still hiding in Mr. Grunwald's dentist's office, was alone there from late evening until morning—the Grunwalds lived outside Warsaw.

Mr. Grunwald's ancestors were German, but his wife was Polish. One evening, my father discovered German food tickets, issued to Mr. and Mrs. Grunwald, lying on a table. It meant that Mr. Grunwald had opted for German nationality; he was no longer a Pole. My father was shocked; he considered Mr. Grunwald to be a careful, intelligent person, a solid citizen and an honest man. Why would he take German nationality, when it was clear to everyone that the Germans would lose the war in the end? There would be no place for the Germans or Volksdeutschen in Poland after the war, and the vengeance of the mob would be cruel. Had Mr. Grunwald done it for the food tickets, or had he been forced to become German by his German relatives? Certainly he did not participate in any Nazi activity, in any anti-Polish or anti-Jewish action.

My father thought of a way to help his misguided colleague after the war and to help himself now. His financial resources were almost exhausted and he had to find a job. Thus he proposed a pact of mutual assistance.

"When the war is over, your life will be in danger, in the same way as mine is now," he said to Mr. Grunwald. "You will be punished for having become a German, a traitor to Poland where you were born and lived all your life, and would like to live until the end of your days. So let us agree that you will help me today, and I will help you after the war. I need false papers in an assumed name, certifying that I am a dental mechanic. I need your references that you have known me for many years as a good and reliable worker, and your help in finding a job for me outside Warsaw. In return, I promise that I will stand by you after the war, and will defend you against any accusation of wrongdoing during the occupation."

Mr. Grunwald agreed, and the two shook hands.

I was still left without a place to go. My mother encouraged me to visit Zofia Chemska, who had worked for us as a maid and governess years ago. She now lived with her husband and their little daughter, Marynia, in Warsaw on Jasna Street.

Zofia had kept in touch with us by phone when we were imprisoned in the Ghetto, and inquired from time to time about our well being. It was obvious that she cared about us and wished us well. That made it even more difficult for me to impose myself on gentle Zofia, to intrude upon her peaceful life. But I had no choice: I could not sleep on the street, and Zofia was my last resort.

When I knocked at her door, she recognized me immediately and was glad to see me alive. We were alone in the apartment and could talk freely, so I explained that I had no place to go, while my mother and sister had already found a home, as had my father. She looked at me with great compassion and sadness.

"When I met your parents and started to work for them, I was poor and had nowhere to go," Zofia said. "I met Karolina and you, two little, well-behaved children, and I envied you. I was an orphan and had no parents to help me. But you had two professional parents. You two were so well protected — if anything had happened to one of your parents, the other would be able to take care of you. You would never know distress and want, the way I had known them. And now, here you are, in a worse position than I have ever been in. How could that happen? It is frightening to think that life can be so bizarre, so unpredictable. I want to help you, Irene, and I will."

Dear Zofia, she was still young, in her early thirties. She was beautiful with her thick, black hair and warm, brown eyes. I remembered her very well as the tall, slender and fine young woman, who accompanied Karolina and me for daily walks in our long-gone pre-school years. She was a very devout Roman Catholic and had to visit the church every day. She took Karolina and me into the church where she could kneel down and pray for a few moments. We liked Zofia so much that we followed her without making any fuss.

The church, though mysterious and inviting, was somber. As she prayed, Karolina and I stayed next to her, patiently waiting for her to finish.

On December 29, 1943, I moved in with Zofia, her husband, and young Marynia at their main-floor apartment on Jasna Street. Mr. Chemski, Zofia's husband, did not like me, a non-paying guest. The apartment had two rooms, a kitchen and a toilet, and was constantly visited by the Chemskis' friends. There was no question of my remaining in seclusion. I was introduced as Zofia's cousin visiting Warsaw. The wife of the janitor called on Zofia daily, and looked at me suspiciously. A visitor does not stay all day in the apartment; I had to go out.

I walked the streets as long as possible, in spite of the bitter cold, to avoid the Chemskis' friends, and to be out of Mr. Chemski's way. I pretended that I had eaten in town, although in fact I did not. I was often hungry, yet I considered myself fortunate, because I had not been hurt physically so far. I thought about so many others who were hungry at that time, and about so many mistreated or tortured.

While aimlessly strolling through the Warsaw streets, I saw emaciated Russian prisoners with blood on their swollen faces, visibly beaten and tortured, walking barefoot in the cruel Polish winter, their uniforms dirty and torn. No one could come near to give them a piece of bread or a cigarette, because they were guarded by Germans in uniform with long rifles ready to shoot. I also saw poor Polish children running the icy streets barefoot and selling newspapers.

But though I counted myself lucky in many ways, I had my own serious problems. I had to leave Zofia's home soon, since my presence was too dangerous for my hosts. But Zofia was determined to protect me, even at the risk of her own, her husband's, and Marynia's lives. She wanted me to stay at her home. At the same time she told me, "Irene, if you survive the war, which I wish for you with all my heart, do not come back here to tell the janitor's wife and my other friends that I have helped you, that I have hidden a Jewess at my home. My friends and neighbors would not understand, they would look down on me, I would be ostracized. I cannot live without friends, please understand, Irene, please."

I felt stabbed in my heart. Then I thought how much I too craved to be liked and accepted by my teachers and my classmates. So I understood Zofia's dilemma and promised her solemnly that I would never betray her noble heart, never.

Zofia tried to make me look more Polish. She told me to cover my hair with a kerchief in the fashion of a simple country girl, and never to appear in public without it. She insisted that any time the janitor's wife came, I should talk or, even better, read the newspaper out loud. Zofia believed that my good Polish pronunciation and my way of speaking would endear me to people and save my life. Thus, when the nosy woman came, Zofia said, "Oh, Irene, I was too busy to read the newspaper today, why don't you read for us, so we can relax for a while."

I read, and the woman stopped eyeing me and after a moment forgot about me. I read, and our minds went away to other places and other people.

Zofia told me that Janka Elterman had come to see her husband and offered him a substantial sum of money if he got rid of me and took her mother and her instead. Zofia was outraged and promised that she would never let me go, no matter how much money Mrs. Elterman was willing to pay her husband.

Determined to save me, Zofia worried not only about my physical survival but also about my soul. Her religion inspired her to give, to share, and even to sacrifice her life for a worthy cause. Saving my life was such a cause for Zofia. But she would have been happier, for my sake, if I were Christian.

"Irene, did you become Christian since I left your home and are you Roman Catholic now?" she asked me. "Please tell me the truth, I will try to help you, I will never abandon you, your religion will change nothing between us," she said and her eyes implored me to tell the truth.

"Zofia," I said, "I have been baptized, but under most unusual circumstances. I doubt if I have become Christian, for you know that my family has always been Jewish." And I told her what had happened.

In the Ghetto there were two beautiful churches on Leszno Street. We heard that converted Jews visited the church near the corner of Leszno and Karmelicka. And a few priests managed somehow to enter the Ghetto, and to keep in touch with the parishioners. Catechism and religious lessons were given in this church to comfort baptized Jews, or those seeking conversion.

My father thought that Karolina and I should learn something about the Catholic religion, in case we should one day succeed in leaving the Ghetto and need to pretend to be Christian Poles. He hoped, of course, that the war would end before that. So

Karolina and I attended church for a short time in the early evenings.

Then, on July 22, 1942, the mass deportations began, the pattern of our lives disintegrated, and the church services stopped. The church then blessed and pronounced baptized all the Jews who had attended the lessons. There was no official ceremony, nor was the presence of the people to be converted requested at their "baptism." Now those converted in absentia could die in the Christian faith.

I explained all this to Zofia, and she seemed delighted, embracing me with tears in her eyes. She truly cared about me and wanted to save my soul. I felt profoundly touched. Later, when I was alone, desperately fighting for my life, I entered the church and prayed; the memory of Zofia's love and her pure, unspoiled faith encouraged me.

Zofia had two nieces, Zosia and her younger sister Lucyna, who had been working in Lorraine since 1940, the year when this part of France had been annexed by Germany. Zosia had been there with her husband Mundek and their three-year-old-daughter, Krysia.

I told Zofia that I too would like to leave Poland to go to work with other Polish slaveworkers. Zofia turned pale. "Irene, you don't know what you are talking about. You know nothing about life and how heartless people can be. They would destroy you. I will not let you go."

But my mind was made up. I asked her to help me find a way, no matter under what conditions. I preferred to be a slave than dead.

Zosia, Krysia and Lucyna had come back to Warsaw to visit their family, while Zosia's husband had been left behind in Lorraine to guarantee their return. It was the last time the Germans allowed this extraordinary privilege.

Lucyna did not want to return, and Zofia thought that this might create the opportunity I was looking for. I would go back instead of Lucyna, and take her place as a slave worker in Lorraine.

Zofia introduced me to her niece, who agreed to the plan. Lucyna would remain in Warsaw; I would travel to Lorraine using her pass, and on arrival I would be introduced to Lucyna's boss as her replacement.

My father was appalled by my decision, and so was Zenon. They were afraid for my safety, afraid that, as a young woman, I would be easy prey among the mostly male, forced laborers. However, they could not find a better alternative, and they accepted the inevitable.

I prayed silently for a miracle — that Zenon would come with me. Somehow, I felt that he would be safer in Lorraine than in Warsaw. Those were my dreams, for I was a young woman in love. And I cherished them secretly in my heart. He said goodbye to me warmly, and gave me a small ivory elephant for good luck. I looked deep into his eyes and for years to come tried to remember his charming, noble face.

To be near me, my father spent the last night before my departure in Zofia's apartment. He wanted to give me a little money to sew into my clothes, but I refused. I was afraid that people would discover the money and become suspicious. I was supposed to be a poor girl, an orphan, who had worked as a maid in Warsaw, had lost her job, was hungry, and decided to work for the Germans to get food.

I never saw Zenon again. He died during the Warsaw uprising in the fall of 1944, killed by a bomb, the death he feared so much. He was with his brother and a friend when he saw a German plane above their heads and a bomb falling directly toward them. He panicked and ran to the other side of the street. The bomb deviated from its course and fell on the building where Zenon had just taken shelter. His brother, Czeslaw, and his friend survived the war.

I too survived, and never betrayed my dear Zofia. Nor was I able to thank her for all she had done for me. She was murdered when recuperating in a hospital in Warsaw in 1944, after minor surgery. The Germans came and told the patients to leave the wards and go downstairs. Then they shot them dead. Zofia must have been thirty-five years old at the time. I heard that her husband died in 1945. I don't know what happened to Marynia.

Around January 10, 1943, I presented myself with Zosia and her daughter, Krysia, at the Transit Center. It was located in a pre-war school building on Skarszewska Street in Praga, a section of Warsaw, on the other side of the river Vistula. We had to wait there a few days for the transport to Germany and then to Lorraine. We were among a multitude of people, most of whom had been caught in roundups in the Polish countryside, and torn abruptly from their homes. Some were coarse, some were rude, but many were nice, simple, naive and frightened people. Most had never been on a train and a number had never even seen one. The girls cried; they were scared and wanted to return to their villages, which they had left for the first time in their lives. But there was no way back, no means of escaping the expatriation and the slave work awaiting us all.

Whether bold, frightened, or resigned, everybody alike was crammed into the seriously overcrowded Transit Center. The constant roundups brought scores of new victims every day.

Inside the center, people were hungry and noisy; we received little food. Zosia asked me if I had money, but I had none. I had my wristwatch and one box of my favorite milk chocolates, called "Krówki," with little cows on the wrapping paper. My chocolate disappeared overnight, and I had nothing left to ease my hunger.

Men and women slept in a number of separate, very large rooms, which were in fact pre-war classrooms. They were packed to capacity with three or four levels of bunks made of wooden planks. The nights were quiet, except for the muffled crying of desperate girls.

The second day I noticed a young girl clowning around. She had long, thick, dark hair, brown eyes and a petite figure. She improvised vulgar dancing and bowed to the crowd, showing her upper legs and behind. Her strange behavior puzzled and disgusted me; it seemed most inappropriate in this gloomy place. Yet a lot of people enjoyed her performances and applauded her.

We were thirsty and at one point a container of water was brought in, but I had no glass in which to get some. The dancing girl had an aluminum cup she shared with people around her. When everyone else was satisfied, she stood alone near the water, the cup dangling in her hands, and I timidly asked if I could borrow it. I expected an arrogant rebuke, since I had not spoken to her before and had not applauded her dancing. But she looked into my eyes, and I saw in hers great sadness, a kindness I never expected. She said politely, "Yes, of course, take it."

Who was this girl? Was she really a vulgar woman or was she pretending? I was puzzled.

I felt a sudden urge to see my mother, who stayed with my sister in Bernerowo, to say goodbye to her, to embrace her for the last time before my departure. I forgot about the girl, I just wanted to see my mother. Somebody told me that it was possible to obtain a pass to leave the building. I had to ask the German in charge, but when I looked for him, he was not available.

I went to the toilets to hide my tears. As I was leaving, determined to find the German in charge, I heard people calling, "Jewess, Jewess, a Jewess among us." Was I recognized, were they calling me? I stood motionless, not daring to look, not daring to breathe. I waited for hands to seize me and take me away. The crowd continued to shout, "Jewess, Jewess among us." Cautiously, I asked what was going on.

"Don't you know? someone said, "The dancing girl is Jewish, she has been kept here for two weeks and the Germans made checks and caught her. They will shoot her."

I felt nauseous, I wanted to scream my pain and rage; this doomed girl had valiantly fought for her life, pretending to be a common girl, hoping her true identity would not be recognized.

I abandoned my plan of approaching the German supervisor and would not be able to see my mother. Later, I went again to the toilets to hide my sorrow. Nobody was there, and I thought about the girl and tried to control my feelings. Life was too ugly, too cruel. The Germans seemed undefeated and I couldn't bear it any longer. Then the door opened, and someone walked in. I did not believe my eyes: there stood the lovely Gienia Mitelberg, a classmate from grade one until the war, another Jewish girl in disguise. We embraced warmly, wished each other good luck, and parted quickly before anybody found us together.

Later, I often wondered what happened to Gienia. After the war I learned that she had survived. She now lives in Toronto, a happy mother of three children and a grandmother of six. We keep in touch and feel as close as when we were two young students.

Still at the Transit Center we had to pass a medical examination before a German doctor. All the women were herded together like sheep, and had to take their clothes off, and wait, totally naked. Then, one woman after another presented herself for examination by the doctor. I don't remember any nurse being present, only the doctor and a male interpreter standing near by. The room was unlocked and men from the staff entered it freely, unabashedly watching us and leering.

The examination was rather superficial; the women were ordered to turn around so the doctor could look at their skin and general appearance. Then he examined the women's hair and ordered them to stand on a stool and looked carefully into their pubic hair. I don't remember what happened to the unfortunate women who had lice.

Many women were very poor and had skin problems. While their faces were smooth, once they undressed, their skin blisters, lacerations, rashes, and pimples were visible. My unblemished body attracted the doctor's attention. He stopped the line of women waiting for examination, ordered me to remain on the stool and told all the women to look at me. I had to turn round and round on this high stool, so all the women could see my clean body. I was considered an unusual case, a noteworthy specimen.

I forced myself to remain calm, awaiting what would happen next. The doctor had absolute power over us. He could choose to probe with his fingers inside me, or order me to stay naked on this stool for hours. But he let me go; I was not molested.

On January 15, 1943, we left the Transit Center to board the train. It was bitterly cold, and we had to walk a short distance to the Warsaw East train station. I was so cold and tired that I could hardly walk, and had to muster all my willpower not to faint. Zosia, loaded with bundles, carried Krysia in her arms. I tried to help her, but I was too weak; I could hardly walk myself. Zosia saw that, and showed no anger for not helping her.

We boarded a passenger train, not a freight train. Our section, consisting of a number of compartments, was locked. Two soldiers stationed at each exit guarded us. They did not try to harm us.

I don't remember receiving any food. Maybe we got something to eat, maybe nothing at all. All I remember is that I was hungry.

A Polish family returning from their stay in Poland sat next to me. There were five people; two parents, their two young boys and a little girl, perhaps twelve years old, called Linda. She was introduced as their cousin, but she did not resemble the family at all. Linda seemed very shy, and her large brown eyes had a "Jewish" look expressing sadness and fear. Was she a Jewish child protected by this Polish family? The parents were relaxed and friendly. They gave me a long probing look, then smiled at me and offered me a little of the food they had brought for the journey.

I looked out the window as our train advanced toward the west of Poland, and saw the earth become gradually less frozen and, later, not frozen at all. I was accustomed to the ground looking frozen solid and dead during winter, and I was amazed and delighted to see the earth carrying some life and breath. As we moved further west, the earth began to show traces of green. I watched the peaceful countryside and tried to relax.

After a very long ride, we stopped at a German city, and were taken to spend the night in what my Polish companions recognized as a deserted concentration camp. We slept in the barracks, which were most uncomfortable, but I was glad that we had been left alone, and that no one bothered us. As we went through the streets leaving and returning to the train station, German children followed us, throwing stones and calling us "dirty Poles" and other insulting names. Nobody tried to stop them.

IRENE SLAVE ID   KAROLA SLAVE ID

JOZEF IN 1945 IN POLISH ARMY UNIFORM

EIGHT

LORRAINE: FORCED LABOR

After a long, trying trip we arrived at last at Marten, known before the war as Marthille, in the region of Lorraine. It was a little, three-street village, six kilometers from a small town called Mershingen but known before the war as Morhange. The nearest train station was in the town of Sarrebourg, six kilometers from Marten in the opposite direction.

Lorraine, a region in north-eastern France, had been annexed by Germany in 1940. All French nationals were deported to camps in the south of France, while German families were brought in to take over their properties. The farms were awarded exclusively to married German men. Whether healthy or disabled, a man was considered to be head of the family, a status denied to women. French citizens could remain in Lorraine only if they proved to have German ancestors and opted for German nationality.

When we reached Zosia's home, the news spread quickly that she and Krysia had returned from Poland. The Wagner family were expecting their maid Lucyna to reappear in their kitchen at any moment. She was a good worker, and they were fond of her. I felt afraid, for I could never be a match for this outgoing, pleasant girl. But Zosia took me by the hand and led me to their house, which was only three minutes away from her home. The family of four was in the kitchen. They smiled at Zosia, then looked at me in disbelief.

"Where is Lucyna?" Mr. Wagner asked.

Zosia bowed her head and in a mournful voice explained, "My sister, Lucyna, simply disappeared. I tried very hard to find her. I looked for her everywhere. Please believe me, Mr. Wagner, I was unable to locate her—I could not bring her back. I was so worried, because I knew I had to bring her back to you, Mr. Wagner, and to you, Mrs. Wagner, that I didn't know what to do, I could not sleep. I thought about it over and over. Finally I took the liberty of bringing another Polish girl to replace Lucyna."

The four pairs of eyes turned in my direction. "She is a good, honest girl," affirmed Zosia in a brighter voice.

Irene, Irene, look straight into their eyes, be calm, my inner voice warned me.

"Huh, she is not as nice as Lucyna," Mr. Wagner announced loudly. The family did not try to hide their disappointment. They examined me carefully and I examined them. Mr. Wagner was a man about fifty years old, with one artificial eye and one artificial leg. Loud, brusque and domineering, Mr. Wagner was the Nazi mayor of Marten and wore a large band with a swastika on his arm. He was also the manager of a large and prosperous farm. His wife, a vivacious, chubby, blond woman, looked years younger. They had two children, a daughter around twelve years old, a very pretty, slim girl with honey-blond hair and light brown eyes, and her younger brother, also a good-looking child.

It was very difficult for the German farmers to get enough slave workers as the Gestapo did not assist them much and there was a serious shortage of manpower. Thus, as Zosia knew from the beginning, the family had no choice but to accept me, and they allowed me to stay as their servant and farmhand.

The first day after work ended, Zosia came and took me back to her home. She, her husband, Mundek, and their daughter, Krysia, occupied a single large, clean room. I was given my own narrow bed. There was no running water, sink, bathroom or toilet. We did not even have an outhouse but had to relieve ourselves in the open air like cats and dogs.

Depending on the season, work lasted from 5 a.m. till 11 p.m. or from 6 or 6:30 a.m. till 8 or 9 p.m. After work was done, the Polish slave workers were permitted to move about within the village, although women generally stayed in their rooms in the evening, while the men went out. But they had to be quiet and discreet, and no one had the right to leave Marten without special permission.

There were only six women in our village. Two of them, Zosia and Jola, were married, while Maria, Jasia, Hela, and I were single. My arrival caused a small sensation among the Polish workers. Everybody wanted to meet the single woman who had come to replace the well-liked Lucyna. Zosia and Mundek's many friends arrived to see me the very first evening of my arrival. As they chatted casually, they looked furtively at me and tried to figure me out. Would I be an easy conquest? Who would be my first lover? There were many strong, young, and healthy Polish men in the area and very few single women. The same highly disproportionate ratio of men to women existed in all the adjoining villages.

I pretended to be unaware of what was going on, but I was frightened by the men's curiosity. Would they guess or suspect who I really was? I tried to be calm and to smile. When they left, I relaxed, grateful that my first day in Marten had come uneventfully to an end.

The next day very early in the morning Zosia took me again to the Wagners. Mrs. Wagner communicated with me by gesture, for I did not understand German. Another slave worker was summoned to explain my daily duties. I tried to adjust to my new situation. For me, having come from the Warsaw Ghetto, the transition to a life in a Nazi household was not easy. I was inwardly seething with hatred toward my new bosses, yet I realized that I could not survive, harboring so much hatred in my heart, for this feeling would suffocate and kill me. I wanted to survive; I had to break my shell and open my heart to somebody, to connect myself with a living being in this household, to resurrect in myself some feelings of sympathy, compassion, even love.

But I could not bring myself to like my Nazi boss, or his wife, or even Tilly and Kaltie, their children. I tried to persuade myself to like Mrs. Wagner, even just a little, for with her blond hair she slightly resembled my mother. But in vain: I hated them all. Then, the dog, which had been sleeping under the kitchen sink, woke up. The beautiful animal left his shelter lazily and looked up at me with big, innocent eyes. Eureka! I had found a blameless creature in this Nazi household. I felt my tension release, and I was able to breathe freely again. All this lasted just a few minutes, but for me it was an eternity, as I left one planet for another. I, a Jewish girl, could now live peacefully and gracefully in a Nazi home.

I stayed with Mundek and Zosia for some time. My watch disappeared without any trace on my second or third day there, and within a week all my underwear too had vanished, with the exception of the one pair of panties I was wearing. I asked Zosia what could have happened to my things, and she looked at me, quite amused, and said that she had no idea. Well, I had to do without.

The days passed, and the men visiting Mundek and Zosia started talking with me. They had one thing on their minds — sex — and I was the object of their lust.

At night I heard noises coming from Zosia's and Mundek's bed but did not understand what was going on. I was afraid to move, afraid to breathe, for the strange sounds seemed sinister. I had never heard anything like this before. Fortunately, it did not happen every night and I could sleep mostly undisturbed. But when it happened, the noise from their bed woke me up and frightened me.

One day I dared to ask Zosia what was going on. She gave me a strange, pitying look. "Are you really so stupid? Do you really not understand?" When I understood, I wanted to move out right away. But I had to wait a few months until I was able to speak German and could ask Mr. Wagner to allocate to me a room near his home.

Mundek and Zosia were surprised that I did not bring anything home from the Wagners' kitchen. "Lucyna was very smart," they told me. "She knew how to please her bosses, and steal without being caught." They coached me on how to take food, counting on my cooperation, expecting that I would share the stolen goods with them. But I could not steal. I knew, of course, that the Germans lived on property they had taken from the French people, nor did I forget how the Germans had destroyed my country, openly robbed our neighborhood and emptied our apartments. I certainly had a moral right to take food from the Wagners. But I did not want to become a thief, and dreaded the humiliation of being called one, if I were caught. The very act of stealing, the furtive gestures and look of a thief, were repulsive to me.

I did not mind the hard work, for my life in Marten was better than it had been in the Ghetto. Our harsh existence as social outcasts and enslaved Poles could not be compared with the agony of the Jews. In Marten, we could enjoy the beauty of nature around us. We could breathe the pure air, and we had some realistic hope of surviving the war. But I soon understood that I would never be good at work in the fields and gardens. I had to compensate for it by learning more specific skills where discernment and application would replace strong muscles. The opportunity to test my resolution came one Saturday morning when I was ordered to wash the floors in the Wagners' house. I had to wash the kitchen floor first and then as many others as possible. Mrs. Wagner was supposed to help me and she began by mopping her bedroom floor.

The kitchen was the center of the house, situated between the cowsheds and the stables on the one side, and the family's bedrooms and dining room on the other. The kitchen floor was blackened by layers of filth that covered the wood after years of neglect and constant activity and traffic across it. This was the first time in my life that I had to wash a floor. We had no detergent and very little precious soap at our disposal. I mixed water with a small amount of some coarse, nameless ingredient supposed to clean the wood. When I began scrubbing, I realized that the floor became clean as long as I scrubbed it in the direction of the wood grain; I had to scrub in one direction and not in circles or across the wood. I applied myself, and saw the dirt miraculously disappearing and the beautiful, clean wood surfacing. I forgot about the other floors and spent all my time scrubbing the kitchen floor so thoroughly that it looked almost like new. Mrs. Wagner, in the meantime, sponged or mopped all the other floors

While I was still on my knees finishing my work, she looked at what I had done and called her husband. "Oh, oh," I said to myself, "she must be angry with me." But she was not. Nobody had ever cleaned the kitchen floor so well. The Wagners decided that I was a good worker.

I wondered how much zeal I could put into my work before I would become a German collaborator. After all, my work contributed to my bosses' welfare and I felt uneasy about it. I pondered the whole matter many times and concluded that as long as I did the most menial, dirtiest, and hardest work, I was not collaborating with the enemy and betraying my country.

My favorite work was to look after the animals. I felt close to them and protective of the defenseless beasts. I had four pigs under my care, each in a pen, and I grew attached to them. Were they not, like me, prisoners condemned to die? Only, I would be killed before them if I were unmasked.

I tried to make my pigs' lives as comfortable as possible.

Half-bent, I entered each pen in my farmer's wooden shoes and threw out all the dirty straw. I washed the soiled floor thoroughly and put in dry straw. Finally, I threw away all the left-over food, washed the troughs and put in fresh food. The pigs ate happily.

I also learned to milk the cows. This did not come easily to me, especially because of the young Polish boy, Wacek, whom Mr. Wagner had renamed Jacob, considering it to be a much nicer German name. Jacob did all kinds of odd jobs but spent most of his time in the cowshed, for he was responsible for keeping the shed and the cows clean. He was an orphan, a poor country boy who had come to Marten in 1941 at the age of 11. He never told me whether he had been caught during the roundup in his village or if he had come voluntarily because he was starving in occupied Poland. I knew that life had been cruel to him. And he in turn became cruel, mainly toward the defenseless animals. Harmless as his cows, in Jacob's shrewd evaluation, I was subjected constantly to his nasty pranks.

He knew that I was afraid of a certain rebellious cow and that I always tried, instead, to milk a meek one. Unfortunately, I could hardly distinguish one from another. They were placed in rows, with 12 cows on each side of the shed, and trying to locate the meek cow, I counted how many other cows separated it from the doorway. However, unknown to me, Jacob had changed the position of my meek cow, replacing it with the wildest one. When I sat quietly trying to milk "my" cow, the wild one kicked me mightily, sending my bucket flying. I fled out to safety in the middle of the shed, while Jacob laughed heartily at my misery.

Another time Jacob hid among the cows and then pushed them hard in my direction. The frightened cows ran toward me and I had barely time to jump off my stool with the bucket of milk in my hand.

But even that was not enough for Jacob. He pursued me, yelling, "You coward, why you don't report me to Mr. Wagner? Are you afraid of me? You are a coward, coward!"

The worst was when Jacob had fits of insane cruelty and kicked the cows or broke their tails, screaming, "You see, I am the boss! Look, look, I can do anything I want." His rage could only be controlled by the fear that Mr. Wagner would become suspicious if too many cows were injured. Yet, the "mighty" Jacob looked in fact so small and miserable that I felt as sorry for him as for the mistreated cows.

I had to learn how to milk the cows in spite of Jacob. The only way to outsmart this unruly boy was to come to the stable before him — that is, before 5 a.m. — for an hour of peaceful practice. Thus, I started coming to work at 4 a.m. every day, when the stable was quiet. I put on the light and began learning to milk the cows. I did not know that my bosses had heard me going to the stable and were watching silently. They told me later that they approved my determination to learn. In time, I became a fast, skilful milker.

Depending upon the season of the year, I was ordered to work in the kitchen, in the garden or in the fields. I remember well those days when, after milking cows, washing breakfast dishes, and peeling a whole bucket of potatoes, I was sent to join the men who tilled, hoed, and weeded the beets.

The beets were planted in long rows, so long that we could not see the other end. We had to work very fast, hoeing constantly back and forth the length of the field. But my back ached terribly and I was out of breath and far behind the men. The only woman there, I worked with the three Serb prisoners of war. They were real farmers, strong and healthy, and they helped me. They placed me in a middle row between two men and each one hoed half of my row while at the same time hoeing his own. They laughed good-naturedly at my ineptitude and were glad to assist me while cheating our German boss in the bargain.

But there was a problem: the young and healthy Serbs had been deprived of women for years, and sex was very much on their minds. If they were not worrying about their persecuted families in Serbia, they worried about their sexual urges.

We were alone in the field, the men and I. We could talk and understand each other because our languages, Serbo-Croatian and Polish, are both Slavic. They asked me to repay kindness with kindness — they pleaded, they begged, they insisted that I have sexual relations with them. They teased me mercilessly, singing lewd songs in my ears, and repeating a rhyme: "ñaíowaía dla chíopaków, zostawiía dla robaków," meaning "The woman who does not give herself to men will die leaving her virginity to worms." Every day I had to endure the same demands, the same songs, the same lust in their eyes. But they never tried to assault or molest me; they never touched me, and they never stopped helping me.

In May 1943, I was finally allocated a room next to the Wagners' house. Accommodations for Polish slave workers were relatively easy to find in Marten because there were several empty houses left by the French families expelled from the village. Thus the Poles could occupy rooms in abandoned houses, if they were close to those of their German bosses.

We all longed for Sundays to arrive. There was a church in the village but we had neither permission nor free time to attend the services, which were reserved for the Germans. However, on Sundays we were given two hours off from our labor in order to clean our quarters, wash our clothes, and take care of ourselves.

Shortly after I had moved to my own room, Jacob decided to visit me every Sunday. Just when I had finished my work and was trying to rest, Jacob would present himself nicely dressed and clean saying: "I came here so you would tell me a story. I want to hear a story."

My telling Jacob stories started when we were assigned to work together separating the bad potatoes from the good for winter storage. It was tedious and monotonous work, and Jacob did it much faster and better than I. He could almost smell a bad potato without looking at it, while I had to take it into my hand and turn it around to inspect it carefully before deciding if it had to be thrown out. Needless to say, Jacob felt much smarter than I, and this, combined with the fact that we worked alone together, encouraged him further to tease me and play more pranks on me. He pushed me, pretending to do it by accident, or he threw the bad potatoes on my side, laughing at my confusion and despair. I had to find a way to pacify him and made a bargain with him:

"Jacob, if you will behave and help me with my potatoes, I will tell you nice stories."

Jacob agreed. He loved to listen to the stories. As I tried to remember the legends and books of my youth, he listened, transported into a world where anything and everything was possible. I soon realized that the stories he enjoyed the most were about strong and handsome men, powerful kings and princes who failed in love, were rejected and humiliated. I selected or modified my tales accordingly. Thus the legendary Polish queen Wanda refused the hand of the arrogant and mighty German prince who, in despair, threw himself into the River Vistula and drowned. In fact, it was the beautiful queen who drowned, but in my story she lived forever, admired and loved by her people. In Gone with the Wind Scarlett became a beautiful princess. She refused the powerful King Rhett, who begged endlessly for her favors until, humiliated and rejected, he left his kingdom and ran far away to hide his shame. And there were other, similar tales. Jacob was jubilant and roared with laughter, jumping around me, clapping his hands:

"More, more stories," or "Tell it again, repeat it," he ordered. Fortunately, like a child, he never tired of hearing the same story over and over again, and so my task was easier.

Jacob had lived in the country many kilometers from the nearest school. When he arrived at school, his feet bare even during the severe Polish winter, he was summoned at once by the local priest or the teacher himself, and ordered to do all the chores in their houses. Thus he never went to classes, never learned anything, and never had enough to eat. He told me that one day he found a piece of stale bread, half eaten by a rat, in a corner of his house. He grabbed the bread and finished what the rat had left. Jacob did not speak about his life to complain. He probably did not know that he had a right to complain or that he had any right whatsoever in this world. He just told me, matter-of-factly, stories of his miserable life, the only stories he knew.

Thus Jacob walked into my room every Sunday, moved the chair near to my bed where I was desperately trying to get a few minutes of rest, and commanded: "Now tell me a story. If you are a lady, you will not tell the boss that I came to your room. Tell me a story!"

He did not know the word "please." No one had ever used this word while addressing him.

My German bosses considered all Poles stupid, and me even more so because I did not speak German. I tried very hard to understand German words and to remember them. It might have helped if I'd spoken Yiddish, which I was told was very similar to German. But perhaps it was better that I did not speak Yiddish, as I could easily have confused the two languages. I had to be very careful not to say the few Yiddish words I remembered from my childhood in Warsaw. Once I said the word "brojt," which means bread, and my Polish co-worker exclaimed: "Hey, that's a Jewish word, where did you learn that?"

I felt my blood freeze but forced myself to smile and to answer as casually as I could, "I must have heard it some place, I don't remember." My co-worker seemed to be satisfied and asked no more questions.

After three months I began to speak German. As poor as my German was, I could pronounce simple sentences and be understood. Fortunately, I was not timid at all, contrary to how I felt learning French and trying so hard to please my good Polish teacher. I considered the German language a simple tool, an instrument to communicate with, and I did not care how ungrammatical it was, or how badly I pronounced or mispronounced the words. I spoke boldly and slowly. I wanted only to be understood.

One day, the Gestapo came to our village and assembled all of us in the mayor's—Mr. Wagner's—kitchen, probably to take an inventory of slave workers. We had to stand at attention and each person had to say his or her name. But poor Jacob got confused. He tried to explain that his first name was Wacek but that he was called Jacob, but he did not know how to explain this briefly, and was therefore unable to introduce himself. The Gestapo men began to get excited. The temperature was going up in the room, and the Gestapo men were becoming agitated. Their voices rose, their faces became red, their eyes wild. Sadly, some of the people assembled in the room started to laugh obsequiously to please the Germans.

The great show of beating and punishing Wacek-Jacob was about to begin. I could not stand it, and forgot that I had to remain unseen and unheard and never attract the Germans' attention. Unable to restrain myself, I spoke out: "His first name is Wacek, but the boss calls him Jacob because it is a nice German name."

There was silence in the room, and the Gestapo men said, "That is good, well-spoken. She speaks German well."

After that my Polish co-workers began to believe that I had already known some German before, and I was a liar. I worried that they would become more suspicious of me, but they soon forgot the whole incident.

Soon after I moved to my own room, I felt forced to break my resolution never to steal, for I had to choose between two evils. This is what happened: to my horror, I discovered one day that my head was full of lice. They invaded my hair without warning and spread like fire. In the evening, I sat at the table in my room to check the disaster. When I shook my hair, the table was covered in lice. I wanted to die. Where had these little beasts come from? Possibly I got them while learning to milk the cows since I used to lean my head on the cows' bellies, keeping the bucket between my legs.

There was nobody to whom I could reveal my problem. I remembered that in Poland people used some kind of petroleum product to get rid of lice, but I had nothing like that at my disposal. However, Mr. Wagner had a motorcycle running on a very smelly product which was probably petroleum or something like it. His motorcycle was kept against a wall in the barn.

When nobody was around I stole a little of the liquid from a can beside the motorcycle. Alone in my room at night, I generously applied to my hair what I hoped to be petroleum. It burned severely while I buried my face in the pillow and screamed into it. Crying from pain, I stayed awake for hours to be sure that my "medicine" would be effective. It had to work, for I could not live with the lice in my hair. Finally, I decided it was time to wash my hair. Burned hair and lice fell into my hands. All the lice had disappeared, but so had my hair. The little pests never returned, even though I continued to lean my head against the cows, too weak to sit up straight while milking them.

Nobody noticed my nearly bald scalp because I kept my head covered with a kerchief. In time, my hair grew back, though it was not as shiny and thick as before.

My room on the second floor adjacent to the cowshed was bright and large with a good-sized window facing the street. The deported French people must have left many things behind, most of which had been stolen. But two big beds with mattresses, a large old wardrobe, a stove, two half broken chairs, and a few pillows and blankets remained.

If my sleeping accommodation was adequate, I still had other reasons to worry. The room was in an abandoned, ruined farmhouse. The access through the empty house was scary. I lived alone, my door had no lock, and the house was completely empty at night. Any man could sneak into the house and enter my room. And men expected the single women to be easy prey to satisfy their sexual craving.

One night shortly after I had gone to bed, I heard footsteps. I had no time to jump out of bed and dress before Mundek and his friend Sebastian came in without even knocking. They pretended to be slightly drunk and in a jolly mood, and said that they just wanted to joke with me. They reached out to tickle me, to make me giggle, jump up, and uncover myself. This would have delighted the two men who, excited and full of lust, could easily overpower me. I had to prevent them from touching me, but I was defenseless, except for my tongue. I thought as fast as

I could about what to tell them, sat up on the bed and curled my legs under me, making myself slightly taller. Then I told them most forcefully and clearly in my educated Polish:

"You two beasts, you disgust me thoroughly! You are nothing but filthy, obnoxious, and repulsive swine, and I would rather die than be touched by you."

The men cringed at my words and stepped back. Mundek turned toward the door but Sebastian, coarser and nastier, pointed his finger at me and cursed, "May all you love die, may you survive them all, and be forever alone." Then the two men left. Stoned by his words, I thought about my family and shivered.

Life was not easy for single Polish women slaving in Marten. Each of us labored for a different boss and had to face her hardship and solve her problems alone.

Maria was a very pretty, healthy eighteen-year-old girl. Tall and strong, coming from rural Poland, she was familiar with farm work. Her hair, cut short, was light blonde, but her narrow blue eyes were expressionless, neither sad nor smiling. Although she was a good worker and could work hard without straining herself, her German boss was often displeased with her and frequently beat her. Her boyfriend, Lolek, another Polish slave worker on the same farm, forced her to have sexual intercourse with his friends and also beat her. It seemed that everybody took for granted the right to abuse this illiterate country girl. Dominated by her boyfriend, Maria could not befriend another man. Scared of the brutal Lolek, men kept away from her.

The German bosses did not interfere with our private lives, as long as we worked hard, obeyed them, were quiet, and did not try to escape.

Jasia and Hela shared a room. Jasia was a pretty seventeen-year-old brunette, slightly plump and of medium height. She had attractive, large brown eyes and a very pleasant disposition. She could read but wrote poorly. Nevertheless, she was her own boss and had a number of men friends whom she chose at her pleasure. She was well liked and nobody mistreated her.

Thirty-five-year-old Hela, Jasia's roommate, looked old and worn. A former street prostitute, she was skinny and almost bald. I understood that she continued to be promiscuous, more with the Serbs than with the Poles. The Serbs had been regular soldiers and were now prisoners of war, and as such they received Red Cross packages with chocolate, cigarettes, and other treats with which they were able to reward Hela for her favors. The Polish slave workers, whom nobody helped, had nothing with which to trade. Unfortunately, they knew neglect and frustration too well; most of them came from city slums and had been poor and deprived all their lives.

The Serbs, our co-workers, wore their uniforms instead of civilian clothes as we did. They were guarded and supervised by a German soldier who, carrying his long rifle, escorted them, morning and evening to and from their work. At night they were locked up in a place known as the Stalag. Their guard was on friendly terms with them; he probably appreciated his easy post, compared to the Germans fighting at the front. He kept a low profile, avoided trouble, and was seldom seen outside his quarters.

My mother and Karolina were still at the Kielbas in Bernerowo, and my father had succeeded in finding a job as a dental mechanic with a dentist in a small town at some distance from Warsaw. Strangely enough, letters from Poland arrived normally. My mother took extreme precautions not to reveal our situation when she wrote to me. She told me that Janka Elterman and her old mother had taken my place at Zofia Chemska's apartment and paid Mr. Chemski handsomely for the lodging.

My mother's handwriting was clear and well formed. One day Mr. Wagner grabbed from my hand the letter that had just been handed to me in his kitchen and tried to read it. He could not understand a word, but he asked, "Tell me, Irene, where did your mother learn to write so neatly and clearly? She writes as if she were an educated German lady."

"Be calm, Irene, be careful, Irene," my inner voice warned. I answered, "My mother worked all her life as a maid and seamstress for the rich and educated, and perhaps they taught her to write their way." Mr. Wagner did not press the matter further.

The village of Marten was situated among farms, flat fields, and pastures. At the junction of the two main streets, running water filled a trough for thirsty animals. I remember the stacks of manure, often as high as the second floor, arranged in rectangles in front of the houses. The strong smell filled the air. The Poles and Serbs were assigned to clean the stables and remove the manure to fertilize the fields.

Behind each house was an orchard. In the spring, I enjoyed watching the apple and mirabelle trees blossoming under the radiant, blue sky. The fragrant air made me feel good. The countryside was green and inviting. Contemplating such beauty were my moments of respite, connecting me with the beyond.

At the Wagners' there was an outhouse, reserved for the German family, located just at the entrance to the orchard from the inner court of the house. We slave workers had no right to use it, and there was no place designated for our needs. Being shy and young, having no toilet facilities was a real problem for me. Sometimes I sneaked into the bosses' outhouse in the orchard, my heart pounding for fear of being discovered. Tilly Wagner found me out one day and promptly reported it to her parents. They admonished me severely not to do it again.

We were given little to eat. It was possible while milking the cows, to steal milk by drinking it fast, directly from the bucket, but I could not force myself to gulp down the unfiltered milk, even though I was always hungry.

For breakfast we had sour-tasting, gray bread, made from ersatz or not very clean flour, cut in long, thin slices. They were thinly spread with so-called jam, red and without any sweetness, made partly from beets. To drink, we had a cup of darkish warm liquid, which was called coffee, with no sugar or milk.

I was the only girl at the table with two Polish and three Serbian forced laborers. The men stuffed an entire piece of bread right into their mouths, swallowed it rapidly, and grabbed another piece which they ate as fast as the previous one. I could not do it: I had to eat more slowly by swallowing smaller portions. I tried to put a second piece on my plate but the men forbade me to do so, saying, "One piece at a time, you cannot store food." Before I finished my first piece, all the bread was gone. True, the men were bigger than me and needed more nourishment, but nevertheless, every morning I left the table hungry.

We breakfasted at 7 a.m., having begun work at 5. Very occasionally we were given a little extra food at 10 a.m., if, for example, the boss had some spoiled cheese left. Though he received food tickets for us, he used them for his own family. For lunch we had boiled potatoes without gravy, thin slices of bread, and a cup of the so-called coffee. Supper was the same. We never got any meat as the bosses ate our ration, but we sometimes got watery gravy — very little — over our potatoes.

The greatest physical discomfort was the lack of sleep. We all craved a few extra hours.

As time passed I became closer to the other Polish slave workers. We suffered and labored together, talked and laughed and shared gossip, any time we met out of the view of our bosses. The men buried their anger and frustration and worked, if not diligently, at least adequately. But they constantly fantasized about the day of reckoning when they would avenge themselves against the Germans. The women, more pragmatic, were preoccupied with everyday problems. Zosia and Jola worried about their young daughters, Krysia and Wiesia, who, fortunately, were permitted to stay with them. We, the four single women, maneuvered between the men's attentions and hard labor.

Every morning I worked in the kitchen while Mrs. Wagner rationed out milk to the local people. I watched them come to the kitchen day after day. Mrs. Wagner measured the milk herself and poured it into people's pitchers.

I observed how these people behaved toward the Nazi mayor of Marten and his wife. I noticed Mrs. Martel, who barely spoke any German. She had six young children. Her husband was employed at the railroad station in Sarrebourg and walked to work six kilometers each way. I wondered how the Martels succeeded in remaining in Marten without being deported. They were unmistakably French and thus scorned by the ruling Germans, poor and humble and uncomfortable in the presence of their German neighbors. Mrs. Martel needed milk for her children and came daily to the Wagners' kitchen to get her meager portion. I saw her eyes watching the milk being poured into her container and her wistful, sad look when Mrs. Wagner stopped pouring. I watched out for Mrs. Martel's arrival and if by chance Mrs. Wagner was busy and asked me to replace her for a moment, I always gave Mrs. Martel twice her ration. We did not talk, but our eyes met and hers told me "thank you." That, unfortunately, did not happen often. Mrs. Wagner quickly got back to the kitchen, pushed me aside, and rationed milk to the waiting people herself.

Mrs. Ackerman was another daily visitor in the mayor's kitchen. Her family was the most prosperous and respected in the village. Their business was to sell, lease, and repair farm machinery and tools. As they were the only mechanics in the village, their services were appreciated even more during wartime, when new equipment was unavailable. The Ackermans were in fact French, and they had a sister who spoke only French. She kept a very low profile and avoided any contact with our German bosses. We Polish people knew about this discreet sister and waved to her when we saw her. Mr. and Mrs. Ackerman played their role of loyal Germans well, always greeting their neighbors politely. When Mrs. Ackerman came for her milk in the morning, she smiled in a friendly way at Mrs. Wagner and brought her each time a small gift such as a can of beans or marmalade, and chatted and joked with her.

The Ackermans were also polite to us Polish people and we were not sure what to think of them. Later something happened that shed more light on the Ackermans. It happened some time in 1944: a British plane was found in the middle of the fields near a dense forest away from any town or village. The Germans looked furiously for the pilots, who had obviously escaped since there was no trace of blood or dead bodies. The pilots were in hiding somewhere. But where?

We were frightened that the angry Germans might turn on us and kill Polish men or women for revenge. I had been warned by Zenon Pawlo never to reveal that I was educated, because the intelligentsia were the first target for exemplary or vengeful punishment. That was why I always behaved as a humble, naive girl.

Days passed, and the British pilots were not found. We went to work as usual. One day Mrs. Wagner asked me to deliver some empty jars to the Ackermans who lived near us. I knocked at the front door and nobody answered, so I ventured behind the house into their backyard — and then I saw some strange-looking young men. They did not look like the slave workers or Germans; they were different. I had never seen them before and was surprised. Suddenly Mr. and Mrs. Ackerman ran toward me, shouting angrily that I had no right to enter their property and I should leave it immediately. They were enraged, which puzzled me because the Ackermans had always been so polite to us Polish workers. I wondered what I had done wrong; I had gone only a few steps behind their house. The men said nothing but turned their heads away from me, as if they were embarrassed at the verbal onslaught they were witnessing.

The Ackermans' attitude was as bizarre as the apparition of the unknown men. I was hurt and offended, but some instinct told me not to reveal to my co-workers what had happened, and I certainly knew better than to speak about it to the Germans.

After the liberation we learned that the strangers were of course the British pilots. They all survived, and the Ackermans received heroes' recognition and applause. When I visited the Ackermans, they received me warmly. In their kitchen, a few German prisoners of war in uniform were sitting at a table eating their supper. They were working for the Ackermans. I was invited to dine with the Ackermans at the family table.

The village of Marten had no doctor, dentist, or pharmacy, but it had two pubs or wirtschafts, as they were then called. One pub, at the top end of the village, was owned by a fat, rude woman who was impolite to us but friendly and servile to the Germans. The pub had a grocery attached to it and was prosperous.

Later, in the fall of 1944, when the Allied armies were in our area and the Germans were on the defensive, I overheard a phone conversation between the woman pub owner and the Germans. She paid no attention to me, a "stupid Pole," even though I was right there in her store, but talked freely and loudly. She was informing the Germans where the Allied armies were at the moment, and giving detailed instructions about the latest moves and positions of the Allies.

Most of the Polish workers had been in Marten since 1940 and knew the people of the village and its surrounding areas. They disliked the village schoolteacher, a devout Nazi who paraded in jackboots with a big swastika on his arm. He was married and had two or three children. Unlike the German farmers who had taken over the French farms, he was not physically handicapped or a war veteran, but a good-looking, tall, well-built Nordic type. As a dedicated Nazi, he despised all the Slavic forced laborers, Poles and Serbs alike. He also disliked those villagers who spoke with a strong French accent, and called them "dirty French."

Among the many people the Nazi teacher despised was a very kind widow and her two children. She spoke barely any German, had no land, and was poor. Perhaps her husband was of

German origin, for it was a mystery to us how she had managed to stay in Marten. The teacher would gladly have kicked the widow's two young girls out of the school, but since the family was allowed to remain in Marten, they had the right to attend the school. However, there was no law to stop the teacher from being nasty and abusive. We often saw the girls come home crying and wanted to cry with them.

The teacher was a good friend of my boss, Mr. Wagner, who of course was a fellow member of the Nazi party. Nevertheless, my Polish co-workers spoke well of Mr. Wagner and believed he was a Nazi by sheer opportunism and not by conviction. They sympathized with him, because most of them had been unemployed and poor before the war, as most likely Mr. Wagner was. He had been an indigent and crippled man, but now his life had been transformed as a result of his adherence to the Nazi party. It was a fairy tale for his wife as well. In her new, pleasant life, Mrs. Wagner, whom my co-workers considered a decent woman, shared with her husband a nice house, a farm, slave workers, domestic animals, a cowshed full of cows and a stable full of fine horses. They had pigs and chickens, farm tools, machinery, and rich land to cultivate.

After a couple of good years, Mr. Wagner became bored and craved amusement, a change from his daily routine. A sexual encounter with a Polish slave worker seemed an easy and exciting diversion. However, to preserve the purity of the Aryan race, Nazi law forbade interracial sexual relations. To have intercourse with a Polish woman, Mr. Wagner would have to be careful not to be caught by the authorities, or to antagonize his wife.

By that time I was living alone in the room in the adjoining empty house. One evening I heard a loud noise on the stairway leading to my room, which still had no lock. It was Mr. Wagner, wearing his Nazi uniform with the big swastika, a rifle over his shoulder, and his dog at his heels. He pretended that he was coming to check the house and made noise to ensure that no one would suspect him of a furtive visit to a Polish slave worker. I understood immediately the purpose of his visit and ran across the room to sit on the windowsill. The window looked on to the street and was covered with blackout material to protect the village against Allied bombing. I believed I would be safer there because Mr. Wagner would be afraid of attracting attention; I could scream or try to jump through the window. His wife and children were very close by, and for once Nazi law was actually protecting me.

Mr. Wagner stood on the other side of the room. "You are a nice girl and I like you," he said. "Look here, I brought you a present, you see it is a big piece of ham I have cut for you. Be a good girl, don't be afraid. See, I leave this ham on the table. It will be all yours, just come to me, I will kiss you."

I remained immobile as if I were frozen and looked straight into his eyes. My lips remained sealed. Only my eyes were saying: "Stay where you are, don't touch me!" If I had spoken, my words could have been misinterpreted as coquetry: I heard that men liked sometimes to interpret a women's "no" as "yes." So I kept silent, my back pressed against the window, believing any movement of my body might provoke him. He continued to talk but finally must have realized that the only way to have intercourse with me would be by raping me. He probably considered this unwise, even dangerous. He could possess me only with my consent, my quiet surrender.

He began to retreat. As he turned toward the door with his rifle and his dog, he said, "You can eat this piece of ham I brought you. It's yours."

Then for the first time I spoke. "You are a fine man. Only a real man would act in this way, and I will never forget it. And never, ever, will I mention it to anyone."

He turned his head and smiled at me. Then he left the room. As soon as I heard that he was downstairs, I ate the piece of ham.

In the spring Mrs. Wagner ordered me to dig up the garden, but my rows of turned soil were uneven, too bulky or too thin and never straight. My back ached and sweat ran down my face, which did not improve my work. Mrs. Wagner told me one day that she was putting up with me because I was the first maid she had known who did not steal. I believe there was another reason as well: I always recognized her, not her husband, as my boss. The other workers asked Mr. Wagner what to do and expected him to give the orders. After all, it was he who yelled louder and meted out the punishments. She was calm and always deferred to her husband. But I remembered my proud and independent mother who put my father first in private and in public, although, in fact, it was she who ran the household and jealously guarded her prerogatives. Thus, I always asked Mrs. Wagner what to do and reported to her when I had finished my work or had a problem. I saw then a tiny smile of satisfaction at the corner of her mouth.

Involved with my co-workers' problems and village chatter, I worried less about my tenuous existence. But I was very careful not to utter a word about my family, since I claimed to be fatherless, with no brothers or sisters. Yet I dreamt constantly about my family and my return to Warsaw, and I often heard in my mind the stationmaster's voice announcing loudly: "Warszawa, Dworzec Główny" — "Warsaw, Central Station." These would be the blessed words I would hear first upon my return to Warsaw, words that echoed in my mind like beautiful music.

My mother and sister were still hiding in Bernerowo. My father regularly sent them food packages and money from the small town where he worked for a dentist. But the situation in Bernerowo had deteriorated. It was now the late summer of 1943, and denunciations of Jews and their rescuers were increasingly common in Poland. Even in Bernerowo, a quiet suburb of Warsaw, some Polish families hiding Jews were denounced by their neighbors and murdered, together with the people they had tried to protect. Julia and Walenty Kielba told my mother not to worry, that they would continue to shelter her and Karolina. However, my mother understood that it had become too dangerous for the

Kielbas and that something had to be done. Another hiding place had to be found for at least one of them. But where, where? my mother thought in despair. Finally, she decided that there was no other way but to send Karolina to join me in Marten, and wrote asking for help. The mail functioned well and her letter reached me promptly.

Karolina needed an invitation issued by a German employer to work on his farm. I knew that there was a shortage of labor, and a slave worker was a valuable and useful commodity. I had once overheard Mr. Wagner and other farmers requesting additional workers from the Gestapo who were visiting the mayor. The Gestapo rebuked them loudly, and our bosses became scared and silent.

I approached Mrs. Wagner. "I am happy working for you," I told her, "but I miss my best girlfriend who lives in Warsaw. I would be so happy if my friend, Krystyna, joined me and worked with me for you, Mrs. Wagner."

She reported our conversation to her husband. "Is your girlfriend nicer than you?" he asked, with lust in his eyes.

"Much nicer, much prettier, and much more experienced with men," I assured him.

His eyes sparkled. He decided to prepare proper papers for my sister, whose name was now Krystyna Wanda Stolarska—ostensibly no relation to me. I wrote and told my mother and sister that the papers would be ready soon.

Even before this process was considered, I had worried about them and written to Karolina suggesting that she might join me. I described my life to her in detail, my new friends, and all I knew about the people in Marten. Of course, I wrote carefully and lightly, like a simple girl gossiping with her friend. Now I had a premonition that Karolina would have to remember everything I had written to her about Marten. "Memorize it well," I urged my sister in my letter. Fortunately, she listened to me and did so.

Coming to Marten by the same route as I had done, Karolina too had to stay in the Transit Center on Skarszewska Street for a few days and pass a medical examination. But she was less lucky, and the doctor became suspicious of her. The life of seclusion at the Kielbas had depressed her, and her blue eyes had the sad, "Jewish" look. She did not look like a poor, starving girl who would voluntarily surrender to slave labor. The fact that she seemed refined, even when she stood naked before the doctor, did not help, and he decided to interrogate "Krystyna Wanda Stolarska." Why was she going to Marten? he asked.

My sister, who had memorized the names and even the nicknames of the Polish people with whom I worked, answered plaintively: "All my friends are working for the Great Germany, and I have been left behind. I feel lonely in Warsaw and I am hungry. Please, I want to join my friends. We like to work for the German people, we feel then useful and happy. I want to be like my friends,"

"And who are your friends?" the doctor inquired.

Karolina started to describe them, giving their names and every detail about them. The doctor let her pass, and she arrived safely in Marten.

Karolina, who I now called Krystyna, was a new girl in the village and the men were greatly interested in her. We worked together for the Wagners and slept in the same room, but we had to be very careful so no one would guess that we were sisters. Everything had to be a secret. Our world was a world of fear and lies.

Krystyna's clothes had been destroyed en route from Warsaw by hydrogen peroxide which leaked out of the bottle she kept in her suitcase. She needed it to maintain the blonde color of her hair, which was normally chestnut. I gave her one of the two dresses I had. My own dress was quite worn but still good enough to wear. How I got the second dress is a story in itself.

When I first came to Marten, Polish workers no longer received the ration coupons to buy clothes or other necessities. Some people still had their last one or two coupons left, which were worthless in themselves, for they were insufficient to purchase anything at all. I asked for them in exchange for a piece of bread, a needle, a hairpin, or anything else I could find. Everyone laughed at me; I was giving them something for nothing—they used to throw such coupons away.

But after a while I had enough coupons to get myself a dress. My co-workers suspected me of dirty dealings with the Germans and could not believe in my simple arithmetic calculations. Fortunately, after some nasty insinuations, the matter was dropped and forgotten.

Later our clothing problem became so severe that we ripped the covers off the mattresses left in the abandoned French houses. Somebody made a dress for me with this material out of kindness, for I had nothing left with which to pay for the work. Later a big hole appeared in the back of my "new" and only dress. I had to wear it back-to-front and cover the hole with an apron.

With Karolina's arrival, Mr. Wagner, who never stopped lusting after me, now had two slave girls to choose from—only my sister was no more receptive to his advances than I was. Mr. Wagner became impatient, yearning for sex with any available woman. There were, of course, three other single Polish girls besides Krystyna and me: the inaccessible Maria, guarded by her boyfriend, and Hela and Jasia. Mr. Wagner decided to approach Hela, who shared a room and a huge double bed with her friend, Jasia. Hela, the former street girl, did not mind satisfying Mr. Wagner, but Jasia's presence created a problem. Jasia expected to be paid for her silence, and Mr. Wagner offered her coupons for a pair of shoes, which she badly needed.

Days passed, then weeks, and Mr. Wagner did not deliver the shoe coupons. Jasia felt cheated and became angry. A simple, uneducated girl, she had trusted Mr. Wagner, the mayor of the village, and expected him to keep his promise.

"A bargain is a bargain, and there is no excuse for cheating a hard working girl," Jasia complained. "How can the mayor be so heartless and dishonest?"

In her mind there was no difference between the Polish and German authorities. They were simply the "Authorities." The legality or the morality of a state and its representatives were foreign and remote concepts to Jasia's mind. "Everybody in this world has their place," she reasoned. "Some people are up, and some are down. I am poor and Mr. Wagner is rich, and he should not deceive me."

That was all Jasia could comprehend. She felt so deeply offended by the mayor's breach of promise that she decided to report the incident to the highest Authorities, which meant the Gestapo. She sincerely hoped to obtain redress for her grievance.

To her great surprise, she did not obtain the shoe coupons.

Mr. Wagner was sent to a concentration camp for eight months for disobeying Nazi racial law. His family was disgraced and had to vacate the farm and move into a modest house in Marten.

Hela was executed, shot dead, for having sex with Mr. Wagner.

The Gestapo praised Jasia for her denunciation of the misdeed. Jasia's boss, a devoted member of the Nazi party, applauded her loyalty to the Nazi rules.

Jasia did not feel remorseful about Mr. Wagner's fate, but she badly missed her friend, Hela, and could not understand why she had been killed. She had not expected things to turn out in such a strange way. "How could the Authorities be so unpredictable?" Jasia asked herself again and again.

The Poles and the Serbs laughed at Mr. Wagner's misfortune. After all, he was a Nazi punished by the same Nazis he had trusted and supported, so why should the slave workers worry about his fate? As for me, I felt sorry for Mrs. Wagner. I thought about my mother, whom Mrs. Wagner resembled a little, and thought how terribly my mother would have been hurt if she had been betrayed by my father. I also remembered Mr. Wagner's lust and that, after all, he had restrained himself and I was still alive and untouched, and so was my sister.

Perhaps one good turn called for another—or perhaps I simply pitied Mrs. Wagner and her crippled husband. I met Mrs. Wagner one day on the street and she turned her head away, but I approached her and spoke, although she still avoided looking at me.

"Mrs. Wagner," I said, "your husband never did it. If he wanted to do it, he would have come to me first. I worked for him, and I was much younger than Hela. But your husband never asked me, he never tried anything. Please believe me."

Mrs. Wagner head rose a little and she gave me a furtive look. Then she quickly went away.

A new German family took over the Wagners' farm. Krystyna and I continued to work there and our chores remained the same, but Jacob was greatly upset by Mr. Wagner's fall. He was attached to him, the first boss who had never abused him. His sense of security vanished, and he became totally unbalanced and ran away from the farm and his new boss. Lonely and confused, he approached the German authorities and asked to be granted German nationality and permission to join the German army. For him, as for Jasia, there was little distinction between the Polish and the German authorities; people in power were always so very distant, so high above them. Their orders had to be obeyed, not understood. When Jacob's requests were refused, he did not return to Marten, perhaps afraid of being punished for his desertion. He wandered around the countryside for some time and was briefly seen in various places, hungry and miserable. Later, we heard rumors that he had been shot and killed by the Germans.

Jasia now lived alone in her room in the dilapidated house across the street from mine. She did not look very well and told me that she wanted to leave Marten. She was not articulate and was unable to express how badly she felt about Hela's death and how scared she was of Mr. Wagner's retaliation when he came back from the concentration camp. "It would be good if I could leave Marten, forget what happened, and start a new life," she told me.

Days passed and the end of 1943 was approaching. One day our new boss received an order from the Work Bureau forbidding him to keep two female Polish servants. One of the girls had to "volunteer" to work at a canteen for German soldiers not far from Marten. The girl had to leave the next day. The boss had been with us only a short time, and hardly distinguished Krystyna from me. He did not care which one left his farm; he would still keep one servant. Thus, either Krystyna or I would have to leave early the next morning.

After work was finished, we returned to our room to prepare one of us for the departure. We were terrified by our imminent separation and by the prospect of working among German soldiers; there was no choice but to surrender to fate. Because I looked more like a Polish country girl and had not been suspected so far of being Jewish, it would be safer if I left and Krystyna stayed on the farm. I had to make my bundle and opened the large wardrobe, which had once belonged to the French occupants. There I saw the two winter coats our mother had ordered for us in the fall of 1939. My coat was marine blue and had a nice opossum collar. It looked like new. An idea crossed my mind: "Jasia wants to leave Marten. She is not afraid of men, either soldiers or civilians. She enjoys sex for the fun of it, and not for the little gifts she occasionally receives. She made such a big fuss about the pair of shoes because she had so very few things. If I gave her my winter coat, would she take my place in the soldiers' canteen?"

There was no time to lose. It was dark outside, but Jasia slept just across the street. I took my coat and went to see her. Her door, like mine, was unlocked. She woke up, smiled at me, and listened to my proposal.

"I like your coat, it looks nice and warm. Let me try it," she said, interested. The coat fit her perfectly, and she looked satisfied. "I don't mind trying a new and different job. Why not? The change might be interesting. But one coat is not enough, give me something else in addition," she added shrewdly.

I had one sweater left and quickly offered it to her. "Okay," she said, "bring your sweater and I will go."

But I had to be sure that Jasia really understood what she was doing and would not back out at the last moment. I tried to explain to her what she could expect working in a soldiers' canteen or pub. "Jasia, are you sure you want to go? It will be very different from your life in Marten. You may have to deal with more men than you would care to. The soldiers may be very rough guys."

She smiled at me as if I was a stupid child. Yes, she was sure, she wanted to go. "You see, Irene, men do not frighten me. Their bark is worse than their bite—I know them too well. I am able to take care of myself and no one has hurt me so far. I'll have better food there and no dirty farm work," Jasia assured me with a smile.

I ran back across the dark street to fetch my sweater and to tell Krystyna what was decided, and then returned to Jasia. She prepared her parcel, chatted with me a while and went back to sleep. I stayed with her all night in case she changed her mind. I would then have had to leave Marten quietly, without any fuss; disobeying the German orders was unthinkable.

Early in the morning, Jasia took her parcel, said a friendly goodbye to me, and went to her Nazi boss to announce that she had decided to volunteer to work in the canteen, and Irene would take her place at his farm. The order said that one girl had to "volunteer," and Jasia's boss, a loyal Nazi, obeyed this like any other Nazi order to the letter; he readily approved her decision. Jasia left, and I took her place in her boss's kitchen.

Later we heard from the Polish men that Jasia was happy in her new place. The Polish men passed information around by word of mouth; they knew all about the Allied defeats and victories and about the other Polish slaves in Lorraine. Perhaps some of them had succeeded in visiting the accommodating Jasia — after all, she had not moved very far from Marten. In contrast to the fate of poor Jacob, Jasia's move from Marten was a beneficial one for her, and she survived the war.

My new boss and his family were even more fervent Nazis than the Wagners. They were proud of their twenty-year-old daughter, Eliza, a good-looking, tall brunette, who had become pregnant while serving as a nurse in the German army in Pomerania. Her newborn pure Aryan boy was her gift to the Fuehrer and the Fatherland. Eliza, a single mother, now lived with her baby on her parents' farm in Marten. Her brother, also a devout Nazi, served Adolf Hitler in the occupied countries of Eastern Europe. The family seemed to be contented and settled.

I was treated in a paternalistic way by this new family. As long as I worked hard, ate little, and did not complain, I was spoken to firmly but politely, and I was not physically harmed. But the son's visits frightened me. He was a young man who wore his Nazi uniform even when on leave at his parents' home. He watched me attentively when I worked in the kitchen. Sitting in the next room with the kitchen door open, he fixed his eyes on me. There was no lust in them but a hard and penetrating stare, evaluating me. He must have observed many Jews when he helped to murder them. He would have also seen many Poles during the roundups, and I feared that he was not sure where to place me. Although I always covered my head with a scarf, as Zofia Chemska had instructed me, I did not look exactly like a Polish peasant girl. If our eyes met, I looked straight into his and I never smiled. However, I tried to avoid his gaze, continued my work and pretended not to notice him watching me.

Krystyna and I now had to face another problem: we were the only single, unprotected Polish women in Marten. Jasia and Hela were both gone, Maria was controlled by her boyfriend, and Zosia and Jola were married. The Polish men around us became more restless and more insistent on sex with us. They asked, "Who do you think the two of you are, two princesses? Why are you so different?" We became really frightened. The word "different" was sinister to our ears because, indeed, we were different and if unmasked, we would have to pay for it with our lives.

We ran out of excuses for why we did not have lovers. The pressure on us became heavier, and the men became more and more arrogant in pursuing us. They believed that a woman had no right to stay unattached.

But not everybody was so primitive and cruel. Józef, one of the Polish slave workers, was different, a little shy, less loud and aggressive. His soft brown eyes and his sincere open face, enhanced by thick dark hair, inspired confidence. He was slim, not very muscular, and of medium height. He was twenty-one years old when I first met him, but looked younger. I sensed that he was more refined than most of our Polish co-workers. We enjoyed talking together and after I had moved to my room, Józef visited me often in the evening. His parents were decent, hard-working people. He said that I reminded him of his older sister, and he wanted to protect me as he wished to protect her.

Józef worked for a nasty man, Mr. Renaud, a slave-driver who spoke German with a heavy French accent. Not physically very strong, Józef endured his servitude with great courage. Mr. Renaud imposed long hours of labor with only short breaks and gave Józef little to eat.

Józef tried to help me with my heavy tasks. Moving a large wheelbarrow full of pig manure was beyond my strength. I was ordered to do it fast and to fill the wheelbarrow to capacity, but if I filled it full, I could not move it. So I wheeled the half-empty cart and emptied it as quickly as I was able, and returned to the pile of manure to load the wheelbarrow again. My back hurt badly and I could barely breathe. But sometimes, Józef succeeded in running through our orchard into the farmyard when I was struggling with my work. He arrived any time he could escape

Mr. Renaud's attention, filled the wheelbarrow, pushed it and emptied in no time.

Unfortunately Józef could seldom help me. Strangely enough it was Elza, wife of the German officer and daughter of Mundek and Zosia's German bosses from Bavaria, who often helped me in yet another difficult task. As I milked my 12 to 14 cows twice a day, I emptied one bucket after another into the heavy milk churns through the bolting cloth. Then I put the churns on a handcart and took them to the truck stop, where the milk was picked up to be delivered to the city. Lifting the full churns from my cart onto the truck, I felt out of breath and dizzy, but the slim, muscular Elza had no trouble in doing it. Any time this friendly German woman saw me struggling with my heavy churns, she ran to help me.

But there was no end to our chores. Sometimes in the evening Józef, eager to help, would wash the floor of my room. When our fellow slave workers discovered this, they teased him cruelly for being so meek and generous to a woman. It was contrary to their customs, but I understood that they were also rather jealous of our friendship. When their teasing turned to threats, I had to ask Józef to stop washing my floor. I announced to the rogues that they had won and that Józef would no longer bring dishonor to men. That calmed them for a while.

Time passed, and Józef remained a sincere friend. I trusted and liked him. He spoke often about his family in Poland. His father worked long hours six days a week in an inadequately ventilated tannery and later became a heavy drinker and smoker. He worked hard to support his family of six children, four boys and two girls, but had little time or inclination to play with them. It was Józef's mother's job to take care of the children, to clean, cook, and earn a little money by doing odd jobs here and there. She believed in strict discipline and wanted to protect her children from trouble with the police, which happened easily in their Warsaw neighborhood. She believed that beating was good for the soul and that the child's crying was good for its lungs.

We both stood apart from our co-workers and feared them. Many were brutal and belligerent men with prison records, drifters without families. But we had to hide our apprehensions and pretend to be brave. This created a bond of sympathy and understanding between us; Józef's life was difficult and so was mine, albeit for different reasons. Józef said that I was the first woman he had loved.

But I was not ready to become Józef's lover. I could not even tell him who I was; he could inadvertently betray me, or be killed for complicity if my real identity was found out.

One day Józef gave me an ultimatum: either I married him, or our friendship would be over and he would stop visiting me. In fact we could not get married, since we were slaves without any civil rights, but Józef stubbornly pressed his proposal.

"But how?" I asked. "We are outcasts and the Church is closed to us. We cannot get married there. We have no right even to approach the priest"

Józef, brought up as a Catholic, could not believe that a priest would refuse to help him. He insisted on our meeting with the local priest to ask him to marry us. Neither Józef nor I had ever heard of a civil marriage, and believed that only a priest could issue a binding and valid marriage certificate.

Józef's attitude touched me deeply, even though I did not want to get married, and I did not want to have sex. I wanted to wait until the war was over and I could return to the life from which I had been so abruptly torn. I wanted to finish my studies to become a professional woman, to have my own career before committing myself to a marriage. These were the ideas my parents had instilled in me since my childhood.

But I liked Józef and cared about his friendship, and so I agreed to go to consult with the priest. We waited for an opportune moment, and one evening after work we walked discretely to the priest's house and knocked at the door. He let us in, although he would have been punished if our visit were discovered. And we could have been punished even more harshly for disobeying the law. The priest at that time was German, although our Polish co-workers, who knew everything, said that before the war he had been French. We had heard that his brother was a bishop in the city of Metz.

Józef explained to the priest that we wanted him to marry us.

The priest said that he could not do so.

"If you don't marry us, you will have the sin of our having an illegitimate child on your conscience. We must marry. It is the only way to save us from committing that sinful act," I said. In fact, I was still a virgin, but in my mind having sex with Józef would be the same as becoming pregnant. I was sure that the moment I lost my virginity, I would conceive.

The priest replied, "Child, don't you worry. After the war I will write to your priest in Poland and explain everything to him. You are a good girl, everything will be all right, don't you worry."

I did not like his idea about contacting "my priest" in Poland, since I had none, and I felt deeply worried as we left. I looked at Józef; his head was hanging. He was crushed. His country had abandoned him; he had starved there. Now his church had rejected him, and he felt bitterly betrayed.

It was a clear night, the moon full and the stars brilliant. We were surrounded by majestic trees, the air was fresh and pleasant, it was peaceful and quiet. I remembered then the writings of Jean-Jacques Rousseau, his love and praise for nature. Suddenly, all my concerns dissipated, and I felt the presence of God high above us. No, we were not alone, not totally helpless. I took Józef's hand and, before I realized what I was doing, I said, "Don't worry, I will be your wife. God will bless us." I made this solemn pledge looking at the sky while addressing God, Józef and myself. And so I became Józef's girl.

Of course, we could not live together or even share the same room. We had no right to change our status or to move from one place to another. We could only meet occasionally and briefly after work.

Józef and I announced promptly to our co-workers that we were lovers. We hoped that this would discourage the men from harassing me. Many of them wished us well, but some became very angry, especially with me, and demanded, "Why did you choose Józef and not one of us?" For Józef, intelligent and thoughtful, was not one of them, the bullies who stuck together. They were physically stronger than him, yet it was Józef who got the girl they all wanted, and this they could hardly accept.

One day, two of them stopped me at a corner, barring my escape. One man brusquely asked, "Why is it Józef and not me that you have chosen to make love with? What does he have that I don't have?" I could see that he was not joking, that angry and full of lust, he was ready to assault and rape me. This time again I had to think quickly to find the proper response, which was my only defense. "All right," I said, "I can go with you, but you will have to be the father of my child." The men stepped back. They looked at me, astonished. "A child?" they asked in disbelief. "Yes," I calmly lied, "I carry Józef's child."

Primitive and crude though they were, they did not take lightly the paternity of a child. To play rough with a girl was one thing; to rape a mother-to-be was another. They let me go. But in fact, I wasn't pregnant. Józef and I weren't even lovers as yet, in spite of our announcement.

Krystyna continued to labor for her new boss. I taught her how to milk the cows, and this skill helped her a lot because, like I, she was not very good at hard physical work. Krystyna often caught colds, for she had a delicate constitution, but she never complained and continued to work at the endless tasks assigned to her. She too had to help in the kitchen, garden and field, and milk at least dozen cows twice a day.

The farm needed more workers, and one day a German boy, Helmuth, arrived. Krystyna did not know if this sixteen-year-old boy had been forced to come or came voluntarily. His mother, who visited him from time to time, had black hair, brown eyes, and a light brown complexion. Krystyna's boss could not forgive her such a non-Aryan look, calling her "dirty gypsy," and despising her and her son. The mistreated Helmuth had to concentrate more on how to avoid the boss's blows than how to farm.

My situation on the farm had worsened. Sebastian, who had a criminal record and who had come into my room that night with Mundek, now worked with me. I had taken his friend Jasia's place, and he resented it. He harassed me, while I kept on pretending that I did not hear him well, and never answered him back. In this way, some kind of uneasy coexistence was established between us. Sebastian kept on insulting me as much as he wanted, but never tried to touch me.

I had a very warm country jacket that was a present from Zofia Chemska, who believed that my winter coat would not be suitable for a farm girl. The jacket was not stylish, pretty or new, but it was deliciously warm and most practical. I wore it when going to work from the room I still shared with Krystyna, a few blocks from my new workplace, and so every morning I hung the jacket on a hook in the stable. Sebastian liked my jacket and without asking my permission, began to wear it. I did not want to quarrel with him, but a poor Polish girl would not let anyone take her jacket without at the very least protesting loudly. The situation was delicate. I would have gladly let him have my jacket to avoid trouble, but I had to assert myself, and claim my property. Finally, I found a compromise.

"Sebastian, I understand that you are cold and you like my jacket," I said to him. "You may borrow it and wear it when I am working inside the house or in the stable. But I must have it back when I am going out. Any time I work outside or walk to my room, I will need my jacket."

Sebastian grumbled in agreement, but the look he gave me any time I took my jacket from his back made me shiver.

In February 1944 our devout Nazi boss was called to the army. His family was forced to leave the farm, and a new family arrived. It appeared that all able-bodied German men had already been mobilized and sent to the front, and the government could not find a "pure" German to take over the farm. This time a German-Rumanian family arrived to replace the idealistic Nazi.

The new bosses were greedy and arrogant people. They fed me with their leftovers. They were unclean and sloppy and, in addition to all my previous work, I had to wash their personal underwear and clothes as well as clean up after their meals in the dining room.

Józef and I finally became lovers in December of 1943. I knew nothing about sexual relations, and Józef was almost as naive as I. I needed time to accept our relationship, and Józef's innocent and timid advances endeared him to me. As my feelings for him grew, my life became fuller. A new dimension was added to it, giving me an unaccustomed feeling of inner peace and contentment. My body yearned to fuse with Józef's and to be one with him. I believed that having sex would naturally lead to conception; it was beyond my imagination that it could be otherwise. And somehow, I accepted this as the normal and welcome outcome of lovemaking.

Some time later I began to feel unwell. I felt chilly and hungry as I had never been before, and I tired easily. My German-Rumanian bosses piled more work on me every day, probably thinking that if I was able to do that much today, it would not hurt me to do a little more tomorrow.

At the end of February 1944, I began to suspect that I was pregnant. Although I had been waiting for this to happen, I could not believe it and wanted to be sure. The closest doctor was in Morhange, six kilometers from Marten. We were allowed to see either a dentist or a doctor there only in exceptional circumstances.

I had had a bad toothache for some time, and I used my pass to see a doctor instead.

The Morhange doctor, a man around sixty years old, was well-liked by the Polish slave workers, for he had been kind and helpful to them. A Frenchman before the war, he must have signed some pro-German papers, since he had been permitted to stay in the town, and after the war he was accused of collaboration with the enemy. However, no matter what had been his official allegiance during the war, he had always acted properly toward us and the Polish people trusted him.

I had to have a gynecological examination, the first in my life. I was very shy and frightened; there would be no nurse to assist the doctor, just he and I in the room. I was most apprehensive when he closed the door, and I lay helpless on the examination table. But he was gentle and polite; he examined me with the special, light touch of an honest doctor. I relaxed and breathed more easily. He did not try to molest me, although I was a slave—totally at his mercy. He confirmed the pregnancy and predicted the normal development of a healthy baby. I was twenty years old, undernourished but healthy.

I had expected that I would become pregnant from the day my relationship with Józef began, yet the gravity of the situation hit me hard, and I left the doctor's office in a daze, trembling and desperate. The street was quiet. It was a gray, overcast day with a few blue patches in the sky, the sun trying feebly to break though. Uncertain as to what I should do, I entered a nearby church. It was silent, empty and dim, and I sat alone with my thoughts and fears. The Ghetto came back to my mind in a flash, with the cries of the Jewish children being rounded up for deportation. And here was I, about to have a child. How reckless it was of me to conceive, even if I loved Józef and my body yearned for a baby.

Sitting in the church, I thought things over, dejected and guilty. Who would help me now? Who would save my baby?

I wanted to pray, but I could not address myself to God, since that would have been a Jewish thing to do. As Zenon Pawlo had warned me before I left Warsaw, I had to banish the Jewish God from my consciousness.

My eyes adjusted to the pale light and I saw the big crucifix in front of me and the stained-glass windows all around the church. I turned my eyes away from the crucifix to the windows instead. I began to pray, begging for courage and for the war to end in time for us. I prayed, "Oh Mother of the Crucified, don't let my child die. You understand a mother's heart, you know my secret. Help me. Give me courage and strength."

I felt close to the Mother of the Crucified, as if she were my sister. She was like one of those Ghetto mothers who helplessly watched their children's agony. I felt that she could understand our fate in the Nazi Reich, that my prayer to her might help.

No, I was not the first woman who had conceived a child in this cruel world. Nor was I the only one who had to muster all her courage and her strength to fight for her child's survival.

"Mother of the Crucified, you and I are of the same blood," I prayed. (We were both Jewish, that forbidden word.) "Help me. Give me a sign that my child will live, that it will be spared."

I prayed ardently, hoping for a miracle, needing a miraculous sign to sustain me. I looked at the windows around me, one after the other, waiting for a sign. And it came: suddenly the sun illuminated the window I was looking at, just that one single window, while all others remained darkened. I watched the light until, after a few minutes, it was gone.

I left the church believing that we would be liberated in time and that my child would live. I did not try to rationalize what happened in the church—I did not want to use logic. I simply accepted that I had received a heavenly promise that my baby and I would survive. I started back to Marten, firmly resolved to carry my baby to its full term.

From that time on, Józef became even more dear to me. My love for the baby overflowed and extended to its father. I felt freer to express myself now that my anxiety at becoming pregnant had gone.

In May 1944, the young German-Rumanian boss was called to the German army and the family had to leave the farm, their good times over.

Yet another family, this time from Croatia, came to replace them. The Serbs were enraged. They were prisoners-of-war, their families persecuted at home, their farms burned and destroyed, while their countrymen, the Croats, collaborated with the Germans. And now they had to face this Croat family from their homeland transformed into Germans. The Serbs working for our new German-Croat boss could not restrain themselves from showing their burning anger and promised revenge after the war. The German-Croat boss grumbled back angrily and the matter ended there.

As for me, not much had changed. I got only the scraps from the bosses' plates, sometimes very meager, other times more plentiful. I was forced to work all day on Sunday, and in addition to all my other tasks, I now had to take our cows to pasture. I could hardly control the cows and had no dog to help me. Once in the pasture, they happily ate the fresh grass, then sat and rested for a while. Afterwards, they started to wander and finally ran in every direction so that I had to take off my heavy wooden shoes and chase them barefoot. On rainy days the dampness penetrated my whole body and I shivered from cold in the wet meadows. It was even worse when the cows strayed into another farmer's field while I chased after them, out of breath, unable to bring them back to their pasture. The farmer would arrive to see my cows grazing contently in his field, and he would run toward me, yelling furiously, "Get these cows out of here, take them out immediately!"

"Help me, please help me," I pleaded desperately. "I don't know how to get them out." And the farmer, to save his field, would join me in chasing the cows.

Alone with the herd in the green meadows, I talked to my baby as I began to feel its movements. "Listen, my baby," I murmured, "there is a beautiful sky above us, the Germans do not own the whole world, the war will end right on time for you. Don't be afraid, my baby, it will be all right, we will survive." And one day, talking to this not-yet-born baby, I remembered the blind hatred I felt once when so dutifully, so carefully, I passed the milk through bolting cloth to protect the German public from disease. "If only I could poison this milk instead of purifying it," I thought then. "But what about the little children? Do I want, do I have the right to murder them as well?" I had asked myself, and I thought about the happy German children I had seen on the streets of Warsaw and at the train station, after I had escaped from the Ghetto. The extermination of the Jewish children was almost complete, and their agony—compared with the carefree, healthy German children holding onto their mothers with one hand, clinging to a doll or a stuffed animal with the other, skipping, walking, talking, laughing—was unbearable. I felt a burning hatred for the German children; I wanted them to be dead like ours.

And now I was talking to my half-Jewish child, and that child, still an embryo, unformed, still inside my body, became the center of my life and the focus of my love. I asked myself, "Do you still hate the non-Jewish children? Do you still want to destroy the German children?" The answer came to me, naturally, spontaneously, "No, I don't want to hurt children, I don't want hurt any child at all." I felt peaceful, resigned to accept life as it was. I was carrying a child, and I was glad, and I was hopeful. The blind, all-encompassing hatred was gone from my heart.

One day I had a surprising encounter in the meadows with Linda, the young girl who had traveled with the Polish family on our way to Lorraine. She recognized me first and ran toward me, then stopped. Her eyes implored, "Take me in your arms, befriend me." Her lips quivered, but she said nothing. She was skinny, and hadn't grown at all since we had met, well over a year before.

I took her hands in mine and said, "Have courage, everything will be fine. Be strong, the war will end one day." She still didn't speak, gazing at me and fighting her tears. We parted, neither of us revealing her identity. She was just a child, so very delicate, so very frightened. Did she survive? I wonder, I wish.

Once our group accepted that I was Józef's girl, the men finally stopped harassing me. But as one problem was resolved, another arose. I got weaker as my pregnancy progressed. I was painfully undernourished and I had fainting spells. Herding the cows had become unbearable, both physically and mentally. I feared that my German-Croat bosses would dismiss me as an inadequate worker, and that I would be sent to a concentration camp or killed at the police station.

My situation became most uncertain and I had to find a way out. I remembered what my Polish co-workers had told me about the doctor I had seen in Morhange: he was very humane and had helped Polish slaves before. I wanted to see this doctor again but, as before, it was not easy to obtain permission.

On August 25, 1944, the day after Paris was liberated, my German-Croat boss let me go to see the doctor. The doctor was very sympathetic to my predicament and offered to send me to a hospital in Metz where I could stay until the baby's birth. He gave me a certificate saying that I was in the eighth or ninth month of pregnancy and expected an abnormal and difficult confinement. In fact, I was in my seventh month, but fortunately, the medical profession was respected by the Gestapo and a doctor's word was honored and obeyed. My boss accepted my certificate of disability and I left Marten to go to the hospital in Metz.

I walked the six kilometers from Marten to Sarrebourg and took the train to the historic city of Metz on the Moselle river in northeastern France. In 1944, its population was below 100,000. I went directly to the hospital, walking fast with my valise, hoping

I would not be stopped and asked questions. The hospital was five or six storeys high, large and impressive. It had belonged to Catholic sisters before the war, but now the German authorities had taken over its management. The nuns were permitted to stay and work only as nurses and cleaning supervisors.

I was placed in the special ward reserved for Slavic women, all young, unwed Polish and Ukrainian expectant mothers, the majority being Polish. The ward, completely separated from the rest of the hospital which served German patients, was on the top floor, and we were forbidden to leave it. The nuns disapproved of us unmarried mothers-to-be and showed their disdain.

Two German women, unmarried and pregnant, were placed in our ward. One was a girl of fifteen and another a maid in her late forties. Both were considered immoral and unworthy of the Third Reich: such early and late pregnancies could produce only defective Aryan babies. The mothers "deserved" to be ostracized, and thus were placed with us. They were frightened having their first babies, while being treated with so much hostility. Nobody counseled or comforted them.

I remember the horrible, heart-breaking cries of the young girl during the delivery. Her punishment was to be left unattended for three days and nights, agonizing in her pain until finally she gave birth to a boy. We heard that she was ill and exhausted, but did not find out what happened to her and her baby. Nor did I find out how the older woman fared, because I left the hospital before her confinement.

We received little nourishment and I was always painfully hungry. We were expected to work for our keep; every day I was ordered to wash the toilets, and the tall windows in the long corridor. I was petrified when I had to climb the ladder to reach the upper parts of the windows. Afraid of falling, I clung to the ladder, motionless and silent with my big belly stuck out while a nun kept urging me to get on with my work. But I remained frozen until, to avoid attracting the attention of her German supervisors, the nun finally let me climb down and found another job for me.

The nuns did not abuse us verbally or physically, but they were very cold. Yet they cared about our children's salvation, and saw to it that every newborn baby was promptly baptized.

One day a supervising nun asked why I always wore a kerchief. "It is not done that way in our country," she said. "You are young, take off that kerchief, show your hair." But I refused. Impatiently, she took it from my head. My hair had grown since I had burned it with gasoline. It was clean and light brown. "But you are so different now, you look like an intelligent girl," the nun announced triumphantly.

"Different" — "intelligent" — the words made me shiver. Zofia Chemska's and Zenon Pawlo's voices echoed once more in my mind, "Don't betray yourself; be careful; wear your kerchief all the time." Tears in my eyes, I grabbed it back, looking offended and reproachful at the startled nun. She left me, shaking her head.

A few days later, the same nun came to me and asked me to act as a godmother to a newborn Polish baby girl. "You know, the godchild takes after its godparents. I was looking for an intelligent Polish girl to be a godmother and I have chosen you."

I held this baby, a sweet little girl, in my arms and prayed silently for her. The nun asked me to take part in three more baptisms, and I became the godmother to four Polish baby girls. I was touched when I held these poor little babies in my arms and begged silently the Mother of the Crucified to watch over them, that they grow strong and healthy.

The mothers of my godchildren could not return to their German farms since their overseers did not want them any more, so the nuns arranged to place them, at least temporarily, in the nearby convent. I was ordered to escort them, carrying their newborn babies in their arms, to the convent. Most of the girls came from rural Poland; they had been seduced by their Polish co-workers or simply intimidated into having sex with them. Now the men were unwilling or unable to help them and to recognize their babies.

The young women cried bitterly and each expressed the same anguish: "I will never see my village again. My parents will not forgive me for having this baby. I have brought shame on them and on our parish. The priest will be very angry and will chase me away from our church. Where will I go, what will happen to me?"

I tried to say a few kind words to each young mother I accompanied. When we arrived at the convent's iron gate, the girl trembling and afraid to enter, I rang the bell. A nun opened the door, gave us hateful look, then ushered the mother and child in and shut the door with a loud bang. I returned to the hospital, my head bowed.

We had two serious problems in our ward. Another Polish woman, older than us, sexually abused and molested a number of the young expectant mothers, and no one dared to report her. We were afraid of the authorities, nuns and Germans alike.

As well, many of us were used as laboratory specimens for medical demonstrations. Treated like wax dummies by the medical staff, the unfortunate women were exposed naked, to demonstrate their genitalia and to allow students to poke inside their private parts. Somehow, I was never called for these "medical examinations," and the lesbian bully never approached me, but I expected the worst to happen to me at any time.

One day, when I was on my knees cleaning the toilet floor, the head German Nazi doctor stopped and said, "Stand up and come here."

A tall man, he took my chin into his hands and lifted my head. He looked intensely into my eyes for a long while. I tried not to blink. Then he said to me, or to himself, "What beautiful blue eyes." He repeated this a few times and looked satisfied; then he departed. I tried not to panic, but it was a bad sign. Why should the head of the hospital be interested in the color of a slave woman's eyes? Had something made him suspicious of me? All the signs were telling me, "Danger, danger, run away, leave this hospital as fast as you can!" But it was impossible to run away. I had no money and no right to leave without special permission. I was a slave, previously bound to my workplace and now to the hospital.

There was an additional worry for me. I knew that my newborn baby would be placed in a nursery, not with me. This nursery was open to the same doctors and students who used the defenseless young Polish women as specimens. These medical men could do with my child as they pleased. They would not hesitate to give away my healthy baby for adoption or to exchange it for a sick one.

One day, around the third week of September 1944, panic struck the hospital. We were not told what was going on, but we saw the nuns running up and down, and general commotion. A few nuns came to see us, nervous and confused, and told us that the front line was coming closer and we might be unsafe if we remained in Metz. We should leave the hospital and rejoin our families or friends.

Thus, miraculously, it became possible for me to return to Marten. About eight-and-a-half months pregnant, too weak to carry my valise, I left my belongings, modest but precious to me, in the care of the nuns. With a train ticket given to me by the nuns but without money or food, I walked to the station. There, I was told that the train had been waiting, immobilized, and no one knew when it would move. There was general confusion and the expectation of Allied bombing, and the station would be the first target, a very dangerous place to be. Unwilling to return to the hospital, I took a seat in the train. We sat there for a long time with little hope that it would move. I had nothing to eat, and a German woman sitting opposite me must have guessed my predicament, because she gave me a piece of bread with a friendly smile. I was touched by her kindness; it boosted my morale and my determination to go on. I was grasping at any hope that the world into which my baby would be born was not entirely cruel and that not all hearts had been contaminated by Nazi doctrine.

After many hours the train finally began to move. The journey took only a couple of hours and we arrived in Sarrebourg in the middle of the night. I didn't know in which direction Marten lay, or how to reach it. The place was deserted, the night very dark and quiet. What should I do? Where could I go? Suddenly, Mr. Martel, the husband of the woman who came every day to the Wagners' kitchen to get milk for their six children, appeared out of nowhere. He worked at the train station, and recognized me and invited to follow him. I ran behind him, just as two years ago I had run behind Józef Lautenberg in Zakrzówek. Then, I wanted to save my mother and sister. Now, I wanted to save the child I was carrying. Then I was a girl; now I was a woman.

I found my sister asleep in our room adjoining the farm. She told me right away that all the Polish men, including Józef, had been taken away by the Germans while the women had been allowed to stay in Marten. "Irene, you must rest and try to sleep," she said. "You can do nothing at night."

The next day I would see Zosia, the same Zosia who had brought me to Marten in January 1943, and she would explain to me what had happened.

I don't remember having any food the night I was reunited with my sister. Nor do I remember what I ate the next day when I met Zosia. Neither of them kept food in their room; they ate in their bosses' kitchens. Yet I must have eaten something, because I was still able to walk.

Zosia told me that the Polish men were taken abruptly with nothing more that the clothes they wore. They were under arrest but not locked up, since the Germans had had no time to prepare a prison camp. The women were going to take some clothes to their men, detained not too far from Marten, in a town known before the war as Château-Salins.

I went to see Mr. Renaud and asked for Józef's clothes, but he said that I was not Józef's wife and had no right to take his belongings. I insisted and made a discreet allusion to the fact that the war would end soon. Finally, Mr. Renaud allowed me to take what I wanted. I borrowed a small milk cart, loaded Józef's clothes and some bread I got from somewhere, and went with the other women on the long, twelve-kilometer march.

At last we arrived, and I saw Józef. I will never forget the joy in his eyes when he saw me. "Irene," he said, "it is so good to see you. I lost hope that this would happen. I prayed and said to myself that if I saw you again, it would be a sign from heaven that the Germans will not kill me as they killed my younger brother. I am certain now that I will live to see our child, and that the three of us will survive the war."

Thus, Józef understood my reappearance as a good omen, and like my praying in the Morhange church, grasped at any sign to uphold his spirit.

Toward the end of the day, Józef and I reluctantly parted. I returned to Marten with Zosia and Jola. Too weak to perform the hard duties required by my German-Croat overseers, I did not want to return to their kitchen. My doctor's certificate stating that I should be excused from farm work until the end of the pregnancy was still valid and protected me. But if I did not work for a farmer, I had nothing to eat. I had no money. Krystyna took meals at her farm and was unable to bring food for me. Mr. Renaud, Józef's boss, offered none, although he knew well that I was carrying his slave's baby.

Mrs. Martel came to my rescue and employed me to help with her six children and her heavy housework. Instead of money, she gave me food but not much, because she was herself poor and had little to spare.

Krystyna and I decided it was safer for me to stay farther from our bosses and moved to the end of the next street, occupied mostly by the non-deported, pre-war inhabitants of Marten. We took a nice room in the front of an empty house left by an expelled French family.

Just a few days later, we were awakened very early by a loud commotion. We looked out of our window and saw the Germans moving away in large, horse-drawn wagons. They took almost everything with them, including horses, cows and pigs.

With the Germans gone, the Polish workers would have to feed themselves, and finding food was not easy. We went to Krystyna's boss's house, searching for anything left to eat. To our delight we found a few live chickens in the farmyard. Neither Krystyna nor I had ever killed a chicken but we had to do it now or starve. We decided to kill one chicken together. Krystyna held the poor bird by its tied legs, its head on the chopping block. I positioned the axe just above the neck, closed my eyes, and cut its head off with one blow. Krystyna promptly threw the convulsing animal away and cried, "It's done!" I opened my eyes. We let the chicken bleed on the ground and, when it was dead, took it to our room and cleaned it and plucked it ready for cooking. The Germans had left plenty of wood, so there was fuel for our stove.

Shortly after, the Polish men returned. Mr. Renaud forced Józef to return to work for him; otherwise, he said, he would complain to the German authorities. The war was not yet over, and although the farmers had left Marten, the Germans still occupied Lorraine.

Krystyna and I both helped Mrs. Martel now, and she gave us a little to eat. Józef got up at 4 a.m. to pick some fruit in the orchards to store in our room for all of us. He still slept in his room adjoining Mr. Renaud's house, but each day, after he had finished his work for Mr. Renaud, he also helped out at the Martels. He cleaned, painted, repaired and did all kinds of odd jobs there. In exchange for their work, Józef and Krystyna had, unknown to me, been promised the Martels' baby carriage, which Mrs. Martel believed she would no longer need.

During the moments of rest, I enjoyed the fine October weather. I sat on our front steps, the village before me, and dreamed that

Józef and I were a part of it, that we had our small house right there in the village, that the war was over and we were free. In my daydream, Józef worked with a pleasant farmer to support our child and me. I took care of the baby, played with it, cuddled and hugged it.

Then the Germans were back. Our bosses did not return, but soldiers filled the streets of Marten again. They were followed by a crowd of Ukrainian women, obviously not army whores, but older, hard-working, country women. We did not know what to think of them. Were they slave workers or volunteer camp followers? They cleaned and washed for the soldiers, did not interfere with us, and kept to themselves. We could easily communicate with them, as the Polish and Ukrainian languages are quite similar, but the women, although friendly, remained reserved and did not explain their situation.

The Polish men feared for their lives, for one could expect anything from the Germans, especially since they were losing the war. Our men tried to remain invisible and we, the women, ran all the errands.

One day, Krystyna and I were caught by a German officer on the street next to the farmhouse. He pushed us with his rifle into the empty stable. We knew the place well, since both of us had worked there. It had two doors, one at the front and another leading to the farmyard and the orchard. The German tried to grab Krystyna but in a split second she had a clever idea. Pretending she saw someone at the back door, she looked straight at the officer and said fearfully: "Look, look! There is a man there." At first I didn't understand what she was doing, but she gave me a furious look and I too began imploring the German to protect us from the lurking man.

The officer became frightened; it could have been an ambush. "Where is he, where did he go?" he roared. Krystyna pointed to the back door, and the officer, his rifle at the ready, ran into the farmyard. Krystyna grabbed my hand and we ran into the street through the front door, as fast as I was able until we rounded the corner and reached our room. Then we stopped, gasping for breath, and looked at each other in triumph; we had escaped once more.

As Allied victory seemed very close, Józef and I decided to approach the priest in Marten again, hoping he would relent and marry us now. We still believed that marriage by a priest was required by the law and was the only valid form of betrothal. At last, on October 3, 1944, we were married at the Marten parish church in the Diocese of Metz. Our witnesses were Zosia's husband, Mundek, and Julie Michel, the priest's housekeeper. We were relieved that our baby would now be born in wedlock.

I believed I was now in my ninth month of pregnancy, but nobody had explained to me exactly when the child was due. I was afraid that it might be born any time, and I could not rely on nature alone like an animal. The child must be born with the help of a doctor or a midwife, I thought, and so I walked to our small hospital in Morhange to seek help. Like the one in Metz, it belonged to the Catholic nuns and had been requisitioned by the Germans. Only a few nuns were left to run it, with only one midwife and one doctor available, the same man who had previously sent me to Metz.

The little hospital was primitive and served mostly the slave workers. We heard that before the war it was used as a nursing home. There were only a couple of rooms with beds available for patients, and no operating room, medical students, or orderlies. I found it reassuring.

The nuns let me stay, as the hospital was almost empty. I did not tell them about my marriage, for I had little opportunity to talk with them and did not want to attract attention to myself more than was necessary. Later, when I told the midwife, she simply dismissed what I said as fantasy, and wrote on the birth certificate, "Of unknown father."

One day, I ventured outside my room to look around the hospital. The building was very quiet and seemed empty. I opened a door and saw an elderly lady sitting alone in an armchair. I startled her and she seemed frightened. When I apologized and tried to retreat, she beckoned me to her and looked deep into my eyes as if she wanted to guess my thoughts. Her eyes were kind and sad. I had seen that look before. Not a word was uttered and I left the room. Later, a nun came to me and inquired angrily, "Who gave you permission to leave the quarters reserved for you? Don't you dare to do that ever again." She too gave me this inquisitive look as if she wanted to read my mind. I humbly excused myself for my disobedience until the nun was appeased. Was the hidden lady a Jewish woman? I never found out. But I would like to believe so, because it would prove that the cold, distant nuns could be brave and generous after all.

Time passed and the baby did not come. Perhaps I had confused the dates and had a few weeks more to wait. The nuns told me nothing. I was not examined, either by the midwife or the doctor. His original certificate had advanced the birth by some two months, and I was now completely confused. I missed Józef and Krystyna and on October 27 decided to leave the hospital and walk back to Marten. What a joy it was to be reunited with them. I took over the cooking and we were happy. On Sunday, I prepared a special supper of fried apple cakes as a main dish. We spent a cosy, friendly evening and the war raging close to us was forgotten for a few hours.

Early Monday morning, October 30, I felt the first birth pains; the baby had decided to appear. We all looked desperately at each other, uncertain what to do. I would have to return to the hospital in Morhange: there was no other way. Józef took me by the hand to the main road and we waited for a wagon going to Morhange to take me. Finally, Józef stopped a horse-drawn country wagon and the driver allowed me to get in. The road was bumpy and the pains came on again. When we arrived in

Morhange, the man ordered me to get out in the middle of town. I walked slowly, holding on to the trees and walls of the houses for support until, exhausted and in pain, I arrived at the hospital. The midwife looked me over and decided that I had plenty of time before the delivery. The nuns agreed, and I was left alone in a room with two empty beds. I was not even given a glass of water.

I resolved to concentrate on the safe delivery of my baby. Though I was thirsty, that was not important. I had to conserve every ounce of energy to endure the pain. I was glad now that I had talked with the Polish and Ukrainian women about childbirth, begging them to describe to me, truthfully, the delivery and the pain. I knew that the pains would come and go at shorter and shorter intervals. I knelt on the floor between the two empty beds, then bent and supported myself by my hands. On my hands and knees, no longer hindered by my natural shyness, I listened to my pains. They seized me and became stronger before they abated. The next wave was sharper and lasted longer, but it too abated. This was exactly as the women had described them to me. I knew then what to expect, and each time the new wave of pangs seized me, I breathed deeply until the paroxysm reached its peak and then exhaled while the pain subsided. I breathed in and out, exhaling rhythmically while my pains grew getting stronger and sharper, then weaker. I did not scream, for I was not among friendly people. There was no one I could trust, and I was too proud to cry.

The time passed as, on my hands and knees, I breathed rhythmically and when the pangs became intolerably sharp, I comforted myself, "The pains are approaching their summit. One minute more and they will begin going down." And it happened that way. I had been left in my room at 8 a.m., and now I heard the 12 strokes of the big church clock. The sunshine reached into the room where I worked on the painful rhythm of childbirth. Suddenly I saw the back of the child's head appear between my legs. "It is coming and will be strangled in the passage," was my thought and I started to scream as loud as I could with the strength of an animal fearing for the life of its offspring.

A nun appeared, saw what was happening, crossed herself and shouted to other nuns, "Stop her, stop her, the child is coming" — for at this precise moment the midwife was leaving the hospital. Then the nun returned to me and said, "Child, throw yourself back on the bed, don't close your legs, be careful," and she crossed herself again, her lips moving in prayer for me. I succeeded in getting onto the bed. The nun lifted my legs apart just as the midwife arrived. It took no time before a healthy baby boy came into the world. The church clock struck one on that lovely, sunny day, October 30, 1944.

The midwife gave one slap to the baby and he began to cry feebly: "La, la, la." She cleaned him and put him in a crib next to my bed. Not for a moment did I take my eyes from him, although I knew that he was safe. He never left the room.

The midwife took care of me, then weighed the baby and told me that he was normal, healthy and weighed seven-and-a-half pounds. She wrote out the official record of his birth, saying that the boy was born at 1:30 p.m.

After she left, the nun asked me why I had not cried out before. "I came to the door several times, but it was so quiet I thought you were asleep and I did not want to wake you up." I hoped that she was telling the truth.

My baby and I were left alone. I was still given no drink or nourishment and the baby too received nothing. He slept quietly in his crib, until late in the evening he began his feeble "la, la, la." I did not know what to do. "Maybe he is hungry," I thought. My body felt very weak and my head heavy, but I reached for him and took him to my breast. It was full of milk. Clumsily, I tried to feed my son.

He opened his eyes and I winced. The blue eyes of my paternal grandmother were wide open, looking at me. "Grandmother, grandmother," I murmured, "You were killed, we know why.

My baby cannot resemble you, or he will be killed like you." The child in my arms closed his eyes peacefully and I realized that I was insane from fear. I tried to reassure myself, "Nobody knows your secret. The baby's body is so clean and white, his hair so blond, and his eyes so blue, that he looks like millions of other Polish babies."

The next morning I was at last given some food and water, and the baby was looked after. It was another sunny day and I could see the blue sky through the window. The morning passed quietly. The other bed remained empty, and the baby and I were alone in the room. The nuns did not tell me when and how to feed my son, so I took him to my breast any time he cried. I was very weak and it was difficult for me to handle him. He drank a little and fell asleep again.

In the afternoon we heard Allied planes roaring above our heads. Then we heard machine-guns over and around us, a cacophony of dry sounds like peas falling on the roof, combined with other more violent and louder sounds. The front line was approaching and Morhange was under fire. The nuns panicked and ran downstairs for shelter. Too weak to move, I stayed in my bed, and no-one came for me. I was frightened, thinking that we could be killed at any moment. What would happen to my child if I was killed and he survived?

There was only one way: to live or die together. I took the baby from his crib and put him very close to me on my left side, covering him with my body. If shrapnel or a bullet struck me from my right side, I might still live and the baby, protected by my body, would be unharmed. If the shrapnel or bullet hit the left side of the bed, the two of us might die together. Fortunately, my theories were never put to the test since the hospital was not hit and no one was hurt. Calm returned after two days of shelling, but the German occupation remained in full force.

Refugees began to arrive in Morhange from other parts of Lorraine, telling about the bombardment and destruction of their homes. A few days later Józef and Krystyna succeeded in visiting and brought me some food. I was glad to see Józef, and he was overjoyed when he saw our son. We agreed to name him John Richard, John after my father, and Richard after Józef's brother, twenty years old when the Germans murdered him in Poland in the fall of 1939. The nuns wanted to baptize the baby right away, but Józef and I preferred to baptize him in our church in Marten where we had been married. I had lost hope that the Germans would soon be defeated and wanted our child to have credible Christian or Aryan papers.

Józef and Krystyna returned to Marten, and I was due to follow in a few days. But Mr. Renaud would not allow Józef to leave Marten again, and on November 9 or 10, two Polish men from Marten arrived with a horse-drawn cart to take me home. The old hostility and jealousy that my attachment to Józef had produced was now gone. Everybody seemed to wish us well and welcomed the newborn Polish baby.

Our room was ready for our arrival; Józef and Krystyna had scrubbed it sparkling clean, and everything had been neatly arranged. Mrs. Martel's baby carriage stood in one corner, ready for its new occupant. Mrs. Martel had been sure that producing six children was enough and she would never need the carriage again; in fact, she became pregnant once more and came timidly to ask me if I would return it to her. But my Richard slept happily in the carriage, and she understood that I could not give it back.

The first day of our return to Marten the front line got very close. Marten was under artillery fire and the planes flew low above our heads. Everybody was nervous; a bomb or shrapnel or a machine-gun bullet could hit us at any time. We tried to be calm. I breast-fed the baby and needed rest but could hardly get any.

Józef and I wanted Richard to be baptized right away. I did not want the baby to die without a religion, and the danger of death was very real. Józef went to see the priest, in spite of the crossfire and the danger of walking on the street. The priest was naturally reluctant to leave his house, but he could not refuse to baptize the baby with death lurking in every corner. We had chosen Zosia and the man I had previously feared, Sebastian, to be the baby's godparents. Even with the Allied forces advancing and our liberation seemingly near, I had to be careful to curry Sebastian's favor, if not for us, at least for our son.

Krystyna went to the church to be present at the ceremony, but I was too weak and stayed in our room. On November 12, 1944, Richard was duly baptized, and his father brought him home. Józef told me that the priest's hands were shaking; it was frightening to hear the planes roaring overhead and the uninterrupted sound of the artillery battery so very close. Nevertheless, the priest had performed his duty. Half an hour later, the only bomb to be dropped on Marten fell on the church roof, making a large hole in the ground precisely where the priest had performed our son's baptism. But by then the church was empty, and no one was hurt.

The fighting came even nearer and we moved into the cellar with Zosia, Jola and their families and many Polish men. When Józef, Krystyna and I arrived with our baby carriage, the others shouted at me, saying there was no room for it, but I paid no attention to their insults and threats. The baby needed a place to sleep and that was that. I glued myself to the carriage, ready to defend it with all my might, but no one touched me. Outside, the bullets and shells were flying and the planes were roaring. Our allies were fighting hard but the Germans were not falling back. Some of the men went outside because they could no longer stand the crowded cellar, but they promptly returned. German soldiers were all around and the Allied shelling and machine-gunning continued unabated. Our men had seen a German soldier hit while crouching to relieve himself, his genitalia torn away. Some of them laughed.

On our second or third day in the cellar, we heard shouting and loud bangs on the door. Soldiers were trying to force open the door with the butts of their rifles, and our men became terrified, thinking that the Germans were looking for them.

The banging and shouting became more violent. I was afraid that the Germans would throw a grenade if the door was not opened. Trembling but determined, I got up and threw it open, hoping that the Germans would not shoot if they saw an unarmed woman. I faced the guns and saw behind them the tired, dusty, and sweating faces of fighting soldiers, their heads covered with helmets. Their guns were still at the ready, but their eyes were smiling.

"Are there any men?" they asked.

I shook my head. Then it dawned upon me that the men looked human: they could not be Germans. I turned toward the men huddled against the back wall, as far as possible from the entrance. "I think they are Americans," I stammered.

The men rushed forward and threw themselves into their liberators' arms. Fortunately the American soldiers were not trigger-happy, because they were certainly taken by surprise by the men's sudden appearance. The Americans immediately realized who we were and regarded us with compassion and understanding. They seemed rightly proud and happy over their victory. Despite the general confusion of the situation, we understood that we had just been liberated and were triumphant. Our men immediately searched for Polish-Americans and, to their delight, found some.

I had a sense of immense relief but I was utterly exhausted and could not fully enjoy our liberation. My sister embraced me, and we said to each other, "Goodbye to the German language, we will never speak it again, we will forget it for the rest of our lives." And we did. Today the German language has completely evaporated from our minds.

NINE

LIBERATED—TO BECOME REFUGEES

We left the cellar to find American soldiers everywhere. Marten had become a military zone and we could no longer move about freely, but this did not trouble us; we were so glad to see our liberators. Jubilant, we expected them to hate the Germans as much as we did and immediately avenge us. The Polish men anticipated summary punishments in the midst of the great celebrations. But the Americans looked at us with tired, surprised eyes and said, "War is bad, and we want to go home." Incredulous, we asked, "If you don't hate the Germans, why did you fight?" They laughed at us in a friendly manner, and we were amazed by the brave Americans who had risked their lives to fight an enemy they did not even hate.

Carrying Richard in my arms, I tried to go back to our room, but I was stopped by the Military Police. Our house was now occupied by the American soldiers, and I was allowed to pick up only a few things and then leave.

The German language had magically disappeared. Now all the civilians spoke French and suddenly everyone was a French national. Marten instantly became Marthille, a French village in Lorraine.

The Polish workers were assembled together in the church; there was a lot of noise and confusion. We hoped that the generous Americans, who gave us food, would continue to protect us. Józef, Richard, my sister, and I stayed close together.

Suddenly we heard loud voices, and there was a commotion close to us. Polish men dragged Mr. Renaud by the arms toward us with Mrs. Renaud and another woman following. Three American Military Policemen accompanied them. The Polish men accused Mr. Renaud of having treated his Polish slave worker cruelly, and of collaborating with the Nazis. They insisted that Mr. Renaud, a collaborator, was a menace to the Americans on the front line. The two women begged the MP's to let him go while, pale and trembling, Mr. Renaud seemed unable to utter a word.

The angry Poles were shouting, urging the Americans to execute the traitor instantly. The situation was tense, bordering on hysteria. Mrs. Renaud wanted Józef to testify that her husband was not a villain and pointing at Józef, cried, "Here, here he is."

The MP's addressed Józef, showing by gesture that they were ready to shoot Mr. Renaud. Whether Józef believed that they would do it or not, he shook his head, "No, No."

His gesture was spontaneous; although he hated the man, he would not approve a summary execution. Thus Mr. Renaud was set free, and the two women promptly took him away. The Americans invited the Poles for refreshments and drinks to diffuse their anger and frustration.

That night, large trucks driven by the Frenchmen arrived to take us away from the battle zone. Classified as "réfugiés-sinistrés" — refugees who had lost their homes — we were crowded into these trucks and driven toward the west, to an unknown destination somewhere into France. The unfriendly Frenchmen in charge pushed and shouted at us. But the Americans, who provided the trucks and food, assisted us in every way. Although we were separated from the Serbs, we heard later that they all survived the war.

In our truck the unexpected happened: the men's tempers erupted. The Polish men who had worked so hard and controlled themselves under German rule now revealed a long-repressed, visceral anger. They quarreled violently, accusing each other of collaborating with the enemy, or of having adhered to the political parties responsible for Poland's defeat. They accused each other of being communists or nationalists or papists or fascists. Men who had worked peacefully together and cooperated through years of slave labor suddenly became enemies. They shouted furiously at each other and in their eagerness to fight were on the verge of pushing over my son's baby carriage.

Józef sat quietly, reluctant to get involved in their battle. I threw myself on the carriage to cover the baby with my body, since the men had become completely wild. My gesture seemed to bring them to their senses and no one got hurt.

After several hours, the trucks finally stopped and we were put into a movie house to sleep on the bare, cement floor. The Americans had sent food to be distributed by the French officials who shamelessly opened our packages, and gave us only the half of their contents. They ate in front of us the chocolate sent by the Americans for the children.

In the early hours of the morning, a fire broke out next to the overheated primitive wood stove, installed in the middle of the large room where we were packed. The fire was close to where I was sitting with Richard on my lap. Everybody ran out into the cold. But I couldn't move, overwhelmed by the fear that, once outside, my tiny baby would catch pneumonia. Józef tried to persuade me to run out, but I stayed glued to the floor, clutching the baby in my arms. I would not let Józef touch him. Desperate, Józef doused the fire with his coat. The fire went out, we were safe and no one was hurt, but poor Józef lost his winter coat.

The next day we were told that all Poles would be sent to camps in the South of France, lawless, chaotic places, we heard. I did not want to go to any camp, so I looked for the mayor, and addressing him in French, asked for permission to stay in his town. He was a young, dignified man who had been released recently from a German prison camp. When I explained that I had a newborn baby, he was very sympathetic and eager to help and assigned us a room in a local house.

The two maiden sisters who owned the house became very upset at the idea of Polish people in their home; they were simply afraid of strangers. They tried to discourage me with a warning that the room assigned to us was very damp and would be most unhealthy for the baby.

I began to cry and went back to see the mayor. "Why are you sending us to such an unhealthy place?" I asked.

He turned his honest face toward me and smiled. "Don't worry. The ladies lied to you because they don't want you and don't approve of my requisitioning their room for you. Go there without fear. I am the mayor and I will protect you."

When the four of us arrived, the two sisters looked carefully at Józef and at once relaxed. They told us that we seemed to be decent, civilized people. Józef was not much taller than I and had delicate features. The ladies had been frightened of having an uncouth foreign giant in their house, because they were only two helpless, elderly spinsters.

Our room had a coal stove in one corner and not much furniture. The four of us slept there, the baby in his carriage, Krystyna in a narrow bed, and Józef and I on a mattress on the floor. We ate thanks to handouts from the Americans who were camped all over this small town and had become friendly with the local people. I needed Vaseline and talcum powder for the baby, but we had neither coupons nor money to purchase them. I went to the American infirmary and begged, "Baby . . . Vaseline . . . baby . . . talc." I did not know the words "please," or "thank you." I just kept repeating the words "Vaseline, talc," which are similar in Polish, and I had learned the word "baby." I would not leave until the compassionate American nurse gave me what I asked.

We had not heard from our parents since the Warsaw uprising, which had lasted from August 1st until October 3rd, 1944. It ended in Polish defeat and virtual devastation of the city. And I still had not revealed to Józef who we were, or that

Krystyna was my sister; I lacked the courage to do so. She and I had brainwashed ourselves to forget our past and remain close to the Polish-Christian co-workers with whom we had suffered and survived. We felt united with them, we belonged to the same nation. We believed in a confused way that by acknowledging ourselves as Jewish, we would distance ourselves from and be disloyal to the Poles. Thus, we continued to live under our assumed names, which had become more real to us than our original ones.

Winter was coming and we stayed on in the house of the two spinster sisters. I thought that we could live there until spring and then decide what to do next; Józef could earn a little money by helping our landladies, and possibly some of their neighbors, by cutting wood, carrying coal, cleaning and lighting the stove, and other domestic tasks. But Józef refused. "Don't force me to be a slave again," he said. "I slaved five years under the occupation, and I want to work now like a man with other men. I will look for a job in a factory."

He left on foot for the city of Nancy to look for a regular job, and Krystyna and I continued to live on American charity. Richard, now five weeks old, was developing nicely; I nursed him and had enough milk to satisfy his hunger. But feeding him was hard and painful for me because my breasts were hurting badly. I was hungry and afraid of fainting, afraid that my breasts, heavy with milk, would press against Richard's little nose and suffocate him. Fortunately, I never fainted.

Józef returned after some two weeks, full of hope and very enthusiastic. He had found a vacant apartment and a job, and the four of us moved to Nancy.

The apartment was on the fourth floor of an abandoned, dilapidated house at 11 rue de l'Equitation. Previously occupied by Jews who had been deported, it now stood empty. It had one very large room with two windows facing on to the street and a smaller room which had once been a kitchen. The stove had been removed, and there was no running water and no toilet. We had to carry clean water up four flights of stairs and carry the dirty water down. The first night we slept on the bare floor.

I don't remember how we got in touch with our Polish benefactor, Mr. Wiëniewski, a French-Polish translator and social worker who was dedicated to the Polish people in distress. Mr. Wiëniewski supplied us not only with useful information but also with the material things we badly needed. He gave us an iron stove which had been left in his basement, a double bed, a camp-bed for Krystyna, and a table with three chairs. Somehow we got hold of a few pots and pans and utensils.

Krystyna found a job at the Polish Red Cross and continued to live with us. However, Józef's work at the factory proved to be almost beyond his strength. As he did not understand French, he was given the menial job of carrying iron pipes on his back.

He and Krystyna, like many others, earned only a pittance.

It was a time of austerity for everybody in France, and there was an acute shortage of all goods. Stocks of everything had been depleted and new production had not yet started. People combed their basements and attics for anything that could be repaired and put to use. Older men borrowed their grandchildren's sleds to earn money by carrying people's packages and parcels through the streets of Nancy.

It was a cold winter, and the streets were icy and snow-covered, which made walking difficult and hazardous. Many people were undernourished, even if they had jobs. Food was rationed through a meager system of food tickets. I frequently overheard women in the stores saying, "Avec les Boches nous avions au moins du beurre (With the Germans we at least had some butter)." Those who had money and proper connections could buy food, but we had neither money nor knowledge of the black market. I worried about Richard; I had no washbasin and he could easily catch cold in our cold room while I sponged him. I walked around the streets looking for anything that could serve as a washbasin. To my great joy, I found a very large mustard container lying near a store, still dirty with the frozen remains of the mustard. It was exactly like a miniature of the large, round Polish balia or washtub, made from pieces of wood held together by iron bands. I walked into the store and timidly asked if I could take it. After scrutinizing me for a while, the merchant let me have the discarded container. I was so happy that I did not even think how heavy it would be to carry.

We had run out of coal for our stove and to feed it, we ripped out decayed wood wherever we could find it, in our abandoned building or elsewhere. Learning that impoverished French children stole coal from the freight trains in the siding near the railroad station, I went there. I saw a lot of children on the heaps of coal in the trains. They threw down the coal for their friends to pick up. I stood nearby and looked longingly at the coal on the ground. The children understood; they threw some in my direction, yelling, "Madame, prenez, c'est pour vous! (Madame, it's for you, take it)". I filled my sack with as much as I could manage and I walked home slowly, carrying it on my back all the way up to our fourth floor.

After that, I made regular trips to the railroad yard, and the children never stopped helping me. Since we now had enough coal to keep our small stove going (although the room remained chilly) but not enough food to eat, I decided to try to earn some money: I would wash clothes for the American soldiers. The streets of Nancy were full of American military men, and there were not enough laundries to satisfy their enthusiasm for cleanliness. I carried soldiers' shirts up to our room and washed them in Richard's washbasin. The most difficult task was carrying the water upstairs and delivering the clean, ironed shirts to the soldiers, since I had to carry everything on my back. Józef, who considered all I was doing as woman's work, did not offer to help.

The American soldiers walked idly about the streets, nostalgic for their homes and for their women. The only other family living in our half-ruined building had a pretty young daughter, about twelve years old. The mother, a loud bully in her late thirties, was tall, plump, and attractive. Every day, as soon as her husband went out, she stationed her daughter in their front window. The child, well instructed, smiled to the passing soldiers, waving at them and inviting them in. Once a soldier was in their apartment, the daughter disappeared, and the mother took over making love for money.

We decided to look for a better place to live. Mr. Wiëniewski recommended us to a Polish family who resided some seven kilometers from Nancy. The family occupied one house and rented the adjoining one, which they owned as well.

We carried our belongings on a borrowed cart with Józef harnessed in front like a horse. Krystyna and I pushed from behind, and Richard in his carriage traveled on the top. Thus, we moved to our new home on the outskirts of a village by the side of the route nationale, the highway joining the German border in eastern France and the city of Nancy to the west.

We settled in our new, comfortable home, surrounded by green grass, with a large orchard adjoining it, and Mr. Wiëniewski arranged for us to get clean, new furniture from the American Red Cross or another relief agency.

American military trucks passed on the highway near our house from morning till night. When the highway was quiet, I pushed the baby in his carriage along the roadside bordering the fields. It was peaceful and pleasant.

One bright and sunny day, as we went toward the village, a woman stopped to admire the baby. He had blond hair and a very clear complexion; everybody found him pretty. I said good-bye to the woman and pushed the carriage proudly, when suddenly a group of youngsters appeared and ran behind, taunting Richard and me with shouts of "dirty Poles," and other insults. Some boys started throwing stones at us, and one or two hit the carriage, though not the baby. I turned back home as soon as I could, my heart pounding. The children's animosity baffled me. I would never have believed that it could happen in France.

Krystyna continued to work at the Polish Red Cross in Nancy and Józef in his factory. They each had to walk some 14 kilometers every day. Józef became depressed. It was January 1945, and Józef, born on December 13, 1921, was young and eager to fight the Germans. He wanted to join the Polish Army in England, where the war was still going on. He explained that I would be better off financially, because I would receive a soldier's pension for Richard and myself and could use the precious food coupons he would leave behind.

Mr. Wiёniewski promised to arrange Józef's papers to join the army. "But first give me your marriage license so that I can make sure that Irene and Richard will be provided for," he said. We proudly presented our church marriage certificate.

He looked at us in disbelief. "But you are not married at all. Only a civil marriage in the City Hall is valid in France," he exclaimed.

Józef's face turned white. He saw his dreams of going to England fading away like so many earlier dreams in his hard life.

I felt sorry for Józef. Then, an idea struck me. "If we are not married already, we can get married right away at the Nancy City Hall. After all, we are free people now."

Mr. Wiёniewski promised to help us with the formalities and on February 26, 1945, we were married in the City Hall of Nancy, in the département de Meurthe-et-Moselle. Józef left shortly thereafter for England to fulfill his dream to become a soldier in the Polish Army. But before he left he said to Krystyna, "I hope that war will end soon and I will return. But if in the meantime Richard or Irene will need help, I count on you that you will assist them, that you and Irene will remain close friends." He still did not know that we were sisters and that we were Jewish.

With Józef gone, a new chapter opened in my life. Now, I called my sister by her real name, Karolina, and we felt closer than ever before. On Sundays she stayed home with me, and we took a blanket and sat in the orchard with Richard between us. It was spring, the days were glorious, the orchard was blooming and smelled heavenly. Those were good, quiet moments.

But though the country had been liberated, the war was not yet over and France was in turmoil. My sister and I were totally alone, fending for ourselves in the impoverished and politically divided France. Every day we saw the endless convoys of trucks filled with American soldiers and their military equipment passing in front of our house. I felt enormous gratitude toward our liberators. They looked weary, and their enormous tanks, weapons and armored cars seemed out of place in our peaceful countryside. Far from home, they were steadfastly doing their job. They too could not enjoy a "normal" life in this year of 1945.

France was torn by ideological and political conflicts. There were feuds between the members of the resistance and the German collaborators, as well as between socialists, communists, capitalists, liberals, and democrats. The economy was in deep crisis. The elderly suffered most as the constant devaluation of the French currency had made their pensions or savings almost worthless. From time to time, the newspapers reported silent suicides by lonely people ruined by inflation and devaluation, without any means of support after a lifetime of work. They shut themselves in their apartments and awaited death from starvation. Their bodies were discovered by the neighbors only because of the stench.

One day in 1945, we were shocked by the most unexpected announcement that all francs were to be taken out of circulation and replaced by new ones. Everyone was entitled to exchange a limited amount of "old" francs for new francs at the bank. Many French men and women who kept their money at home "under the mattress" lost their savings.

The economic and social unrest made us more fearful and insecure. Our situation seemed hopeless and the future grim. I saw no doctor and no one advised me when to start Richard on solid food. I badly needed support and guidance in bringing up the child, and I missed my husband — my dreams of a happy family eluded me. But Richard, unaware of what was going on, grew nicely, and at six months old, he was healthy, good looking, and a source of joy for me.

Then, on a sunny May morning after my sister had left as usual on foot for work, Richard was sitting on my bed, quite happy while I cleaned the room. I talked to him as I worked and he watched me with his big, blue eyes, so trustful and loving. Suddenly I heard the church bells ringing loudly and excited voices coming from the village. I opened the window and looked out. What was happening? Another disaster, a fire in the village?

It was Wednesday, May 9, 1945, and the Germans had just signed the act of unconditional surrender.

"Finally," I said to the baby, "finally we have won." But I was too exhausted to rejoice. I took Richard in my arms and found comfort in kissing and hugging him. He put his head against my chest and his little hands touched my face. I sat with him on my bed for some time while the people outside ran and danced and shouted, wild with joy.

The war in Europe was over, but our situation did not improve. The promised wife-and-child support from England had not yet started coming, and the only money in the house came from my sister. I had to help to support us — leave the house and find a job. By working for the Americans, I would be able to bring home some food. Thus I readily accepted the Polish women's advice that the baby should not be breast-fed beyond six months and that it was time to start him on a bottle.

I found work as a cleaning woman for three American officers. They occupied a nice apartment, which I learned later belonged to a deported Jewish family. Now I too began the daily 14-kilometer walk to and from Nancy. I paid my neighbors, middle-aged parents with a couple of children, to take care of Richard in my absence. Their oldest daughter had a baby the same age, and they seemed to be a nice family.

The officers gave me a generous portion of food each day, half of which I brought home for Karolina. I spoke no English and they spoke no French, but somehow we communicated. It was perhaps the tenth day of my work for the officers when, as soon as I arrived at the apartment, I saw they were greatly disturbed. Something had been stolen from them, though I did not understand what had been taken, nor do I remember how they let me know about it. Maybe they showed me an empty wallet, or opened a wardrobe pointing to an empty space, indicating something was missing. Their eyes inquired, "Did you take it?"

Of course I had not, and I became angry. After all, I was not the only stranger visiting their apartment: every morning I saw the lipstick stains on their bed sheets and on the cigarette butts in the ashtrays. I wanted to tell them, "Ask the ladies you are inviting, not me," but I could not speak English, so I pointed to the stained bed sheets and the traces of lipstick and then the apartment around me. I looked back at them with angry, accusing eyes. How could they suspect me, when they were inviting "these sort of women" into their rooms?

The men discussed something in one of the bedrooms, then asked me to go with them in their jeep. They took me to their base to see the interpreter who informed me that I had just been fired. To soften the blow, the officers offered me a ride home to spare me the seven-kilometer walk.

They drove me to the house of my neighbor who took care of Richard. I arrived unexpectedly in the middle of the day—and discovered that my child was crying and no one was paying any attention to him. My heart sank. I felt betrayed, and for many years to come could not forgive myself for entrusting my child to such people. I took him home, held him in my arms, kissed and cuddled him and walked with him around the room, trying to give him all the attention he had missed in the last ten days. I felt bad but didn't cry. I felt so guilty for letting my baby be hurt.

When my sister came home, tired and hungry, we ate the food I had prepared and I told her what had happened. We decided that something had to be done to improve our situation, for we could not continue life in this way. I told Karolina I was going to Paris to look for a job. We had heard that the newly installed Polish communist government had taken over its embassy and consulate in Paris. I would go there to inquire about a teaching job, knowing that there had always been evening schools for the children of Polish emigrant workers who wanted their children to learn the Polish language and culture. Karolina took a few days off from her work and stayed with Richard while I was gone.

The train to Paris was very crowded and all the seats were taken. The long corridor was full of people standing or sitting on their luggage. The corridor opened into compartments, each one normally taking eight passengers, but now, passengers were glad to enter a compartment just to stand. I didn't even manage to get to the corridor but stood squeezed between other people on the platform leading to it. A woman invited me to lean on her upright valise. Everybody was tired and most people were hungry. When a man unpacked a sandwich and began to eat, other passengers eyed him enviously; it was almost indecent to eat in public.

The train had first-class compartments and a dining car reserved for Allied officers, who were mostly American. But there were Russian officers — also our Allies — standing amongst us, as uncomfortable as we were. Although no one spoke Russian, people tried to explain to them that they should move into the more comfortable officers' cars. But the Russians did not want to move and that puzzled us. We knew nothing about orders they had been given not to fraternize with Westerners, so everybody joined in the chorus to persuade them to leave our carriage. Finally, the Russian officers changed their minds and left, giving us a little more breathing space.

We arrived at night at the Gare de l'Est in Paris. The air was pleasantly warm, since it was late May or early June, but it was dark, and I was alone in a big, bustling city. I was very frightened and did not know how to look for a hotel. Terrible stories about traffic in white women and prostitutes came to my mind and the small hotels near the station terrified me. Looking around, I saw a face that looked honest and asked the stranger where I could find a clean, inexpensive place for the night. The man smiled and conducted me to a small hotel just on the other side of the street. I was given the keys and the man claimed the tip which I had to give him.

I spent a most uncomfortable night because I could not find the bed cover; French beds are made in such a way that I lay on the top of the sheets and cover without realizing it. Whenever I heard people walking or opening a door in the corridor, I trembled with fear that I would be assaulted. But no harm came to me and the next morning I went to the Polish Embassy.

A newly appointed communist cultural officer spoke with me. He looked me up and down, a small, undernourished woman wearing American charity clothes. "No, there is no job for a school teacher," the man told me. But I did not believe him, because it was clear that all the Polish schools had been closed during the occupation, and they could not have been reopened and staffed so quickly. So I sat in the hall and waited to meet somebody more sympathetic.

Then two men arrived, obviously very sure of themselves, speaking with excited voices. The cultural officer greeted them subserviently. The men did not bother to go into his office but talked loudly with him in the hall. They seemed to be Polish communists, living in France, and trying to open a Polish school in their district. They had evidently spoken about their problem with the cultural officer before and were visibly annoyed that no teacher had been found.

I remembered my friend and protector Zofia Chemska telling me, "Speak, Irene, any time you have the opportunity to read aloud or to talk. Your educated Polish and your mastery of the language will always please Polish people and benefit you." I rose from my seat and addressed the men in my impeccable, educated Polish. "I have a Certificate of Maturity and one year of medical studies from Warsaw," I said. "I have just explained to the cultural officer that I am highly qualified to teach Polish." I felt very sure of myself and looked straight into the men's eyes.

The men looked at me attentively and seemed impressed. "The matter is settled then, comrade. Here is our teacher," they announced.

The cultural officer frowned at me. "Fine—but do you have with you your academic credentials?"

"Papers? Are you asking for my papers?" I said. "I have just been liberated from the slave labor camp. I have no documents, no papers. Listen to the way I speak, and you can judge for yourself that I am an educated woman."

The cultural officer gave up, and I was appointed the sole teacher and director of the Polish language school for the miners' children in Joudreville, Department of Meurthe-et-Moselle. I did not reveal that I was Jewish.

When the business was concluded, I asked where a refugee could stay overnight and was sent to the Polish Consulate to inquire about the matter. The employee whispered with a colleague. Then he said, "I cannot send you to this place. It is too dangerous for a young woman alone." But I would not go away and, finally, I was given the address of the center.

When I arrived there in the evening I noticed the same tense, quarrelsome atmosphere as in the truck that had taken us away from Marthille (Marten). But I was encouraged as soon as I saw a few families with small children. I took a camp bed right in the middle of a family with three young boys, and began a conversation with the mother, a nice Polish woman.

Suddenly we heard a commotion, two angry French supervisors were yelling at her seven-year-old son, accusing him of stealing something. The boy ran toward his father and the men pursued him, now yelling at the father. Although he did not know a word of French, the man believed that he had to punish his son to appease the Frenchmen. The boy clung now to his mother, crying. She looked helplessly at the men in charge.

In fact, the boy had not stolen anything, but the French supervisors were suspicious and overzealous. The whole place was unsettled and ready to explode like dynamite. I could not remain quiet, and I spoke to the supervisors in a determined tone in my fluent French. "Please, leave the child and his family alone. Calm down, please." The tension was diffused. The grateful parents watched over me as if I was their daughter, and we spent a peaceful night in our corner.

TEN

JOUDREVILLE: A BRIEF RESPITE

Joudreville was not very far from Nancy, but getting there was difficult because there was no train or bus between my place and the village. I hired a taxi and filled it with as many of our belongings as it could take, leaving the furniture behind. Karolina did not come with us but moved to a women's hostel in Nancy to stay close to her work.

The taxi took about three hours to get us to Joudreville, the baby sleeping peacefully in my arms.

Richard and I were received enthusiastically by the two families who had fought for the Polish school, the Iwanickis and the Giereks. Joudreville was a large village built for miners and their families by the mining company. The miners lived in clean, comfortable bungalows owned by the company, and all the bungalows had small gardens and looked alike. They had two or more bedrooms, a toilet and running water. The men's salaries were sufficient to support a family. A doctor, a pharmacy and stores were located in Pienries, the closest town which could be reached on foot.

I felt happy in Joudreville from the beginning. It had been a very long time since I had been with Polish families, with parents and children living harmoniously together, the fathers providing for them, the mothers taking care of the family's needs, and the children attending schools. The children went to regular French schools and spoke French well, while their parents spoke it poorly.

We lived with a Polish family until my accommodation and the school facilities were organized. The mining company had assigned a little house for the school and for my lodging, rent-free, and supplied me with free coal and electricity. The Polish Embassy paid my salary. Richard and I had two rooms upstairs for ourselves, but we lived in only one, with an iron stove in the middle of the room. The other room, unheated, was used for storage. Downstairs was the school. It had two classrooms, a kitchen and a toilet.

Classes were to be held five times a week for two or three hours in the evening. We had no reading material; everything in France at that time was in short supply. I had to improvise lessons from memory. The 120 students who were enrolled ranged from young children to older teenagers. I divided them into six classes. My students were less enthusiastic about the school than their parents and would have preferred to play after their day at French school.

I dreaded the first day of teaching. I had no underclothes—no brassiere, no under-shirt, just my panties under my dress—I felt naked. I wore American gifts of heavy boys' shoes and a pair of socks of slightly different color—which made me feel ridiculous.

The first day arrived. As I stood facing my class, the moment I saw these young faces looking confidently at me, my shyness disappeared as if by magic. I felt collected and in control, and I began to teach . . .

The parents felt possessive toward me. I was "their" teacher, hired by them, unlike the French teachers who were put on a pedestal, for they represented the French government and authority in the eyes of the miners.

One day the father of two of my pupils, two nice young girls, decided to visit our class to check on my performance. He appeared in the classroom visibly drunk, and not only talked insulting nonsense but physically pushed me aside to take my place in the center of the class. His two girls, 10 and 12 years old, must have wished they could disappear into the ground from shame. My desire to protect these two gentle girls gave me the inspiration and the courage to deal with their father.

I decided to appease Mr. Kowal by giving him a royal welcome. "Mr. Kowal, we are glad to see you. Antos, please bring a chair for Mr. Kowal and put it right next to me."

The students, who had begun to giggle, became silent and watched, astonished to see what would happen next.

"Mr. Kowal, we shall continue our class and we would be very glad to hear your opinion. We will value your guidance." I turned toward my class. Mr. Kowal did not know how to express his opinion, or how to guide me. He was embarrassed by being so politely addressed. Barely able to stand on his feet, he left the room.

The class began to taunt his two mortified daughters. But I asked the students to remember that their fathers also drank sometimes and that it was not up to children to criticize their fathers. Somehow, I managed to get our lesson going again.

When the class ended, the two girls approached me with tears in their eyes and just looked at me, trying to say "thank you."

But although I soon had many friends among my students' parents, I could not tell them the truth about myself. I could not abandon the pretence and regain my identity. The Polish miners needed "one of their own" to boost their morale, to prove to their bosses that a Pole could be well educated and speak French fluently as I did. Although most were proud of being miners, they were even more proud of their national identity and sensitive about their Polish honor.

One day there was a big party for all miners, their families and supervisors, with music, dancing and short speeches. The Poles chose me to make a speech on their behalf. I was nervous about speaking before such a varied audience, remembering well that the Poles themselves were not an entirely uniform group;

not everybody shared the same opinions and beliefs. My speech was short: I spoke about the joy of freedom from the German occupation, about the pride of men and women in being good and devoted parents—raising their families well—about the dignity of preserving their language and culture while being loyal to the adopted country, and so on.

I didn't expect such applause. The Poles approached me with pride in their eyes; I was their star and a role model.

One day I visited the parents of one of my students and we talked over a cup of tea. Suddenly we heard a commotion outside. Mrs. Borowicz, the hostess, went out to look and returned, smiling.

"It is Yvonne who used to fraternize with the Germans. Our resistance men have shaved her hair and now they walk her around the streets so that everybody can see her shame. Come, Pani Nauczycielko (Mrs. Teacher), and see for yourself."

She looked at me, the virtuous wife of a Polish soldier, expecting me to be pleased. But I ran into another room at the back of their house and covered my ears with my hands so as not to hear the shouting. I felt nauseated. How dare these men be so cruel to a woman? I asked myself. I hated the Germans at that time with all my heart, but to me a woman's body belonged to her, and I believed that she did not betray her country or anybody, except possibly herself, when she was friendly with the enemy. To me, shaving a woman's head was nothing but a primitive, brutal revenge by jealous and frustrated men and women.

I kept my thoughts to myself. When I returned to my hosts I listened to them politely and left shortly thereafter.

In spite of the distance that separated us and the lack of a telephone, Karolina and I kept in touch and encouraged each other. She finally got her break when she was appointed as an archivist at the Polish Consulate in Strasbourg; she became friendly with the Consul's wife, Mrs. Rutkowska, and enjoyed her new position. The two of us were well established now, although in an unsettled way, still hiding our identity and living every day for news from our parents.

In August 1945, I heard the words "atomic bomb" and did not understand clearly what was going on. I did not read the newspapers or listen to the radio since I did not have one. I had decided not to read the newspapers after Józef's departure. News about the war, the social and political unrest in France, and the trials or executions of ex-collaborators was too upsetting for me. I wanted to have a peaceful life and thus chose to live in my corner and was glad to stay there, for I had to preserve every ounce of my energy and sanity for my baby's survival, as well as my own.

Some parents asked me about the atomic bomb. I knew something about atomic energy, of splitting the atom and its potential for producing a bomb, but I could not understand why they constantly asked about a bomb, when I was talking about atomic energy. I concluded that the Americans must be conducting experimental research on the bomb. I was completely unaware that atomic bombs had been dropped on Hiroshima and Nagasaki.

Just before his first birthday, Richard started to walk. What a joy it was to see this little person walking around the room. But we had to be very careful because there was a hot stove in the middle of the room that intrigued him very much; there was something red inside that he wanted to inspect. However, no accident ever occurred, as I never left him alone.

My financial situation had greatly improved. I had two sources of income: one as a teacher and the other from my husband, a soldier in England. The money arrived regularly and I could pay our maid and even buy some clothes, although they were difficult to find. Life was still hard in France.

But we had no news from our parents. Karolina continued to write to the Bernerowo address, but there was no answer.

I often thought about Józef. I had finally admitted to myself that we were incompatible, that his background and outlook on life were completely different from mine. Love was not enough. I felt I had to follow my mother's footsteps and become a professional woman, while as far as Józef was concerned, we had to start a family. I would have had to take care of the children and help support the family by doing any kind of menial work.

And I had never told Józef who I was. He would have been most embarrassed to learn that I was Jewish, and I did not have the courage to face his rejection. I thought about it over and over again, trying to find a solution. At last, I came to the conclusion that it would be better for both of us to seek a divorce. This made me sad; I would have preferred a different outcome.

One day, I received a telegram from Karolina telling me that our parents were both alive and living in Bernerowo with the Kielbas. Shortly thereafter, Józef wrote to me that he was returning to Warsaw. He did not offer to join me in Joudreville as he was anxious to resume his life in Poland.

Karolina insisted that we return to Poland as soon as possible. She was eager to enter the university and to continue her medical studies and when she came to Joudreville, I could no longer resist her wishes and my own longing to return. I told my students' parents I had to leave. They understood how much I wanted to join my parents, although they were disappointed that I could not stay until the end of the school year. I felt uneasy about their displeasure and hoped that my students and their parents would forgive me, for my nine-month stay in Joudreville had been happy.

In March 1946, Karolina, Richard and I left for Poland. The international trains were not yet running, at least not regularly and not for everybody, and we returning refugees were loaded into open freight trains. They were crowded with the masses of deported people trying to return home. Men, women, and children together slept on the clean straw that was spread on the bare floor. Both the trains and the food were supplied by the generous Americans, who helped us from the day of our liberation and never abandoned us. There are no words to express my gratitude to the American people and the military for the help they gave us.

We were all very excited, and triumphant at having survived the war and now to be returning home. The train was noisy but people were friendly and well behaved. I took a small heater and some methyl alcohol to warm a bottle for Richard, clearing carefully a space in the straw to avoid a fire. Understandably, people were nervous and unhappy when they saw me lighting the heater with a match. But Richard was the only one in our wagon who was so young — barely seventeen months old — and they let me heat his milk.

It was a long, slow journey, lasting ten days, and Richard had to be constrained to lie down, stand up or sit. He could not run around or walk because of the lack of space, and by the end of our journey he had forgotten how to walk. We had no toilets, and as our train often stopped in the middle of nowhere, we got out in search of a place in the bushes to relieve ourselves.

Karolina easily caught colds or other viruses and now she was getting feverish. I had to take care of both her and Richard, kneeling on the floor most of the time to attend to them as they lay or sat on the straw. But the Americans continued to keep us well provided, and we were neither hungry nor thirsty.

When we passed through Germany, farmers waited for us at the stations begging young men and women to come to their farms and help them with the work. Needless to say, they were received with insults, for we could not believe that they had the nerve to approach us. The Germans seemed not to comprehend our anger and made generous offers to the prospective workers. But it never came to blows and our people were content to shout and laugh at them. We felt victorious, relishing the great future and reward that awaited us. Did our past sufferings not entitle us to such expectations?

Finally, the slow train neared Poland. We would reach Warsaw very soon, and my heart beat in joyful anticipation.

Then, at the last moment, we were told that our train would have to deviate from its course and that we would arrive instead in the south of Poland, near our border with Czechoslovakia. This was unexpected and certainly unwelcome news. We would have to change trains with Karolina unwell, the baby in my arms, and all our luggage to be carried.

We arrived at a small station in the south of Poland and sent a telegram to our parents in Bernerowo, asking them to meet us at the Warsaw train station in 12 hours. The telephone at the Kielbas had not yet been restored; in 1946 the country was still disorganized, quite different from pre-war Poland where the trains, telephone, and post office had all worked extremely well.

We boarded the train to Warsaw before it was full. Its long corridors opened onto small, eight-passenger compartments, each one with a door. I laid Richard down with his little pillow and blanket, almost taking up a whole bench. People started coming in. They were very friendly toward us and admired the baby, seeming sincerely touched to see him and the two of us returning home from forced labor. Karolina and I felt welcome.

Then something happened: I saw Jewish men, wearing yarmulkes and long coats, pious Jews who had survived the war in Russia and were returning home. Our nice fellow-passengers stood up and barricaded the door. The Jews tried to enter through the window, which was promptly pulled down and locked. "There is no place for Jews in our compartment," the Poles shouted.

"I'll hold the baby on my lap. We can make room," I suggested.

"No, no, this is a Polish child coming home. We will not let him be disturbed."

I saw the desperate Jewish faces again. The trains were terribly overcrowded, and I wondered how many times these men had been pushed out. Karolina and I kept quiet. We could not risk being recognized, and in any case, this would not have helped the Jewish men. The train started. Our fellow-passengers went out of their way to be nice to us and would not let me move Richard. He occupied almost the whole bench till the end of our journey, which lasted 14 hours. We arrived at night at the Goods Station, a long way from Warsaw's Central Station, so that I never heard the station-master's announcement I had dreamed of for so long.

There was no sign of either our father or Mr. Kielba. We felt tired, abandoned and scared. When we inquired how to get to Bernerowo, we were urged not to leave the station until the morning.

"Young ladies, don't let anybody drive you at night. It is very dangerous. In the morning, you can hire a small farmer's wagon which will take you to Bernerowo. Don't forget to settle the price before you board and don't pay until you get home." We understood.

Looking around, we saw people sitting in small groups with men holding long sticks sitting or standing in front. We found a small place near a group with children and tried to relax. Three of the men approached us. "Young ladies, you cannot sit here all night with the baby. Our wagon is right there, and we will take you home."

"No, thank you," we told them, "we are waiting for our father."

"You will be home before your father arrives. We want to do you a favor because of the child. There are many people around begging us to take them, but we want to help you."

That gave me a cue. "Why don't you take the people who beg you since we don't want to go with you? Look, I see there" —I indicated with my hand—"the men looking in our direction. They look angry, they must be ones begging for your service. Take them and leave us alone. We are staying put right here."

The men left. Karolina looked at me and smiled. Richard slept peacefully.

Suddenly the light went off. It was pitch dark inside the station, and the air was filled with fear and loud voices. My sister and I kept close together with Richard between us and waited. After some time, the electricity went back on. Everybody breathed more easily and the mood became more relaxed.

Eventually we saw daylight coming through the windows. "Maybe you could start looking for a wagon," Karolina suggested. She looked pale and very tired. While she stayed with Richard, I went to look around. As soon as I stepped out of the building, I saw a lot of drivers with their country wagons waiting for passengers. Unsure of which to choose, I walked around when, out of nowhere, I saw Józef.

He was as shocked as I was. His first question was, "Where is Richard?" Then he asked, "What are you doing here?"

"And what are you doing here?" I was incredulous to see him. He had just stepped out of the train, he said, returning from a trip to the northwest in newly annexed Polish territory. He explained to me that "everybody" was going there to bring some of the goods left by the Germans into the devastated city of Warsaw. Józef did not look to me like a prosperous merchant; I knew he was not cut out for this kind of business.

Józef wanted to see Richard. He took him into his arms, and the child awakened and started to cry. Reluctantly, Józef handed him back to me.

I asked Józef to help us find a driver and together we went out and hired a wagon. I saw that he had very little money with him. "Do you want to ride with us?" I asked, for he had said that Bernerowo was in his direction, and that he would get out before us and walk home.

We did not talk much. Józef offered to take Richard and me to his parents' home, but it was obvious that he had neither the money nor a situation to support us. I knew that if I joined him, it would be worse than in France. Not only would we be poor again and dependent upon his family, but I would also have to continue to live under an assumed identity. Even if my being a Jewess was "forgiven" by my in-laws, it would still have to be hidden from their friends and relatives. Of that I was certain. I shook my head.

"We are going to join our parents in Bernerowo. I will be in touch with you soon."

It was a cool March morning and since I had no gloves, my hands had turned blue. Józef saw that and took off his gloves to give them to me, insisting that I put them on. I felt warmer and better. But what about Józef? I loved Józef and forced myself not to cry. I felt very bad. I felt guilty. But I had to think about the future, Richard's and mine. I needed a new start, a new beginning. Our marriage was over.

Józef left us as he said he would before we reached Bernerowo. I did not give him our address but he gave me his, although I knew it already.

ELEVEN

RETURN TO POLAND

It was still early in the morning when the wagon stopped at the Kielbas' house in Bernerowo. Our arrival took everybody by surprise. The telegram had not been delivered — it arrived a week later.

Our parents ran toward us, trembling with joyful excitement. The Kielbas cried, "The children have arrived, the children are back home!" My parents looked at the baby with tears in their eyes, and my father clasped him in his arms and carefully kissed his forehead and hands. Richard, pale and tired, wrapped in a surplus American blanket, did not protest. He smiled and seemed to accept at once his grandfather's love and embraces.

We went into the house where the five people waiting for us inside greeted us in chorus. Maryla Rozyki, the Kielbas' daughter, stood next to her parents beaming with joy at the sight of Karolina, her friend from the time she had stayed in Bernerowo.

But where was Witold Rozyki, Maryla's husband? And what were Janka Elterman and her mother doing here? I asked myself. The two women seemed unchanged. The years in hiding and humiliation had left no traces on them. They smiled at us and looked curiously at the baby. Mrs. Tran searched my face with silent questions: Would the baby boy be brought up as a Jew? Would he be circumcised? I pretended not to understand the unspoken words. I did not want my son to be circumcised or brought up as a Jew, but I was not ready to say so openly. Did the old lady understand my embarrassment? Perhaps, because she turned her eyes away, while she extended her arms to take me into hers and kept me there for a long moment.

We all had breakfast together; everybody was very excited and talked at the same time. I would have preferred this first meal to be more private and intimate, just with my family. The communal atmosphere and my parents' deference to Julia and Walenty annoyed me, even though our hosts were older and we sat at their table.

Both my parents were working and supporting the whole household. They acted as if the country was still occupied, as if the others needed help now and it was their duty to provide it. But above all, they had become sincerely attached to Julia, Walenty, and their daughter, and gratefully were trying to repay them for sheltering Mother and Karolina during the occupation.

Mrs. Tran and her daughter had no one else to help them, and my parents adopted the two widows as substitutes for their murdered family. I didn't tell my parents, then nor thereafter, that Janka had tried to oust me from Zofia Chemska's apartment on the Aryan side of Warsaw to hide there with her mother. I did not want to break a friendship so dear to them. Besides, the war was over, and Janka Elterman, now a destitute widow taking care of her old mother, was harmless and needed our support.

The house was certainly too small for all of us. It had four rooms, a kitchen and one bathroom. The basement floor was beaten earth and could only be used for storage. Half of the house was occupied by my parents' dental practice, which they opened right after the liberation. It had a separate entrance through the garden. One room was used as the office and the other as the waiting room. My parents already had many patients.

Family life was centered in the living/dining room. I sat there on a couch with the baby in my arms, expecting my parents to sit with me, but they disappeared into their office where their patients were waiting. Julia and Walenty went to their room, and Janka left the house.

Maryla and Karolina went to the kitchen for a private talk.

Pale and sad in her black dress, Maryla spoke about her husband, Witold. He had been killed during the Warsaw uprising, she told Karolina, sometime between August 1 and October 3, 1944. On Tuesday, the first day of August 1944, he had left home to go to work as usual in the city. The uprising began about 5 p.m. in Warsaw, and took people entirely by surprise; thousands vanished without a trace. For a whole year, Maryla hoped and waited for Witold's return — in vain. Now she knew that he never would be back, that he had been murdered with other innocent bystanders. Maryla had no children and, although she was still very pretty and only thirty-five years old, she felt that life had passed her by, and that her chances for happiness were gone.

During this ill-fated uprising, Julia Kielba had lost her sister Anna in the most tragic circumstances. August 15, 1944, was the feast of Assumption, an important holiday for Polish Catholics, and Anna had gone to visit her sister Victoria. They were in good spirits, even though the uprising continued unabated. The fighting seemed far away from Victoria's apartment in a majestic, old wooden frame house on 65 Wspólna Street in a quiet Warsaw neighborhood.

She was busy in her kitchen preparing a meal when the Germans stormed into Wspólna Street and began setting the houses on fire one after the other. Before Victoria understood what was happening, the old apartment house caught fire and rapidly the flames reached the stairway of solid oak. Anna, who had difficulty walking, screamed for help, but she was too heavy for Victoria to carry. At the last moment, as the stairway was engulfed in flames, Victoria ran from the house. Anna perished in the fire, and Julia refused to see Victoria ever again, losing thus both her sisters.

Mrs. Tran, by then in her nineties, sat in a chair opposite me and shook her head as she watched me with the baby. She said nothing, but her wise eyes were telling me, "My child, I feel sorry for you." I tried to avoid her compassionate look and played with the child, inwardly asking myself: "What is going to happen next?" This was not the reception I had awaited and hoped for so long.

Mrs. Tran began to talk, telling me calmly that Julius, her only son, had been killed. "Do you recall, Irene, that it was Marta, Julius's wife, who gave Janka the address of the Pawlos at the Zakrzówek cemetery?"

"Yes, I had not forgotten. And Marta wrote to the Pawlos recommending us to them."

Mrs. Tran continued, "Julius seemed safely established in Austria. Zenon and Czeslaw Pawlo had arranged the Aryan papers for Julius and sent him to work in an Austrian town. Everything went according to plan almost until the end of the war. Then one day there was a brawl in a pub, and my Julius was there, just by chance. The police were called and arrested everybody, including my son. He never returned. I wonder if the Gestapo found that he was circumcised. That would indicate that he was Jewish, for, as you must know, the Polish Catholic do not practise this ritual."

Mrs. Tran became silent, then resumed pensively. "Was my son tortured to reveal the whereabouts of his family and the names of his friends? He probably was, but he betrayed no one."

The old lady, calm, almost stoic, had more to say. "My son's wife, Marta, and their two daughters survived the war in Zakrzówek and now live in Warsaw. Marta decided to abandon her Jewish origins and cut all her contacts with the past. She and the girls continue to live under their assumed Christian identity. Marta, my poor daughter-in-law, has lost all her family, even her Aryan-looking sister, Alice, who worked with the Polish Resistance. But Marta cannot leave Poland. This is her country and she has no relatives abroad."

"Mrs. Tran, do you blame Marta for having renounced Judaism? Are you angry at her?"

"No, I am not. You see, Irene, I have not enough money or strength to help Marta and my two granddaughters. She will stay in Poland and will do what she considers the best for the future of her daughters. I am so sorry I cannot help them." Mr. Tran bowed her head. "Irene, I can still be useful to Janka, the only child I have left. She needs me. She has no children and no one left to love her. You certainly have heard that her husband, Dr. Elterman, a medical doctor and colonel in the Polish army, was murdered with the other Polish officers in the Katyż Massacre of 1940."

Night came, and it was time to go to bed. Julia and Walenty Kielba had their own room, but the eight of us had to manage as well as we could. Janka and her mother were installed in the waiting room, Mrs. Tran on a couch and Janka next to her on a camp bed. Maryla slept on a narrow couch in the dental office. My father set up a camp bed in the kitchen while my mother, Richard and I occupied my parents' double couch in the living/dining room.

Karolina had to sleep on the dining room table which only a short while ago had served as our dinner table. She hated this arrangement, complaining, "What is happening to us? The war is finally over, but we still continue to live the same miserable life as during the bombing and occupation. When will we leave our past behind, and start a normal life?"

Our parents did not seem to mind this situation. After all, they reasoned, "There are so many people who have lost their entire families and their friends during the occupation. We are grateful that we have survived the war, that we are reunited again, and that we have such devoted and sincere friends who are glad to share their comfortable home with us. Indeed, we are very lucky."

This was the same house where my mother and Karolina hid during the occupation and my father visited them regularly until he left Warsaw to work for a dentist. Sometimes, coming to Bernerowo, he took the last tram before the curfew (9 p.m., if I remember). As the tram stopped at the outskirts of Warsaw, he had to walk across the fields till he reached the suburb of

Bernerowo. By then it was past curfew and he had to be careful, ready to jump into the bushes at the slightest noise for fear of being caught by the German patrol.

One evening my father heard the sound of an approaching car. It could only be German. He hid in the bushes, afraid even to breathe. The car stopped not far from him and a man emerged and pointed out a direction with his hands. My father recognized him as Mr. Byczek, a Pole from Bernerowo. Mr. Byczek spoke in a heavily accented German which my father had no difficulty understanding. "You will find them by turning left. The Jews will be right there at the Palewskis." Mr. Byczek repeated the Palewskis' address, then turned to the right and walked away. The car drove off.

In the morning it was discovered that the two families, the Palewskis and the hidden Jews, had been taken that night and executed shortly thereafter. The Kielbas and my parents knew with certainty who the denouncer was. He and his family moved into the empty house shortly after its occupants had been murdered. Mrs. Byczek wore furs and jewelry which she never had before.

As soon as the war was over, Mr. Byczek found new sponsors. He became a secret agent for the newly established Polish Communist government and continued to spy on his countrymen and women. He was as dangerous in 1946 as he had been during the occupation.

During her years in hiding, my mother stayed away from the windows so as not to be noticed by a neighbor or a passer by. However, the bathroom window was small and high and she sometimes peeped through. She could see the back windows of the house next door to the Kielbas and noticed two men, a woman and a child. They never left the house and stayed mostly in the back room. My mother saw that before each meal the people rinsed their fingers in a small glass vessel and dried them on a towel that sat on a sideboard near the table. There was no doubt in my mother's mind that these people were performing the Jewish ritual of symbolically washing their hands before eating bread. Hence, they were certainly hidden Jews. She spoke about it with the Kielbas, who confirmed her suspicions: the neighbors were only two people and the four others were strangers.

Mrs. Kielba, the only practicing Catholic in her family, went to church daily and prayed for her neighbors and their guests' safety.

Every morning, my mother peered at the neighbors' house and felt reassured to see the Jewish people well and alive moving about. She talked with them in her mind to assuage her loneliness. But one sunny day German cars stopped right before the Kielbas' neighbors' house. They must have known the exact address. They must have been well informed. They arrested all five adults and the child, the hidden Jews and the noble Christians sheltering them, and shot them all dead, either on the grounds of the Pawiak prison or at the Gestapo quarters.

Bernerowo was no longer a safe place to hide and that was the reason why, four years before, my sister had left to join me in forced labor in Marten. My mother remained the only one hidden by the Kielbas. Maryla and her parents tried to reassure themselves and my mother. "Let us be calm. We have survived so far. We shall see the end of the war together," they repeated.

But Witold Rozyki was apprehensive. He was young and did not want to be killed. My mother understood his fears and decided to leave her hiding place at the Kielbas, even though she had nowhere to go and not much money in her purse. One afternoon, when the house was quiet, Maryla and Witold were out, and Julia and Walenty were having a short nap in their bedroom, my mother put on her coat and hat, and went to the door on tiptoe. As she turned the knob, she felt a strong hand holding her arm.

"And where do you think are you going?" Julia Kielba asked loudly, almost hysterically. Walenty came out of his bedroom. "We will live or die together, do you understand?" they said, both speaking at the same time. "We will never let you go out, never,"

"But you have to consider Maryla and Witold. You are four people and I am only one. Let me go," my mother pleaded. But they did not let her go.

When the war was over, the denunciations were left unpunished. The Communists and certain segments of the population did not want to pursue those who had denounced the Jews and their rescuers.

Not long after we arrived, we were all woken up in the middle of the night. The house was surrounded by Polish soldiers with rifles ready to shoot, as if they were storming an enemy bastion. They demanded access to the house and a number of them rushed in and ran from one room to another, pointing their rifles at us, without a word of explanation. The baby, woken up and sensing our fear, began to scream. I held him and tried to calm him down. The soldiers ran madly back and forth, in and out of the house. Finally, after about an hour, they left. What had caused such a savage intrusion? No one told us, but perhaps someone wanted to frighten the Kielbas for being friends with us, the Jews.

The following days were calm, and we continued to reminisce. It was my father's turn to tell his story. Thanks to Mr. Grunwald, he had found a position as a dental mechanic with an Ukrainian dentist in a town close to the Russian border. When his boss became incapacitated by an accident, he took over the practice and was able to generate enough income to support his employer's whole family. He was also able to send food packages and money regularly to Bernerowo, and this made his separation from the family more bearable.

As soon as he was liberated, my father remembered the promise he had made to Mr. Grunwald to defend him against accusations of having been disloyal to Poland by taking German nationality during the occupation. He had to hurry to rescue his colleague from reprisal. But neither the trains nor the buses were running, and he had to ride from town to town on farmers' wagons until he finally reached Warsaw. He arrived just in time, for some Polish dentists were ready to lynch Mr. Grunwald, accusing him of being a traitor.

The sudden apparition of Jan, the Jew, astonished my father's pre-war colleagues. He amazed them even more when he stood up to defend Theodor Grunwald and did not mince his words: "Are you accusing Theodor who has risked his life to save me? Whom did you save? Are you judging one of our colleagues who has been more courageous than any of you? Isn't it rather shameful?"

Mr. Grunwald was forgiven for having taken German nationality. That was his only sin. Their pact of late 1942 had worked. He was left unharmed and remained my father's good friend for the rest of his life.

My father told another story. When the newspapers announced the public hanging of a few German murderers in the port city of Gdansk, reclaimed by Poland after the war, he felt an irresistible desire to see the hanging. "Maybe they were the ones who had murdered my mother," he said. Again the journey was difficult, partly on foot and partly with rides on trucks or farmers' wagons.

Walking through the countryside, my father saw a mob closing in on a young German soldier in uniform, only sixteen or seventeen years old. The boy was on his way back to his home in Germany.

The mob was getting hysterical, their anger and lust for revenge about to explode. The forlorn young soldier stood there repeating in German, "Please, I want to go to my mother, let me go to my mother, please."

"I saw before my eyes the two of you, my dearest girls," our father said. "Maybe you were now walking across Germany, barefoot, hungry and alone, trying to reach your mother. Maybe some good Germans pitied and helped you. I had to help this boy, I just had to."

Father pushed himself to the front of the crowd near the boy-soldier, and cried as loud as he could, "I am a Jew and I lost my mother and sisters and have no news from my two deported daughters. I, a Jew, ask you to let this boy go back to his mother. Do it for me, please."

The mob looked at the speaker, first in disbelief, then in understanding, and the boy was let go. Perhaps the young soldier succeeded thereafter in reaching his mother. My father hoped so.

"How about the hanging, Father, did you see it?" I asked. "Well, I got there too late. When I arrived it was all over," he replied, hiding his relief.

Watching my parents, I sensed their pain and confusion. In spite of the hardships and humiliations inflicted upon Jews by some Poles, my parents remained attached and faithful to Poland. But in a secular way, they felt deeply Jewish. They were sensitive to any anti-Semitic remark; they considered it as an insult to the memory of their murdered family and to the destruction of their world.

Our daily life was subdued; Mother was busy with her patients, and Father had to leave home often to go to Warsaw and use somebody else's dental laboratory, or to look for dental material which was hard to find, or to contact old friends.

Mrs. Tran insisted on helping in the kitchen. She had been an excellent cook, while Julia Kielba had always hated preparing meals. If Mrs. Tran had been younger, Julia might have felt uncomfortable about it. But as it was, Julia was only amused and gracefully accepted the ninety-year-old lady's leadership in her kitchen.

The house cleaning was divided among the three of us. Julia had to clean her and Walenty's bedroom, Karolina took care of the two rooms used as dental offices and I was responsible for the rest of the house — that is, the bathroom, the kitchen and our large living/dining/bedroom.

I worked hard, day after day, and strained my back. I was in great pain and could not walk for three days. Even then, no one, including myself, thought that the work was too heavy for me. After all, I had to be at home with Richard; thus I should not stay there idle. While I kept busy washing all windows, scrubbing the floor on my knees, and washing endlessly, by hand, all our linen, clothes, and the child's diapers in a portable washtub, Walenty Kielba walked outside with Richard. Walenty had no grandchildren of his own and loved Richard, enjoyed taking care of him as well as feeling useful in this busy household.

So life continued. Richard brought joy to my parents, especially to my father. He watched his grandchild lovingly, too shy to cuddle him in the presence of others. He adored Richard the moment he saw him, the grandson to take the place of the son he always wanted but never had. At the same time, he was a little embarrassed at becoming a grandfather at such a young age. He was forty-four years old in 1946, still a handsome man, his blond hair still thick, his blue eyes sparkling and his smile engaging. He dreaded getting old.

Richard was getting solid food now but still no one guided or advised me on how to bring up a baby; the three mothers living in the house, including my mother, seemed either not interested or had forgotten how to deal with it. Did they believe that since Richard was healthy, there was no reason to worry or to seek professional guidance? I felt I could only rely on myself; I had to follow my intuition and common sense in bringing up my son.

Sometimes I sat with Richard in the garden and watched the neighbors across the fence. One of them was a young girl, Miss Kislak, studying and laughing with her girlfriends. I envied her, for I had forgotten how to laugh; I worried how I would support

Richard and myself, and whether I would ever be able to finish my education. My son was the center of my life, and I wanted him to be happy, but I also wanted to become an independent, professional woman. Only then, I believed, would I regain my self-respect and be able to provide adequately for Richard.

My parents worshipped Julia and Walenty Kielba, Maryla Rozyki, Czeslaw Pawlo, his mother Mrs. Pawlo, and the memory of Zenon Pawlo. These people represented for my parents a microcosm of humanity and a reflection of God's beneficence. Needing to believe in human goodness, they became compulsive in praising their benefactors and putting themselves down. That troubled me a great deal. I admired the beautiful friendship between my parents and their rescuers, who had been heroic without expecting reward. But my parents considered rewarding their rescuers to be their sacred duty, a way of justifying their survival. "Life has a meaning only when one is giving and loving," they told us.

I needed to talk about how I felt, whether it was anger or sorrow or hope. I had survived the war, taking my chances in the open, not hidden in the closet. I had survived through incredible good luck, through our friends' help, and through my own courage. Now I wanted to go on with my life and stop worrying all the time about others. I resented my parents denying themselves and Karolina and me the right to pursue happiness, insisting, "Fulfilling one's duty is the essence of life, everything else is secondary." That made me feel selfish and confused.

Karolina was the first among us to wake up and claim the right to live up to our potential and abilities. Now twenty-four, she wanted to finish her medical studies as soon as possible. But going to Warsaw for the day and back to Bernerowo was exhausting. She had to be on her feet all day, running from one place to another, searching for papers, matriculations, locating friends or just simple information. Transportation was by means of old trucks, filled beyond capacity with passengers. Food was scarce, and there were no cafeterias or restaurants for a quick meal.

It came time at last for the five of us to move from Bernerowo; the Kielbas needed their house for themselves. There were not many sound houses left in Warsaw, so my parents began to look for a skeleton of a house to rebuild an apartment. They found a burned-out building—empty and sinister—reduced to a shell. It was located on Narbutta Street, in a section of Warsaw called Mokotów. It was less damaged because it was inhabited by the Germans during the Occupation.

My parents' second-floor apartment was one of the first to be rebuilt. Others followed their example and in a relatively short time, the whole building was occupied.

In June 1946, my parents moved back to Warsaw. With three large rooms, a spacious entrance hall, a kitchen and bathroom, the apartment seemed to us luxurious; it had electricity and running water. There was no central heating: as usual, the apartment was kept warm by white tile porcelain stoves, attached to the wall and fed with coal and wood, as was the kitchen stove. The only hot water was in the bathroom, from a water heater operated by electricity, a much-appreciated luxury.

The family's activities were centered in the large, bright dining/living room which was converted into a bedroom at night. My parents beautiful pre-war furniture—the dining room set removed in 1939 from our apartment on Pawia Street—had been returned intact. We could hardly believe our good fortune that it survived destruction and had now been gracefully returned by the charming Janina Zenkowska.

At night, two camp beds were set up in for Karolina and me, and my parents slept on a large couch. Richard's crib was in the next room, which was both his bedroom and the dental laboratory. The dental office was in a separate room and the large entrance hall was used as a waiting room.

All the rooms had high ceilings and large windows which gave plenty of light and sunshine. To us and to our friends, this was a luxurious and enviable dwelling. Once more my parents became popular and well-liked dentists and enjoyed a pleasant social life. They entertained their loyal friends every Sunday, and people often dropped in during the week.

I cooked for the family and helped Karolina clean the apartment. It was primarily her responsibility and she did it with enthusiasm and skill.

I longed to see Pawia Street, where I had lived before the war. It was far from our new home and I had to use a transportation truck, as the tramways and buses were not running yet. The trucks were so crowded that I was glad to get standing room in this one. It was high and there was a small ladder to climb in. More and more people filled the truck. Since I was small, I was pushed around and nearly toppled over. I could hardly breathe and there was nowhere to move. Then a tall, strong countrywoman spoke out for me: "Let this young lady breathe! Hey, move over, give her some air. Don't you people have any shame?" I was allowed to move to the side of the truck where there was nobody in front of me and I could get some fresh air.

The truck stopped on Leszno Street and I ran toward Karmelicka Street; I could not wait to see Pawia Street. My heart beat rapidly and memories of our pre-war life rushed into my mind. But when I reached Karmelicka Street I saw nothing but mounds of debris and rubble. There were no buildings left, not even a shell in what had been the Ghetto, except for the two churches on Leszno Street. All the houses had been reduced to ashes. The streets, covered with dust and broken bricks, were impassable even on foot. Only Leszno Street itself had been cleaned so that the traffic could move.

Grief-stricken, I stood for a long time looking at what had been my neighborhood. Then I slowly turned back to the freight truck to return to Narbutta Street.

I felt like a stranger in Warsaw. My friends and neighbors were gone, and the city I had known had ceased to exist. I felt as if the ground I was walking on was saturated with human blood, and the air filled with cries of agony.

My father advised me to get out of the house, to see people and to continue my studies. The family would keep an eye on Richard for me. I wanted to work and to become independent financially, but it was not easy to find work, especially for an unskilled applicant. My Matura was no better than a high school diploma for the purpose of getting a job. My parents offered to continue supporting me and Richard while I finished my education. I decided to be pragmatic and study pharmacology.

My life had begun to take shape when the news of the pogrom in the Polish city of Kielce hit us. Why the liberated Poles had attacked the small group of surviving Jews in such a barbaric way was a mystery to us. Well over forty people — men, women, and children — were murdered in Kielce in just one day, on July 4, 1946.

My father considered it an isolated incident, an aberration which would never be repeated. Nothing could shake his love for Poland and its people. He was happy with his Christian Polish friends and tried to ignore the undercurrent of anti-Semitism.

But my mother, Karolina, and I felt differently. We were unable to lie to ourselves any more: anti-Semitism was a fact of life in Poland.

Another example of the precarious situation for Polish Jews was the murder of my pre-war friend, Lucynka Nasibirska, and her father. They survived the war only to be killed after the Liberation, presumably by the Poles who took over their property. The crime was left unpunished; the police were unable to find the culprits. Yet my father hoped that the anti-Jewish sentiments would fade away, and one day soon would simply disappear.

The academic year began in October. The days were cold and windy. The students were first asked to help clean the Old City, the historical part of Warsaw, now lying in ruins. Every day we arrived, shovels in hand, to the piles and mounds of debris, accepting our task dutifully and determined to restore our capital to its pre-war glory.

Perhaps life would be good again, I thought. So far, Józef had not insisted on seeing Richard, and I went to meet him at his parents' home to discuss our divorce. He was there with his youngest sister, Tania; his parents were out. He was polite and visibly embarrassed at being unemployed and unable to support his son. I still loved Józef and tried to avoid hurting or humiliating him. He agreed not to contest the divorce and to let me keep his name. I promised not to ask for alimony or child support. We parted, both sad, both resigned to go our separate ways.

Fortunately there was a new law allowing the dissolution of "war" marriages, that is, marriages contracted during the war, on the grounds of incompatibility, without the necessity of proving the fault of either party. As much as I wanted the divorce, I would have been unable to accuse Józef of any wrongdoing. There must have been thousands of others in the same situation, and I appreciated the government's wisdom. It helped us to start a new life.

Józef insisted on visiting rights, which were granted to him, but he did not use them, probably because he had no money to bring anything for his son. He was jobless and poor. And I was now an unemployed, divorced woman with a child to support. I considered myself a failure to be dependent financially upon my parents. It did not even occur to me to be proud of my healthy baby, born under such difficult circumstances.

At the university we had fulfilled our contribution to the cleaning of the Old City and classes now began. Our classes and labs were held in any place that could be found, since not many buildings had been restored in our ruined city. Students had to run from one corner of Warsaw to another.

Some of my colleagues seemed very nice and I would have liked to have known them better, but I had to rush home to take care of my baby as soon as classes were over. At home I found him smiling and I loved to be with him. He was an energetic child and enjoyed exploring every corner of our apartment. He was frightened only of the electric vacuum cleaner. Otherwise, he was a bold and curious little person. I would have preferred to postpone my studies and be able to give him all my attention. Pharmacology interested me very little and running from one boring lecture to another was not fun. But as a single mother, I had to be realistic and acquire a lucrative profession.

The gradual reappearance of those Jews who had miraculously survived, mostly in Russia, added a new dimension to our life. We were registered with a Jewish organization that kept the names and addresses of all the survivors. People constantly searched for relatives and friends, and the organization was the first place of inquiry. We had many unexpected visits and encounters.

At the same time many Jews were leaving Poland, and my mother, Karolina and I were impressed by their courage in doing so. We longed for a life without the constant tension between Christians and Jews. But my father did not share our feelings. He was happy with his work, his family, his patients, and his friends.

And it happened that one day in November of 1946, I came home to find my mother and my sister waiting for me impatiently. They had exciting news: an unexpected opportunity had presented itself, a collective passport for eighteen Jewish students, granted by the government. It was an unusual favor, for people could not leave the country easily at that time. The leader of the group had allocated a place for one of us. Thus, either Karolina or I could join the group and leave Poland.

My mother wanted me to go. I had lived in France and I still had my permit to stay there. I had helped the family before when I had obtained the Aryan papers, found a place to live for everybody, and convinced Father to leave the Ghetto. Better I should go, my mother reasoned, than Karolina, who was close to obtaining her medical degree. It would be unwise to interrupt her studies even though Karolina wanted to go; Paris seemed very attractive to her—but so was her medical degree. Anyway, soon the whole family would leave Poland, my mother and Karolina concluded, and I would be only the first to leave, to encourage them and lead the way.

My father was consulted. He frowned at me. "Why don't we all stay in Poland?" he asked.

As for me, I did not want to leave. I had only just begun to adapt myself to my new life. If I left, I could not take Richard with me. He would have to stay with my parents. I felt a stabbing pain in my chest even at the thought of our separation. We had never been separated before. But if we stayed in Poland, Richard could be hurt in the future. One day Józef might claim his son. And Richard could not belong to both of our two different worlds, as they existed then in Poland. To which world would he belong? He could not be Józef's Jewish son; he would have to keep his Jewish identity secret for the rest of his life, and be afraid, even ashamed, to reveal the truth about his maternal family.

All these anxious thoughts rushed through my head. I wanted to stay in Poland but I was apprehensive. I did not want to lose the opportunity of returning to France, but I was not sure what I would do there. Obviously I was not ready to leave Poland. I still loved my country.

My father understood my distress. He shared my anxiety about Richard's future and advised me the only way he knew how. "Irene, don't make a hasty decision. Wait, just wait. There will be other opportunities for us to leave Poland, and maybe it will never be necessary. Perhaps the country will settle down, and anti-Semitism will just die away. Irene, please don't go."

The next day when I went to the University I had a pleasant surprise. Two of my colleagues, a young, good-looking man and a pleasant woman I had noticed before, approached me and invited me for a walk between classes. Finally, I said to myself, I will have some friends. I felt happy and hopeful.

We sat on a bench and the man spoke. "We have watched you for some time and we have gotten to like you. You seem to be a serious, intelligent and responsible young woman. We would be very happy if you agreed to join our group."

"Your group? You mean a students' fraternity?" I asked in joyful anticipation.

"No, not exactly. We have in mind other, more serious activities. Poland needs our help. We want to chase the Russians away from our land. We want to get rid of them. We will not hesitate to plant bombs and derail the Russian trains passing through Poland," he said.

The woman added a few words describing the future plans of their terrorist group. I could not believe what I had heard. I was speechless for a moment. Then I responded, "Are you out of your mind? Did we not bleed enough? Must we continue to fight endless battles we cannot win? I believe that we should heal our wounds first, get stronger, and wait for a proper opportunity to reclaim our country. I don't understand you, I don't agree with you."

They looked at me calmly, said nothing more, and we parted.

As soon as I got home I asked my father to join my mother, Karolina and me in a serious discussion of our future.

"Father," I said, "Mother's foresight when she sent me to the Pawlos to get the papers saved our lives. You did not want to leave the Ghetto, and now you don't want to leave Poland. There is a time to stay, and there is a time to move. We simply cannot live in this country."

The four of us talked for a long time. My father finally agreed, albeit reluctantly, that we should all move and soon. I had to take advantage of the present opportunity and leave Poland now. They would follow at their first opportunity. In the meantime my parents would take care of Richard as if he were their own son. Karolina promised to help. She sincerely loved the child, I knew that.

In bed, I thought over my coming departure. I was in a daze; the Ghetto, Aunt Rosa, little Hania, the helpless, crying Jewish children loaded into the trucks that took them to the Umschlagplatz rose before my eyes. The time had come again for me to do something concrete for my child, for my family, for myself.

My parents could do more for Richard than I could. I was giving him what was most precious for me: my own parents. He would be happy, I reasoned.

As for me, why should I expect to have an easy life? And the screams of the Jewish children came back to me. How could I dream of a happy life with my child and my family intact, forgetting what had happened to my people, to my country?

An ugly superstition came to my mind: my immediate family had been spared and I had given life to a healthy child — that was too much luck. An oblation had to be made, a sacrifice to avoid the reversal of our fortune. I had to suffer so that my child would be spared. I had to pay for his future happiness.

I did not know how I got this superstitious fear; it was primitive, it was stupid but it was very real to me. I could not find reason, just as there had been no reason why my family, my friends and millions of others had to perish so brutally, so painfully. The only reality surrounding me was pain and suffering. It seemed that I could not escape it.

My head became heavy with thousands of thoughts contradicting each other. Slowly a decision emerged. It became clear to me that we must leave Poland to live in a country where we would not be afraid to reveal who our ancestors were. I had to provide such a place for my son and for myself.

Thus I agreed to leave Richard with my parents for a short time before they joined me in France.

On the day of my departure, I could not bring myself to leave the room where Richard was playing on the floor. I watched him and I could not move. Then, when he turned his head from me, engrossed in his toy, I ran out of the room.

My father went with me to the gathering place from where the eighteen people—mostly young Jews—would depart. Some were a little older and obviously not students, but the authorities checked only the number of the travelers and not their credentials.

Seeing these people, the determination and hope in their eyes, my father for the first time warmed to the idea of our family's future departure. He saw Jews who were not afraid to claim their right to be themselves, even if they had to pay for it by leaving their ancestral country.

The moment for boarding the trucks arrived and I had to part from my father. He held me in his arms for a long time, as he had done four years ago when I left for the forced labor in Lorraine. The war was over, but peace still eluded us. We had a long and arduous road to travel and, once more, I was leaving my beloved Warsaw.

The trucks took the passengers to the train and the train carried us south to the border and into Czechoslovakia. Poland was left behind. Yet another chapter of my life opened. I had left my baby and my heart was broken. "I had to do it, I had to do it," I repeated to myself, but my eyes overflowed with tears and I could not stop them.

My fellow Jewish travelers were annoyed with me, for I was the only one in the group whose immediate family remained intact and yet I was so unhappy.

They asked me, "Are you crying for Poland?" They introduced me to a woman whose husband and child had been murdered by Poles in the pogrom in Kielce—in liberated Poland with the

Germans gone. Now, alone, she traveled with us toward an uncertain future. "Look at her and stop crying," they said.

I looked into the sad eyes of the pale, bereaved woman. She tried to smile at me. But her courage and composure did not alleviate the pain of leaving my child. My misery was deepened by the fact that I was unable to hate Poland. It was my country. Its language was my language. I felt as Polish as I felt Jewish, for I was a Jewish Pole.

Unfortunately, such national identity was not recognized. I had to be either one or the other.

We reached Paris in December 1946. I was twenty-two years old.

POSTSCRIPT

The five of us were reunited in the United States.

Karolina received her medical degree and married William Bein, an American citizen. They left Poland and thereafter she practiced her profession in New Jersey.

My father was heartbroken for Poland and never stopped longing for his beloved country, yet he succeeded in making new friends and a decent living for himself and my mother at their new home in the United States.

I struggled for years but finally I achieved my goal, and with my degrees in law and library science, I began an academic career as an instructor at Rutgers University, New Jersey, in 1957.

Richard grew up to become, in his turn, a lawyer. He has two children, Aaron and Anna and the family lives in Oregon.

Józef, Richard's father, remarried, and he and his wife, Wanda, still lived together in Warsaw. They had two married daughters and six granchildren.

Mrs. Tran died at the age of 98. Janka passed away in her late eighties. The two women never left Poland.

Each survivor's story is different, and each sheds new light on human nature. I have witnessed the atrocities of the Nazis side by side with the immense courage of the victims and their rescuers. And many decades later the image of Halinka Herszhorn, the young Jewish girl who was selected to go to the Umschlagplatz and to her death, remains vivid in my mind. There was no anger in the sad eyes illuminating her ashen face as she looked at us, who remained in the Ghetto and still had a chance to survive, while she had none. Thin, in her outgrown, worn-out dress, her back hunched, Halinka Herszhorn, abandoned by the whole world, appeared to accept calmly her fate. She knew that the oppressors could destroy her body but not her young soul untouched by their inhumanity.

And I will remember the Jews who resisted by their everyday struggles to survive with dignity, ordinary Jews born with the expectations of a normal, uneventful life who became heroes without knowing it, without asking for it. And I will remember the Jews who took the arms and fought bravely, even when they knew they had no chance to win.

And I will remember the valiant Christians who risked their lives to save the Jews. These rescuers' nonviolent and heroic resistance to Nazi inhumanity has proven that human spirit and decency are not easily destroyed, that they can survive the worst oppression, and that not all has been lost.

During the years under Nazi rule, I said to myself:

> Don't let your enemies defeat you.
> Keep moving, keep walking —
>   not everyone wishes you harm.
> Don't freeze up, go ahead,
>   for one day you will meet people
>   willing to befriend you.
> Continue your journey
> Don't lose courage,
> Don't lose hope.

KAROLINA AND IRENE 1930

PAWIA 1945

HELENA — 1946

JAN 1946

KAROLINA IN WARSAW IN 1946

MOISHE DOBREJCER
(SURVIVED — IRENE'S FIRST COUSIN NOW IN MELBOURNE)

RICHARD 1946

UNCLE HENIEK — JAN'S BROTHER SURVIVED AND
EMIGRATED TO ISRAEL, A LOBOR LAWYER AND JUDGE

IRENE IN CASABLANCA 1955

JOZEF AND RICHARD MEET FOR "FIRST" AND LAST TIME
IN 1984 IN WARSAW

PROFESSOR IRENE BESSETTE   QUEENS 81

Upper Ontario Law Sociaty — 85

Irene's grandchildren Anna and Aaron in 1980

Irene with grandson Aaron in 1994

IRENE AND GRANDAUGHTER ANNA IN KINGSTON IN 2004

THE REMAINING FAMILY — PORTLAND 2009 — 85TH
BIRTHDAY — ANNA, RICHARD, AARON AND IRENE

CHRONOLOGY OF RELEVANT EVENTS

1896:

Author's mother, Riva Helen Dobrejcer, born in Mohilev, Russia.

1899:

Author's maternal grandparents, Grunia and Aron Dobrejcer, leave Mohilev and settle in Warsaw with their younger children.

1902:

Author's father, Jan Borman—Bakowski, born in Lublin, Poland.

1921:

Helen and Jan married in Warsaw, Poland.

1922:

Karolina, author's sister, born in Warsaw.

1924:

Irene (author), Jan and Helen's second and last child, born in Warsaw.

1939:

July/August:

Helen, Karolina, and Irene vacation in Brok on the river Bug, in Poland.

September 1:

First day of the war. Bombing of Warsaw.

September 2:

France and England declare war against Germany.

September 6:

> General Staff abandon Warsaw.

September 7:

> — Polish government fly abroad. The defense of Warsaw continues, headed by General Walerian Czuma and the city's Mayor/President Stefan Starzyriski.
>
> — Massive exodus of men fleeing eastward from Warsaw. Athor's paternal uncle Henryk joins the flight (He survives and settles in Israel after the war).

September 17:

> The Soviet Army crosses the frontier to occupy Eastern Poland. Hitler and Stalin ratify partition of Poland by formal treaty on 28 September.

September 24:

> Author's grandmother, Grunia Achlomov Dobrejcer, dies of pneumonia in shelter.

September 26:

> Warsaw loses water and electicity.

September 27:

> Warsaw surrenders. Bombing stops.

September 28:

> Capitulation of Warsaw officially signed by General Tadeusz Kutrzeba.

September 30:

> — Curfew imposed in accordance with the act of capitulation. Restrictive hours change during the Occupation, more severe for Jews than for Poles.
>
> — Possession of guns, weapons, arms, ammunition, explosive materials, and the like forbidden in the occupied Poland.
>
> — German soldiers enter Warsaw.

October 15:

> Mr. and Mrs. Szmit, dentists, come to live with author's family.

October 20:

>All radios owned by the non-Germans in the Occupied Poland are confiscated. The population of Warsaw ordered to deliver their radios to police stations.

December 1:

>Jewish men and women ordered to wear a white armband at least 10 centimeters wide with a blue Star of David, on the right sleeve. Children up to 10 or 12 years old exempted.

1939/1940:

>— Jewish schools, libraries, cinemas, theaters, and cabarets closed. Public and private dances forbidden for the Jews.

1940:

November 16:

>Warsaw Ghetto sealed, its gates closed.

December:

>Author begins clandestine lyceum-level studies leading to a baccalaureate degree.

1941:

>— Underground medical school, under cover of "Sanitary Courses for Fighting Epidemics" opens in the Ghetto. It lasts until July 20, 1942.
>— Quarantines for typhus and the use of sulfur for disinfection increase in the Ghetto.

June:

>Order to black out Warsaw to protect it from Allied air attacks.

June 22:

>Germany initiates surprise attack on the Soviet Union, beginning war between these two nations.

Fall:

> Territory of the Ghetto reduced by the closure of part called "Little Ghetto." Its population resettled in the remaining, diminished Ghetto.

December 7:

> Surprise Japanese air attack on Pearl Harbor.

December 8:

> United States declares war against Japan.

December 11:

> Germany and Italy declare war on the U.S.

1942:

> — Dr. Hanarin, after purchasing Argentinian passports, is taken with his family to the Pawiak prison, never to return.

January 4:

> Final date for Jews to surrender furs.

July 22:

> The "Final Solution" or mass deportations from Warsaw Ghetto to Treblinka death camps initiated by the Nazis.

August 3:

> Author, her parents and sister taken to the Umschlagplatz.

August 5 or 6:

> Dr. Janusz Korczak and the children taken to the Urnschlagplatz and deported.

August 7:

> Author and her family rescued from the Umschlagplatz.

August 9:

> Jozef Lautenberg leaves the Ghetto for Zakrzówek with author's mother, Mrs. Tran, and Janka.

August 12:

> Rosa Lautenberg and daughter Hania taken to the Umschlagplatz and deported.

August 14:

> Author, Karolina, Janka Elterman, Gustaw Lautenberg and his family leave the Ghetto for Zakrzówek.

October:

> Zakrzówek Jews are deported during the first two weeks of October.
>
> Author, her mother, sister, Mrs. Tran, and Janka flee Zakrzówek back to Warsaw.

Late October:

> Jan, author's father, escapes from the Ghetto.

1943:

January 15:

> Author deported from Warsaw for slave labor on a farm in Marten/Marthille, Lorraine.

January 18:

> Second wave of deportations from the Warsaw Ghetto to Treblinka begins.

April 19:

> Ghetto Uprising begins. It is crushed May 16, yet armed resistance lasts until June. The hunting-down of those still hiding in the ruins continues until August 1943.

September:

> Karolina joins author for slave labor in Marten.

1944:

June 6:

> D-Day — First day of the Allied forces landing in Normandy, France.

August 1:

> First day of the Warsaw Uprising, lasting 63 days. The act of capitulation signed October 2.

August 25:

> Liberation of Paris.

October 3:

> Jozef, a fellow slave worker, and author marry clandestinely at Marten parish church.

October 30:

Their son, Richard, is born in Morhange, Lorraine.

November 14 or 15:

Village of Marten/Marthille liberated by the American Army. So are all Polish slave workers, including author, Józef, Karolina, and baby Richard.

1945:

February 26:

Jozef and author re-married in the City Hall of Nancy (Meurthe-et-Moselle).

March:

Józef joins the Polish Army in England.

May 9:

Second World War ends in Europe.

July or August:

Author arrives with Richard in Joudreville to take the post of director and sole teacher of the evening school for children of Polish miners.

August 6 and 9:

Hiroshima and then Nagasaki destroyed by U.S. atomic bombs.

September 2:

Japan formally surrenders to the Allied powers.

1946:

February:

Jozef, officially demobilized, returns to Poland.

March:

Karolina, author, and Richard return to Poland.

December:

Author and Jozef obtain a non-contested divorce in Warsaw. Author leaves Poland for Paris, leaving Richard "temporarily" with her parents.

1949:

July 16:

> Karolina marries William Bein, an American citizen, in Warsaw working for JOINT relief agency.

1950:

March 3:

> Karolina obtains her medical degree and leaves Poland to rejoin her husband first in Marocco and then in the United States.

1957:

> The surviving family—Jan, Helen, Karolina, Richard, and author—reunited in the United States.

1968:

> The author leaves for Queens University School of Law in Kingston Ontario where she meets and marries Professor and author Gerard Bessette (D Feb 21, 2005).

2008:

> The Author returns to the United States and joins Richard in Portland, Oregon

NAMES MENTIONED IN THE TEXT

For a variety of reasons some of the names in this memoir have been changed.

"Murdered" is used when the fact is known with certainty by the author. "Believed killed" is used to indicate persons presumed dead, and "Fate unknown" for those who had disappeared without trace.

No indication is given for people whose lives were **not** in danger.

For those whose lives were in danger but, to the knowledge of the author, survived, it is so indicated.

It should be noted that the masculine and feminine forms of Polish family names are slightly different. For example, the surname of the author's mother is indicated as *aka* Bakowska, her father's *aka* Bakowski. The surname of Mr. Cygie's wife is Cygowa.

(Chapter numbers in parentheses indicate the first mention of the name in the book.)

Abel: a five-year-old Jewish boy abandoned together with his three-year-old brother, Sam, by their starving mother in the Ghetto street (IV). Murdered.

Abram Laufer: *See* Laufer, Abram.

Ackermans: an influential local family from Marten (VIII).

Ada: a newborn girl. Stayed with her mother, a Christian Pole, at the superintendent's apartment on 38 Pawia Street. Died from malnutrition during the bombing of Warsaw in September 1939 (II).

Adam Birman: *See* Birman, Adam.

Adam Himelfarb: author's friend during the Occupation. A fervent zionist. Committed suicide together with his parents in the fall of 1942 (IV).

Adam Silnicki: see Silnicki, Adam.

Ala: *See* Eisenstein, Ala.

Alex: Pola Eisenstein's Christian friend who proposed to marry and save her (IV).

Alice: Marta Tran's sister, actively engaged in the Polish resistance movement under assumed Aryan identity (XI). Murdered.

Altman, Mrs., DDS: had graduated from dental school together with Dr. Bakowska. Escaped with her young daughter to the Warsaw Ghetto in 1942 (IV). Both were murdered.

Ania (Maczacka): author's colleague; studied with her at the underground Lyceum courses in the Ghetto (III). Murdered.

Anna: Julia Kielba's sister and Janina Zenkowska's grandmother. Perished in the fire in August 1944 (XI). **Aunt Rosa:** *See* Lautenberg, Rosa.

Bakowska, Helen, DDS: author's mother assumed name **nee** Dobrejcer, referred to as Dr. B. or Helen (I). Survived.

Bakowskis (*Borman — pre 1942*): refers to author, her parents, and sister, Karolina based on their wartime name. All four survived.

Bein, William: U.S. citizen. Director of the American Joint Distribution Committee in Poland after the war. Married Karolina in 1949 in Warsaw (Postscript).

Bela Eisenstein: author's best friend. Had two sisters, Ala and Pola (II). Murdered.

Bernerowo: a Warsaw suburb where author's mother and sister hid at the Kielbas' house during the occupation (VII).

Birman, Adam: former pupil of Dr. Janusz Korczak. Learned the trade of dental mechanic at Jan's laboratory and became his friend (III). Murdered with his mother and sister.

Blumstein, Mr.: PhD in mathematics. Pre-war director of author's Gymnasium and Lyceum (III). Fate unknown.

Blumstein, Mrs.: PhD in Sciences. Wife of the director of author's Gymnasium and Lyceum (III). Fate unknown.

Borman-Bakowski, Jan, DDS: author's father, referred to as Jan (I). Survived.

Borowicz, Mr.: a miner from Joudreville. Father of five children. Lost three fingers in mine accident (X).

Brams, Mr.: PhD in History. Author's professor before and during the war (III). Murdered with his wife and their young son.

Byczek, Mr.: a Christian Pole. Denounced the Christian couple who hid a Jewish family. Both families were executed. He survived the war and worked as an agent for the Communist regime (XI).

Chemska, Zofia: author's rescuer. A Polish Christian woman, mother of Marynia (VII). Murdered in 1944 while in a Warsaw hospital.

Chemski, Mr.: Zofia's husband, Marynia's father.

Cukier, Mrs.: Lived with her husband and a young daughter on 38 Pawia. The Bakowskis' neighbor (V). Fate unknown.

Cygie, Mr.: PhD in Mathematics. Mrs. Cygowa's husband. Author's professor in the Ghetto (III). Murdered.

Cygowa, Mrs.: PhD in Natural Sciences. Author's professor before and during the occupation (III). Murdered.

Czerniakow, Adam: the president of the Warsaw Ghetto's Judenrat. Refused to cooperate with the Nazis in the deportations of Jews that began on July 22, 1942. Committed suicide on July 23 (V).

Czeslaw, Pawlo: Zenon's younger brother. The Bakowskis' rescuer (VII). Survived. *See also* Pawlos.

David: Zygmunt Frydman's nephew, nineteen-year-old David was author's first date; they danced together at a private party in the Ghetto (IV). Murdered.

Dobrejcer, Aaron: author's maternal grandfather. Grunia's husband. Teacher. Died in 1917 (II).

Dobrejcer, Freda: Monos's wife, Jadwiga's mother, and author's aunt (III). Murdered.

Dobrejcer, Grunia Achlomov: author's maternal grandmother. Died of pneumonia in September 1939 (II).

Dobrejcer, Jadwiga: daughter of Monos and Freda. Author's maternal cousin (III). Murdered.

Dobrejcer, Monos: author's maternal uncle, Freda's husband, and Jadwiga's father. Teacher (II). Murdered.

Dobrejcer, Mosze: author's maternal cousin. Grisza and Dora's son, brother of Aron, Estera, and Bernard. The only one from his family who survived—now in Melbourne, Australia(photo).

Dr. B.: Riva Dobrejcer (Helen Borman Bakowska), DDS: Author's mother. Survived.

Dworecka, Rena: author's pre-war friend and classmate, her guest during their vacation in Brok on the Bug in 1939 (I). Murdered.

Eisenstein, Ala: Bela's oldest sister (III). Murdered. **Eisenstein, Bela:** author's best friend (II). Murdered. **Eisenstein, Mr.:** Bela's father (III). Murdered.

Eisenstein, Pola: Bela's middle sister (III). Murdered. **Elcztein, Mietek:** *See* Mietek.

Elterman, Janka: close friend of the Bakowskis. Journeyed with them during the Occupation. Took care of her other, Mrs. Tran. Sister of Olga and Julius. Marta Tran's sister-in-law. Nelly's aunt (II). Janka and her mother survived. Marta and her two daughters survived but her husband Julius Tran was murdered (XI). Olga and her daughter Nelly were killed during the bombing of Warsaw in September 1939 (II).

Elterman, M.D.: Janka's husband. Colonel in the Polish Army. Murdered in Katyri (II).

Eliza: A young German woman and unwed mother, staying with her baby at her Nazi parents' home in Marten—where author slaved.

Elza: a young German woman from Bavaria. While her husband, an officer, was called to the German army, she stayed with her parents—Mundek and Zosia's bosses in Marten (VIII).

Emilia, Koska: see Koska, Emilia.

Ewa: *See* Mrozik, Ewa.

Fela: author's family's maid for a short time in 1942. Was present during the Bakowskis' arrest in August 1942 (V). Presumed deported and murdered.

Frankel, Mrs.: had working papers while her friends had not. Refused to be separated and went with them to the *Umschlagplatz* in 1942 (V). Murdered.

Fryd, Mrs.: Lily Lautenberg's mother (VI). Survived. **Frydman, Zygmunt:** Jan's dental mechanic and the family's friend. David's uncle (IV). Murdered.

Ghetto: with capital letter, refers to the Warsaw Ghetto. **Gienia Mitelberg:** author's pre-war classmate and friend (VII). Survived.

Gienia Sztucberg: Karolina's friend. Underground librarian in the Ghetto (IV). Murdered with her parents.

Grunia Achlomov Dobrejcer: *See* Dobrejcer, Grunia Achlomov.

Grunwald, Mr.: Jan's friend and professional colleague. Polish citizen but ethnic German. Adopted German nationality during the occupation. Jan's rescuer (IV).

Gustawa Jarecka: *See* Jarecka, Gustawa.

Hanarin, M.D.: advised Jan to purchase Argentinean passports from a Jewish middle-man in the Ghetto. Bought them for himself and his family (IV). Murdered with his wife and their young daughter.

Hania (Hannah) Lautenberg: *See* Lautenberg, Hania.

Hela: thirty-five-year-old Polish slave worker in Marten. Had a sexual encounter with Mr. Wagner, the mayor of Marten (VIII). Murdered.

Helen: author's mother, Dr. Bakowska, referred to as Dr. B. (I). Survived.

Heller, Mrs.: a courageous German woman who hid and saved her Jewish husband (V).

Henia Zawoznik: *See* Zawoznik, Henia.

Henryk: Jan's brother and author's uncle (II). Survived.

Herszhorn, Halinka: a young Jewish girl who lived with her parents at 38 Pawia Street. Showed great courageand moral fortitude when selected to go to the *Urn- schlagplatz* for deportation (V). Murdered.

Himelfarb, Adam: *See* Adam Himelfarb.

Hirszfeld, Ludwik: medical doctor and scientist of international reputation in serology, epidemology, and bacteriology. A Jew, converted to Roman Catholic religion, he was forced to enter the Ghetto. Author's professor at the underground medical school under cover of "Course to Fight Against Epidemics" (IV). Survived with his wife and daughter.

Inka Szekman: Karolina's pre-war classmate. Studied English during the bombing of Warsaw in 1939 (II). Murdered.

Irka Silnicka: *See* Silnicka, Irka.

Iwanicka, Mrs.: author's Christian Polish friend from Joudreville. Mr. Iwanicki's wife. Mother of author's two young students, Richard and Irene (X).

Iwanicki, Mr.: a miner from Joudreville, Mrs. Iwanicka's husband (X).

Jacob: a young Polish slave worker from Marten. Renamed Jacob from his real name, Wacek, by his German overseer (VIII). Murdered.

Jadwiga: author's maternal cousin. *See also* Dobrejcer, Jadwiga.

Jan: author's father, Dr. Jan Bakowski (I). Survived. **Janina Zenkowska:** *See* Zenkowska, Janina.

Janka: *See* Elterman, Janka.

Jarecka, Gustawa: a distinguished woman writer. Taught Polish and French literature at author's underground Lyceum studies in the Ghetto. Murdered with her mother and two children. Her husband's fate unknown (III).

Jasia: seventeen-year-old Polish Christian slave worker in Marten (VIII). Survived.

Jerzy: *See* Sliwa, Jerzy.

Joe: worked for the woman coal seller in the Ghetto. Moshe's brother (IV). Died of starvation.

Joint: American Joint Distribution Committee or AJDC (III). **Jola:** *See* Kardan, Jola.

Józef: author's husband and Richard's father, a slave worker in Marten (VIII). Survived.

Józef Lautenberg: *See* Lautenberg, Józef.

Józio Szwed: *See* Szwed, Józio.

Judenrat: Jewish Council run by the Jews but dominated by the Germans. Administered daily life of the Jewish communities and implemented German orders. **Julia:** *See* Kielba, Julia.

Kaltie: *See* Wagner, Kaltie.

Kardan, Jola: a Polish Christian slave worker from Marten. Stayed there with her husband, Kazik Kardan, and their daughter, Wiesia (VIII). All three survived.

Kardan, Kazik: Jola's husband, Wiesia's father (VIII). Survived.

Karolina: author's sister *aka* Krystyna Wanda Stolarska. Referred to in the text also as Krystyna (I). Survived.

Kielba, Julia: Walenty's wife, Maryla Rozyki's mother. Polish Christian friend and rescuer of the Bakowskis (VII). Survived.

Kielba, Walenty: Julia's husband. Maryla Rozyki's father. Polish Christian friend and rescuer of the Bakowskis (VII). Survived.

Korczak, Janusz: pen name of Hirsh/Henryk Goldszmit. Medical doctor, educator, writer, and director of the Jewish children's orphanage, known as the Orphans Home (III). Murdered with the children in the first week of August 1942.

Koska, Emilia: a teenager daughter of the Koskis (VII). **Koski, Mr.:** Mrs. Koska's husband, Emilia's father. Assisted author in bringing false Aryan papers to her family in Zakrzowek (VII).

Koska, Mrs.: Mrs. Szmit's loyal Polish Christian friend. Visited her in the Ghetto. Was sympathetic to author and her family. Took their furs for safekeeping (IV).

Krystyna: assumed name of author's sister, Karolina.

Laufer, Abram: a Jewish soldier who lost one leg during the German invasion of Poland in 1939. Son of the refugee dentist Mrs. Laufer, who rented a room on 38 Pawia Street (III). Believed killed in 1942.

Laufer, Mrs.: the refugee dentist who came to live at 38 Pawia Street with her husband and their son, Abram (III). Believed killed in 1942.

Lautenberg, Gustaw: Ignacy's brother, Rosa's brother-in−law, Lily's husband (V). Survived.

Lautenberg, Hania: author's paternal cousin. Deported when six years old with her mother Rosa (V). Murdered with her mother.

Lautenberg, Ignacy: Rosa's husband and Hania's father. Died in the Ghetto from typhoid (enteric) fever in June 12, 1942 (III).

Lautenberg, Józef: Ignacy's father, Rosa's father-in-law (III). Survived.

Lautenberg, Lily: Gustaw's wife. Rosa's sister-in-law. Mrs. Fryd's daughter (VI). Survived.

Lautenberg, Rosa: Jan's sister and author's aunt. Ignacy's wife, then widow. Hania's mother (III). Murdered with Hania in August 1942.

Lewin, Mr.: owner of the 38 Pawia building where the Bakowskis lived, and of the adjoining Opus factory (III). Killed.

Linda: a young girl travelling with a Polish family to Lorraine. Author met her then and again on the meadow near Marten (VII). Fate unknown.

Lolek: a Polish slave worker in Marten, Maria's brutal boyfriend (VIII).

Lorraine: a region of eastern France. Annexed by Germany in 1940. The village of Marten, where author and her sister were enslaved, was in Lorraine.

Lucynka Nasibirska: *See* Nasibirska, Lucynka.

Luka, Mr.: Polish Christian neighbor of the Bakowskis from 38 Pawia. Tadek's father. Arrested by Germans in 1939 for having been a foreman in Opus, a Jewish enterprise (III). Survived.

Luka, Mrs.: Friend and rescuer of the Bakowskis. Mr. Luka's wife, Tadek's mother (II). Survived.

Luka, Tadek: Son of Mr. and Mrs. Luka. Stood with Samuel Rotein on the roof of the 38 Pawia building to protect it from the fire during the bombing of Warsaw in September 1939 (II). Survived.

Magidson, Franka: author's French teacher in the Ghetto. Ida's sister (III). Murdered.

Magidson, Ida: author's chemistry teacher in the Ghetto (III). Believed killed in 1942.

Maria: eighteen-year-old Polish Christian slave worker in Marten. Mistreated by her boyfriend, Lolek, and by her German boss (VIII). Survived.

Martel, Mrs.: a French-speaking mother of six children. A pre-war Marten resident. Friendly to author (VIII).

Marten: German name of Marthille, the village in Lorraine where author and her sister were deported for forced labor (VII).

Marthille: French name of Marten (VIII).

Maryla Rozyki: *See* Rozyki, Maryla.

Mershingen: German name of Morhange, a small town in Lorraine, where Richard, author's son, was born.

Mietek Elcztein: author's childhood playmate and neighbor. Worked for the *Judenrat (IV)*. **Murdered.**

Mirka Nusbaum: author's co-student at the underground Lyceum courses in the Ghetto (III). Murdered. **Mitelberg, Gienia:** *See* Gienia Mitelberg.

Mitnik, Mr. and Mrs.: Intellectual and artistic couple. Aunt Rosa's friends. Had a young daughter named Stela (V). Murdered.

Mitnik, Stela: a graceful, affectionate girl, seven or eight years old in 1942. Sent for safety outside the Ghetto by her parents (V). Fate unknown.

Monos: *See* Dobrejcer, Monos

Morhange: called Mershingen during the Occupation. A small town in Lorraine where author's son, Richard, was born.

Moshe: worked with his brother Joe for the woman selling coal by buckets (IV). Died from starvation.

Mosze Dobrejcer: *See* Dobrejcer, Mosze.

Mrozik, Andrew: a Polish Christian. Became insane during the bombing of Warsaw in September 1939; killed his two children and himself (II).

Mrozik, Ewa: Andrew's wife, and Dr. Sliwa's sister. Survived (II).

Nancy: a city in North-Eastern France.

Nasibirska, Lucynka: author's pre-war friend. Murdered with her father, both Jewish, shortly after the war—possibly because they tried to recover their property. The crime has not been solved (XI).

Nasibirska, Mrs.: Lucynka's mother. A lawyer. Killed herself after the murder of her husband and daughter (XI).

Nelly: Janka Elterman's niece. Killed, together with her mother Olga, by a bomb in September 1939 (II).

Olga: Mrs. Tran's daughter, Janka Elterman's sister, and Nelly's mother. Killed with Nelly by a bomb (II).

Opus: men's shirts and dry cleaning factory located at 38 Pawia and the adjoining building. Owned by the Lewin family (III).

Osak, Mr.: a dentist. Dr. Bakowski's presumed friend. Had his dental equipment stolen (VII).

Ossowska, Krysia: Zosia and Mundek's daughter. Lived with her parents, slave workers, on a farm in Marten, Lorraine (VII).

Ossowska, Zosia: Mundek's wife, Krysia's mother. Lucyna's sister. Zofia Chemska's niece. Zosia brought author to Marten (VII).

Ossowski, Mundek: Zosia's husband, Krysia's father (VII).

Palewskis: Kielbas's Polish Christian neighbors from Bernerowo. Murdered with a Jewish family they hid in their house (XI).

Paul: the refugee hairdresser in Warsaw Ghetto (III).

Pawlos family: remarkably courageous Polish Christians — mother, father and two sons. They selflessly helped a number of Jews. The two brothers, Zenon and Czeslaw, were inventive, effective and generous rescuers. They befriended the Bakowskis (VI). The family survived, except for Zenon who was killed by a bomb during the Warsaw Uprising in 1944.

Pola: *See* Eisenstein, Pola.

Rosen family: the Jewish family whose Warsaw apartment was emptied by Germans (III). Fate unknown.

Roszewski, Sebastian: a Polish slave worker in Marten. Became Richard's godfather (VIII).

Rotein, Samuel: stood with Tadek Luka on the roof of the building on 38 Pawia to protect it from fire in September 1939 (II). Fate unknown.

Rozyki, Maryla: The Bakowskis' friend and rescuer. Kiel- bas only child. Married to Witold (XI). Survived.

Rozyki, Witold: Maryla's husband (XI). Believed killed during the Warsaw Uprising in 1944.

Rutkowski, Mr.: a miner from Joudreville. Became Polish consul in Strasbourg in 1945. Karolina/Krystyna worked at his Consulate for six months until March 1946 (X).

Samuel Rotein: *See* Rotein, Samuel.

Schultz: the owner of the German Ghetto workshop that was supposed to shelter its Jewish workers from deportation (V).

Silnicka, Irka: author's friend and neighbor from 38 Pawia Street. A talented pianist (IV). Murdered with her mother and younger brother, Adam.

Silnicka, Mrs.: the Bakowskis' neighbor from 38 Pawia Street, mother of author's friend Irka and of young Adam (III). Murdered.

Silnicki, Adam: younger brother of Irka Silnicka, author's friend and neighbor from 38 Pawia Street (IV). Murdered.

Sliwa, Jerzy, DDS: Mrs. Szaloska's nephew and adopted son. He and his wife were loyal friends and rescuers of the Bakowskis (II). Survived.

Stefa, Redke: the Bakowskis' maid. Stayed with them until the Ghetto was sealed (III).

Stolarska, Krystyna Wanda: *See* Karolina.

Szekman, Inka: *See* **Inka Szekman.**

Szmit, Mr.: a dentist and Jan's colleague. Rented a room in his apartment on 38 Pawia (III). Murdered.

Szmit, Mrs., DDS: Mr. Szmit's wife (III). Murdered.

Szwed, józio: a young idealistic Jew who, with his friend Zosia Zatorska, tried to distribute pamphlets among German soldiers to convince them that Hitler was wrong. Was imprisoned in Pawiak, tortured, and murdered (III).

Szwedowa, Mrs: Józio's mother (III). Murdered.

Tadek Luka: See Luka, Tadek.

Tania: Józef's sister (XI).

Teacher: German Nazi who taught in Marten and was known as Mr. Teacher, Wagners' friend (VIII)

Tilly Wagner: *See* Wagner, Tilly.

Toebbens, Walter C.: the owner of the largest German Ghetto enterprise, called a workshop, that was supposed to shelter its Jewish workers from deportation (V).

Tran, Julius: Mrs. Tran's son and Janka Elterman's brother. Marta's husband (VI). Murdered.

Tran, Marta: Julius's wife and mother of their two daughters. Janka's sister-in-law. Alice's sister. (VI). Survived with her daughters.

Tran, Mr.: Janka Elterman's father. Injured during the bombing. Died from his wounds in December 1939 (II).

Tran, Mrs.: mother of Janka, Julius, and Olga. Survived to live close to 100 years (II).

Trojanowski: superintendent at 38 Pawia (II).

Victoria: sister of Julia Kielba and Anna. Janina Zenkowska's grand aunt (XI).

Wagner, Kaltie: a young son of Mr. Wagner (VIII).

Wagner, Mr.: a German Nazi and Mayor of Marten. Author's overseer. Father of Tilly and Kaltie (VIII). **Wagner, Mrs.:** Mr. Wagner's wife. Stepmother of Tilly and Kaltie (VIII).

Wagner, Tilly: Mr. Wagner's daughter (VIII).

Wisniewski, Alexander: a French-Polish translator and a social worker. Assisted author and her family during their stay in Nancy in 1945 (IX).

Zaleski, Mr. and Mrs.: Mrs. Sliwa's parents who owned a variety store in Warsaw. Invited Karolina to stay in their home, risking their lives for her (VII). Survived.

Zawoznik, Henia: author's pre-war classmate. They met for the last time at the *Umschlagplatz* in August 1942 (V). Murdered.

Zenkowska, Janina: the Bakowskis' dear and loyal Polish Christian friend. Kept their dining room set during the whole Occupation and returned it intact (III).

Zenkowski, M.D.: Janina Zenkowska's husband.

Zenon Pawlo: the Bakowskis' friend and rescuer (VII). Killed by a bomb in 1944. *See also* Pawlos family.

Zloto, Franka: Jan's friend. During the Final Solution, shared her one room on the Toebbens factory premises with Krystyna—her daughter—author, Karolina, and their father (V). Survived.

Zloto, Krystyna: Franka Zloto's pretty 16-year-old daughter (V). Survived.

Zofia Chemska: *See* Chemska, Zofia

Zosia Ossowska: *See* Ossowska, Zosia.

Zosia Zatorska: a young idealistic Jewish woman who, with her friend Józio Szwed, tried to distribute pamphlets among German soldiers to convince them that Hitler was wrong. Was imprisoned in Pawiak, tortured, and murdered (III).